LANDSCRIPT IS A PUBLICATION ON
LANDSCAPE AESTHETICS INVITING AUTHORS
FROM DIFFERENT DISCIPLINES TO INVEST
SOME THOUGHT ON ESTABLISHED MODES OF
PERCEIVING, REPRESENTING, AND CONCEIVING
NATURE. STEERED BY AN EDITORIAL BOARD
COMPRISED OF INTERNATIONAL EXPERTS
FROM VARIOUS FIELDS OF VISUAL STUDIES,
LANDSCAPE DESIGN RESEARCH, AS WELL AS
SOCIOLOGY AND PHILOSOPHY, ITS GOAL IS
TO ACT AS A REVELATOR OF CONVENTIONAL
PERCEPTIONS OF LANDSCAPE AND TO
CULTIVATE THE DEBATE ON LANDSCAPE
AESTHETICS AT A SCHOLARLY LEVEL. THIS
DISCUSSION PLATFORM AIMS AT REKINDLING
A THEORETICAL DEBATE, IN THE HOPE OF
FOSTERING A BETTER UNDERSTANDING OF THE
IMMANENCE OF LANDSCAPE ARCHITECTURE
IN OUR CULTURE, FOCUSING CRITICALLY ON
THE WAY WE THINK, LOOK, AND ACT UPON
SITES AND NONSITES TODAY.

T0313572

Professor Christophe Girot, Albert Kirchengast (Chief Editors)
Institute of Landscape Architecture ILA, D–ARCH, ETH Zurich

SUBMISSION GUIDELINES

Manuscript proposals are welcome in fields appropriate
for *Landscript*. Scholarly submissions should be
formatted in accordance with *The Chicago Manual of
Style* and the spelling should follow American convention.
The full manuscript must be submitted as a Microsoft
Word document, on a CD or disk, accompanied by a
hard copy of the text. Accompanying images should be
sent as TIFF files with a resolution of at least 300 dpi
at 8 × 9-inch print size. Figures should be numbered
clearly in the text. Image captions and credits must be
included with submissions. It is the responsibility of the
author to secure permissions for image use and pay any
reproduction fees. A brief letter of inquiry and author
biography must also accompany the text.

Acceptance or rejection of submissions is at the discretion
of the editors. Please do not send original materials, as
submissions will not be returned.

Please direct submissions to this address:

Landscript
Chair of Professor Christophe Girot
Institute of Landscape Architecture ILA, ETH Zurich
Wolfgang-Pauli-Strasse 15, HIL H 54.2
8093 Zurich, Switzerland

Questions about submissions can be emailed to:
kirchengast@arch.ethz.ch

Visit our website for further information:
www.girot.arch.ethz.ch

LANDSCRIPT 2

Filmic Mapping

LAN
RIP

DSC
T 2

FRED TRUNIGER

FRED TRUNIGER is a film scholar and curator.
He studied Film and German Studies at the University
of Zurich and the Freie Universität in Berlin and
received his PhD from the ETH Zurich. He is head of the
research focus "Visual Narrative" at the School of Art
and Design of the Lucerne University of Applied Sciences
and Arts.

FILMIC MAPPING

FILM AND THE VISUAL CULTURE OF LANDSCAPE ARCHITECTURE

For Kristina Trolle

In Memoriam Rüdiger Neumann (1944–2007) and
Gerhard Benedikt Friedl (1967–2009)

[II]
Filmic Land Survey

Appendix

Introduction: From the Aesthetic to the Dynamic Landscape

The theory of landscape was changing at the end of the twentieth century. Well into the latter part of the century, the discussion was dominated by considerations of concrete, formal problems, seen primarily from the standpoint of landscape as a natural environment. An aesthetic and small-scale, garden-related nature was of primary concern and interest. In Switzerland, for example, the use of non-native plants in Swiss gardens was a favored topic, as was the debate about whether a garden should be considered "architectural" or "natural" (Weilacher 2001; Stoffler 2008).

The consideration of larger, more abstract relationships, in which landscape might also be understood, was largely forgotten in this context. The growing recourse of humankind to its spatial (and therefore also landscape) resources, which over the course of the twentieth century came to include increasingly larger portions of the earth's surface, was mostly ignored for quite some time. Nonetheless, as early as 1950, John Brinckerhoff Jackson had started a periodical entitled *Landscape*, in which he attacked the idealization of the landscape, still widespread at the time, and focused instead on his immediate, everyday environment. He concluded that this "vernacular landscape" had long ago been comprehensively reconfigured by humans. This fact raised questions of form and identity, with which society would need to come to terms sooner or later. In a brief passage from his 1984 book, *Discovering the Vernacular Landscape,* he describes his vision for the future role of the landscape architect in a world formed by human beings:

> I would like to think that in the future the profession of landscape architecture will expand beyond its present confines and concern itself with making mobility orderly and beautiful. This would mean knowing a great deal about land, its uses, its values, and the political and economical and cultural forces affecting its distribution. The environmental designer should be concerned with the spatial changes taking place. It is precisely in the field of land use and community planning that a trained imagination, an awareness of environment and habitat can be of greatest value [...]. Environmental design is not simply a matter of protecting nature as it is, but of creating a new nature, a new beauty. It is finally a matter of defining landscape in a way that includes both the mobility of the vernacular and the political infrastructure of a stable social order (Jackson 1984, 155).

Jackson's work introduced a paradigm shift. He not only described the city, but also the landscape as a space for social interactions, which assumed communicative functions within society. Within Jackson's tradition, it has been identified as a preferred location of ideological controversy (Mitchell 1994), as a projected space of societal utopias (Schama 1995) and of subjective states of being (Vöckler 1998), or as a corporeally experienced space with specific atmospheric qualities (Böhme 1995).

These new approaches take into account not just the landscape as topography, but also the perceiving, interpreting and socially interactive human being as actual producer of that landscape. Whilst this theory was regarded for most of the twentieth century as a serviceable, moral structure for the design of the landscape, today it has developed more in the direction of a discipline within the social sciences. The *scenic landscape*—1 of the nineteenth century—to which significant moral-pedagogic functions were attributed, in addition to the aesthetic—has given way to an understanding of the landscape in constant transformation, largely detached from originary nature

1   The concept "aesthetic landscape" is used analogously to the English concept "scenic landscape," for which no exact translation is given in German. The "aesthetic landscape" as an approach is described exemplarily in Joachim Ritters' *Landschaft. Zur Funktion des Aesthetischen in der Gesellschaft* (1963).

and dominated and reconfigured by human beings. Landscape is a cultural construction—both in material and in mental terms—which enables the human being to access and possess the space in which his everyday life takes place. To denote the contextualizing and spatially based understanding of landscape in this work, I use the term *dynamic landscape*.—[2]

This work examines how the shift from aesthetic to dynamic understanding of the landscape has affected the visual culture of the landscape—particularly landscape theory.

When the basis of an entire profession is revised, one can assume the presence of transformations reaching down to its deepest layers. If, as in the case of landscape architecture and its theory, images are omnipresent, it lies close at hand to trace the paradigm shift in the visual culture of landscape architecture as well. Given that landscape architecture cannot avoid having to adapt its use of image-based representation to the changed givens of reality, this study addresses this fact based on the fundamental premise that film and video (or more generally, the moving image) represent perhaps the most important source of images. They provide appropriate imagistic forms with which to address the paradigm shift. Stated in different terms: film and video are better suited than other media to representing the processes of the dynamic landscape. This book is written with the aim of indicating new ways of reading film, so that it can fully develop its potential as a means of representing landscape. The reasons for choosing the moving image are described in the book's first section.

The uncertain basis of my thinking is the insight that there is no real genre of landscape film,—[3] to which I will refer in my undertaking. This situation allows me the freedom to attempt my own—admittedly experimental— definition for this not yet existent film genre. I therefore

2 This is a variant on the terminology used by J. B. Jackson, who speaks of "systems of man-made spaces on the surface of the earth […] always subject to change."

3 It is established that there is no actual genre of landscape film, but rather, only groups of films (albeit many of them) at different locations and times that approach the topic of landscape (Pichler/Pollach 2006, 9). In this work, I nevertheless use the term "landscape film"; I do not give this title only to films that *depict* landscape but rather also to those that *narrate* landscape. As a genre designation, this use of the term cannot (yet) be definitive, but as an effective designation for the particular, focused landscape interest of each film and as a contribution to the discussion about a later definition of the genre "landscape film," however, I do not want to relinquish the term.

push the concept of landscape film in part further than would normally be the case by not emphasizing the image of landscape.

A semi-pragmatic work on the influence of the landscape film must first make a fundamental decision: it either chooses to approach its subject matter by means of the feature film and therefore to deal with films that potentially reach the greatest audience, but also are also subject to strict rules in terms of cinematographic narration. The other option is to assemble a body of films that can broach the abstract topic of landscape without being beholden to dramatic narration, and are therefore not bound to use this topic as collateral to the staging of action. In the former case, it seems possible to derive persuasive force in favor of the pragmatic influence of the film from its capacity for societal transformation, a capacity rooted in its wide distribution throughout a population. John Ford's Westerns are certainly the most well-known examples of such a capacity, achieved through sheer broad-based presence within western society. In no small measure, the Midwestern United States as the locale of the historical frontier owes its position in collective memory to its representation in Ford's films from the nineteen-thirties to the nineteen-sixties (of which the most important is perhaps *Stagecoach* of 1939).

The focus on little-known films thus occurs at the expense of the advantages gained from the widespread societal acceptance that an idea can achieve through film. I have decided in favor of this alternative and have based my study largely on experimental and documentary films. This decision was based on the conviction that the films chosen represent one or the other (or several) aspect(s) of the landscape with particular purity, because they are not obliged to respect normative filmic forms. Their production outside of institutional contexts and without anticipatory concern for audience statistics gives them the freedom to risk formal experiments and to plumb the possibilities of filmic representation of the landscape in every regard. They transform the way in which we see and create images of our environs by *extending the repertoire* of both seeing and image production.

In choosing the examples, it was important that their understanding of landscape should match the level of complexity of the dynamic landscape. They all share a primarily open form, which *pre*-interprets the landscape for the viewer by means of a precise reading of visible and invisible clues, but do so without enforcing a single interpretation. It is the author's artistic freedom not to attribute meaning to the evidence stringently, but rather to leave the viewer room for his own interpretation. These films address active viewers, who question critically what the film offers and are able to integrate information into a more broadly conceived framework of interpretation so that in the end they develop their own, *mutable* image of the landscape portrayed.

The target audience for these films is not as broad, as is the case with feature films, but it includes, generally speaking, film aficionados and specialists. In relation to the representation of the landscape, these are influential professionals who, in their daily work, *actually* change the face of the world day by day. There is a clear affinity between their efforts and those films that focus on the landscape thematically and formally, above those that use it only as a narrative instrument, but in the process achieve a greater degree of audience penetration. The few exceptions prove the rule. I am persuaded that the films described here are more interesting in many respects, for their pragmatic approach within the field of landscape theory, than their fictional counterparts, which enjoy greater audience success.

The same is true of this book. If it can reach these specialists and film lovers, and influence their ways of seeing, then the films discussed here will certainly, in one way or another, have an impact on the way society deals with landscape.

Filmstill from *The Searchers* (USA 1956) by John Ford

When considering whether or not to include a film in this study, it was not a decisive factor that landscape as image be represented in a particular, or particularly prominent, way. Instead, the criterion was the inclusion of factors that relate to the definition of the dynamic landscape and are at least equally important to the representation of the landscape. These are, on the one hand, the social, historical, economic, and societal contexts in which landscape and its representation are embedded. On the other hand, these are also the haptic qualities of a film, which can provide the viewer with an entrée not only to the image of landscape but also, as I will argue, enable an actual landscape experience in the movie theater. Ultimately, the film analyses in the second half of the book have implications beyond the cinema for the practice of landscape perception—which today is closely associated with the moving image.

These two thematic emphases—the contextualized view of the landscape and the experiential quality of filmic representation—underlie this book's ambition to describe an adequate (although certainly not the only) form of depiction, with which to gain an understanding of the dynamic landscape. This incorporates the role of theory in creating the basis upon which the necessary modifications of the visual culture of landscape architecture can be implemented. To this end, my study offers some indication of which insights can be gleaned from film. It simultaneously represents a contribution to a new understanding of the visual culture of landscape and brings a series of highly relevant, if little-known, films into the discourse by means of detailed analyses.

The first chapter, *Landscape Theory as a Complex Science of the Images*, sets out in search of a new self-identity for landscape theory. For the past decade, landscape theory has engaged in a quest intended to find a new locus for a societally relevant area of theory. This search is fraught with problems, especially because of the seemingly strange status of the discipline of landscape architecture at technical universities—at least in Switzerland where this study was conceived—and the relative youth of its theory, which is based in the social sciences. I would like to demonstrate that the theory of the dynamic landscape may be understood as a complex science, which unifies insights from both positivist practices and from social scientific-hermeneutic methods. This is the case because the paradigm shift from an aesthetic to a dynamic understanding of landscape reflects nothing other than a more universal reorientation towards complex models of knowledge in the sciences. The foundation of the understanding of landscape used in this book is both pragmatic and tailored to the practical work of the landscape architect, who makes spaces that are intended to (and must) satisfy aesthetic motivation, as well as the need for an immediately usable environment for human beings. The user of the landscape experiences these spaces in ways that are atmospheric, subjectively filtered, and imprinted with prior personal knowledge and individual dispositions.

The characterization of the dynamic landscape leads me to the question in the second chapter, entitled *Working with Images*, as to how this kind of landscape can be adequately dealt with in visual terms. The visual culture of landscape must undoubtedly confront changed demands. This chapter focuses on the actual application of images in both landscape architecture and landscape theory and demonstrates the image's dominance. It becomes clear that the use of images mostly follows a paradigm that does not meet the contemporary requirements of the discourse. A "catalogue of requirements and demands" thus collates the factors relating to the desired representation of the dynamic landscape. The chapter concludes with three theories about the societal relationship to landscape, which in the recent past is increasingly influenced by its secondary communication through media and technology.

In the third chapter, entitled *Filmic Landscape Communication*, the results of the search, which I describe exemplarily in the two first chapters with reference to the visual culture of landscape, are compared with film theory and the parameters of filmic representation. I wish to demonstrate that film offers an appropriate representational medium for the dynamic landscape, because it communicates three primary aspects: *constant transformation, sublation of the polarity between city and country*, and *immersion*. The third chapter's conclusions form the basis for the examination of case study analyses in the second half of the book.

This second half collects film analyses, in which specific aspects and focuses of the landscape film are highlighted.

The fourth chapter is dedicated to the filmmaker Rüdiger Neumann, who died unexpectedly in 2007. The second half of the nineteen-seventies marks the beginning of his rapprochement with the filmic image of the landscape, which became his sole interest for nearly twenty years. It is worth noting that Neumann's early work marks an attempt to use formal dictates and chance operations to limit the gaze in such a way that the cultural aspect of seeing ceases to play any role in the act of filming. In the course of his career, however, Neumann turned away from the stringently standardized, quasi-positivistic or scientific gaze intended to make disparate landscapes aesthetically comparable. He gradually replaced chance with trust in his own gaze, that was well-trained (by chance operations). Neumann undergoes a personal and artistic transformation, which, as far as I can see, illustrates exemplarily the movement from the classic-aesthetic to the dynamic understanding of landscape.

The fifth chapter is dedicated to a particular view of landscape. Its topic is *The Pedestrian's Gaze*, a fundamental and nonetheless singular form of perceiving our environment. Unlike the experience at high speeds, as in a car or train, the pedestrian perceives himself as part of the landscape. The characteristic of his gaze is its corporeality. This chapter describes films that translate the specific, physically influenced perception of walking into their medium and represent the particularities of this gaze.

The telling of stories is an ancient and fundamental cultural technique, and also has a function in landscape: "strata of memory" (Simon Schama) overlay individual and societal consciousness of the landscape and often prevent the human being from seeing what *really* is to be seen. The sixth chapter, *Narrating Landscape*, is dedicated to the function of the narrative form for this kind of depiction, and collects films that tell stories about and based upon landscapes, and set out to lend importance to a specific reading, often based upon a subjective position. If Simon Schama's observations that cultural memory plays a decisive role in the evaluation of our environment are accurate, then film can be understood as having the potential to influence the formation of this collective memory bank. The power of the medium to propagate images and stories is treated as a factor that can help to determine the value allocated by society to a landscape.

The book's conclusion, like the beginning of its second part, studies in depth the work of a single filmmaker. James Benning, similarly to Rüdiger Neumann, devoted nearly all of his creative production to the representation of landscape. As in Neumann's case, his approach has changed constantly over time from 1971 to the present. The chapter entitled *James Benning: Panoramas of the American West* concentrates on Benning's oeuvre of the last twenty years and demonstrates how narrations of the landscape can assume the most subtle form, in contrast to which the traditional usage of the concept of narration is inadequate. In his work, narration often occurs through image clusters and thematic sequence. The analysis of the effect of time and duration, and the role of process-based development in both topography and filmic seeing, round off this inconclusive set of observations about the representation of the dynamic landscape in film.

The films that remain on my table are those that would have warranted mention in this study but could no longer be included. Thus, for example, films such as *Vom deutschen Rand* (On Germany's Border, GER 1999) by Volker Köster or *Gallivant* by Andrew Koetting (GB 1996)—both of which document a trip along each country's border—could be described in terms of our abstract, often mythically imprinted relationship to our native countries. Ursula Biemann's work on economic geographies in *Performing the Border* (CH 1999), *Remote Sensing* (CH 2001), *The Black Sea Files* (CH 2005), *Sahara Chronicle* (CH 2006/07), and *X-Mission* (CH 2008), among others, would also be a rewarding subject for more exacting examination. These films are precise analyses of the way space is structured by political and economic hierarchies. Finally, films on the politics of space, which is in fact strongly determined by actual national and international power relations or through the exercise of discursive power definitions, would also be within the scope of this work. Left unmentioned are the films *Limes: Bioborder/Park/ Spektakel* (Limes: Bioborder/Park/Spectacle, AUT 2001) by the artist group WR and *Unternehmen Paradies* (The Business of Paradise, GER 2002) by Volker Sattel, both of which portray landscape spaces as the scene of power enactment.

Films act upon our relationship to the world by transmitting information and by forming habits of seeing in the long term. Using the analyses collected here, I would like to demonstrate that the medium possesses analytical and communicative qualities, which enrich the discussion surrounding the dynamic landscape and can point to a way forward for it within the field of the visual. This study suggests the reading of films within a methodical framework, which in turn can allow this reading to become an extremely productive undertaking with regard to a professional engagement with landscape.

[I]

Understanding Landscape and Visual Culture

Landscape Theory as a Complex Science of Images

Complex Science

Complexity within the sciences is not only increasing within individual fields of study: today, research is becoming increasingly transdisciplinary among established research trajectories. Transdisciplinary research makes sense in those areas in which a line of questioning transcends disciplinary boundaries, and is therefore itself transdisciplinary from the outset. Those problems can themselves be considered transdisciplinary; they have outgrown disciplines and therefore demand *transdisciplinary research trajectories*, in which the disciplinary knowledge relating to more than a single scholarly area must be developed across respective boundaries (Mittelstrass 1998, 107). Notably, environmental problems belong in this category. They cross boundaries because their medium, nature, itself represents a tightly interwoven multiplicity. Much that we find in nature cannot be *explained* as positivist science would have it, but demands first of all to be *understood*.—[4] Given the impossibility of a comprehensive view, it is not possible for any single branch of knowledge to offer universally valid certainties (and thus explain the world). Forms of knowledge within the humanities gain significance in this context, since they are based upon the rhetorical structure of stable intellectual architectures, which help human beings to understand social behaviors

[4] The differentiation between "understand" and "explain" draws upon the hermeneutics of Wilhlem Dilthey. See Mittelstrass 1998, p. 123 and 1997, p. 81.

5 See for example Haraway 1988; Nowotny, Scott et al. 1994; Nowotny 1999; Nowotny, Scott, Gibbons 2004/2001.

and to orient themselves in their world. Insights draw their validity at least in part by proving themselves correct in everyday life, a quality that seems to be gaining *in importance.*—[5] "Reliable knowledge" gives way to the "social robustness" of research results, as Helga Nowotny, Peter Scott, and Michael Gibbons propose in their book *Re-Thinking Science: Knowledge and the Public in an Age of Uncertainty.*

The essential points of the paradigm shift in scientific theory are reflected by developments in the contemporary landscape theory of the past three decades. The "system of man-made spaces on the surface of the earth," as J. B. Jackson described landscape (Jackson 1984, 156), is an object of study that is full of social contingency. Jackson's theory of the dynamic landscape entails an increase in complexity, compared to earlier approaches: in his paradigm, the study of everyday spaces requires the inclusion of social scientific methods that enable an understanding of topographic transformation as a component of real political power relations. Arguments are developed accordingly in transdisciplinary discourse; the boundaries of traditional aesthetic and natural scientific approaches to the landscape are broken down.

Of course the transformation of landscape theory into transdisciplinary scholarship, integrating the methods of the social sciences and the humanities, has consequences for it hermeneutics. It is not only urbanism in the nineteenth century, that was a "purely technical matter" (Sitte 1965, 2): the development of the landscape, too, oriented itself for many years primarily towards facts derived from such natural scientific research areas as plant sociology, water management, traffic and infrastructural planning, or topology. From the outset as regards the forms of knowledge known today, the functionalist understanding of landscape architecture saw itself more as a part of technical research (which explains its frequent location at technical universities and colleges within the European tradition, and at land grant universities in the United States); scholarly interaction with interpretive, hermeneutic methods and their "unfocused" insights must first be (re)learned.

"Landscape Two" and "Landscape Three"

The transformations within landscape theory over the past decades reflect real-world restructuring processes as they have gradually developed over the course of industrialization in the past two centuries. As a tendency since the Renaissance, which was also fortified during the Romantic period, the predominant societal understanding of the landscape has been one that prioritized *aesthetic* qualities. Landscape as a concept defined (and developed) in painting—[6] described an aesthetic reference to the natural space whose ideal was considered as the harmonic relationship between the human being and the nature of the depicted natural landscape. The French painter Claude Lorrain created the frame of reference, which remains valid today. Arcadia—the locus of the Golden Age in Greek mythology—is the progenitor of visions of an ideal, which are associated with the aesthetic concept of landscape.

Industrialization in the nineteenth century put an end to the fine-grained landscape development typifying the agrarian age, and with it to one of the fundamental prerequisites for the ideal of Arcadian architecture. A process of homogenization established itself and remains up until today. In our time, this development has assumed global proportions—[7] and ever larger areas of the earth have taken on the appearance of an increasingly homogeneous surface, which is reconfigured in ever shorter periods: our landscape has become more and more a "system of man-made spaces on the surface

6 The concept "landscape" derives from early sixteenth-century painting (see Gombrich 1966, 109 and especially 112). The ideas associated with it, however, are much older. Gombrich establishes that Pliny, as early as the first century AD, mentions a specialty, or "specializing artist," who anticipates the idea of landscape painting. The theme of a happy life within idyllic nature has recurred in literature ever since and became a model for landscape painting.

7 Sieferle (2003, 64). In this essay, Sieferle references an earlier book publication (1997) and takes a decided position against a view of landscape that still treats nature as a criterion. For Sieferle, it is no longer possible today, given centuries-old reconfiguration by human beings, to imagine the appearance of a landscape that is untouched by humans. It should not be forgotten that nature within the classical agricultural landscape honored by the Arcadian ideal had already been reconfigured by humans.

of the earth" (Jackson). The natural processes of growth and decay have been replaced by the will and action of mankind, which controls the earth's surface much more completely today than ever before in the history of the world. Jackson soberly calls this form of landscape, produced by mankind's constant reconfiguring, "Landscape Three." This process has affected not only the natural and cultural landscapes that had formed a large part of the earth's surface in the nineteenth century, but also those forms created by mankind for other purposes other than agrarian as they increasingly extend into open land: suburbs, traffic infrastructure, industrial zones, and recreational areas.

"Landscape One" and "Landscape Two" in Jackson's model refer to the chronology of earlier landscape concepts. The first is the virtually ahistorical space with a social and political character and later, the aesthetic scenery deriving from Arcadian poetry. "Landscape Two" has proven a particularly successful and influential model. Guided by it, mankind has appropriated its environment for centuries, even beyond the point where the actual environment has ceased to have the form of "Landscape Two."

The attractiveness of the Arcadian approach to landscape lies in its capacity to unify art so harmoniously with nature that the viewer tends not to see the former as such. The ordered beauty of depictions (and of many actual landscapes) in which nature has lost all capacity to threaten and everything seems made for the human being allows us to forget the mercilessness with which nature reclaims that which has been wrested from her through gardening or agriculture. Human artifacts are naturalized in "Landscape Two" (Smith 1991, 65) so that, in the eye of the beholder, they become elements of that particularly biblical relation to the world: "Be fruitful, and multiply, and replenish the earth, and subdue it" (Genesis 1:28). For what at its core is the landscape described in Genesis if not an agricultural landscape? The Bible places the origins of our environment in the active hands of human beings, who master "the herb yielding seed," "the tree yielding fruit," and are master "over the fish of the sea, and over the fowl of the air, and over the cattle, and over all the earth, and over every creeping thing that creepeth upon the earth" (Genesis 1:10, 11, 26). The garden of paradise occupies the center as a privileged zone, seemingly unaffected by the force of nature that first must be tamed in order to become truly beautiful.

Mankind thus received its license to domesticate landscape from the highest authority. As a part of God's creation, however, nature absolutely has its own purpose to serve. Ruins, for example, are favored witnesses to its reconquering force. The beauty of decay demonstrates not only the confluence of "originary" mankind's cultural achievements and the work of nature, but also, the fact that culture and nature must not necessarily be understood as opposites. Within the agrarian and idyllic ideal of "Landscape Two," the results of this reconquest—picturesquely ruined stone buildings, often framed by the splendor of voluptuous plant life—do not threaten human culture but are instead a memento mori. They recall a long-lost age in which the bucolic ideal was considered a reality. It is towards this age that the landscape gardens of the eighteenth and nineteenth centuries strove.

Meadows near Greifswald, painted in 1820 by Caspar David Friedrich, in which the silhouette of a city is represented with exaggerated height on the horizon, subtly suggests the naturalization of human constructions: city and landscape are sharply separated into background and foreground. However, it is not only the city, but also the open meadows before it where the horses play, which are the result of intensively cultivating the meadows. There are nonetheless a few elements that convey to the viewer a feeling of virginity: the horses' suggested gallop implies wildness, and the gentle movement of the terrain in the foreground, crisscrossed by a scanty growth of the stalky "weeds", are perhaps the remainders of an earlier, unshaped topography. Through this implied wildness,

Caspar David Friedrich: *Meadows near Greifswald* (1820–22)

the agrarian plain outside the city retains the nimbus of (idealized) naturalness.—8

The interplay between the man's capacity to create and nature's capacity to reappropriate is always in the end decided in favor of nature as soon as man abandons his work. His inexorable "defeat" is implicit in the ideal of "Landscape Two", but it can be given a positive slant if understood as the culturally determined human's yearning for the state of nature. Originary nature is, in the concept of "Landscape Two," no longer necessarily an indispensible element of representation. Its hybrid concept of nature has instead such a strong integrative power that it is capable of naturalizing countless man-made artifacts, thereby making culture's traces in the landscape nearly invisible.

Citylandscape

Consideration of the urban, which is the most obvious cultural artifact affecting the landscape on a large scale, entered into landscape theory long before Jackson. The city had already been part of the debate for hundreds of years.

Seventeenth-century painting developed the veduta as a playful form for landscape painting: it conformed in formal terms to classical "landscapes", but differed from them on the one hand in its attempt to deliver a true, detailed image of an actual situation, and, on the other, in its capacity to offer aesthetic views of the city. The urban silhouette proved to be as appropriate for aesthetic representation as open land.

With the appearance of Jean-Jacques Rousseau's texts, however, the city acquired a bad reputation as a place for human habitation. In the eyes of society, the city air no longer made one free—9 but rather, ill—and the hygiene and social conditions were actually in decline. Therefore,

8   This pictorial construction is repeated in Friedrich's work many times in a similar manner. New Brandenburg in *Morning Fog* (1816/17), for example, shows the city in the middle ground in front of a gentle chain of hills. In the foreground is a meadow with low vegetation. The scene is, as so often the case in Caspar David Friedrich's work, observed by two strolling men who are represented in the extreme foreground amid a seemingly natural undergrowth and replace the "wild" horses in the Greifswald painting. Also compare the painting *Moonlit Landscape at Morning light (Lonely Tree)* of 1822. A variation on this theme is also found in *Hills and Harvested Field near Dresden* (1824/25) and *The Evening Star* (ca. 1830), in which the city in the middle ground is partially obscured by a hill. In both paintings, freshly plowed fields and poplar allées indicate the traces of human work even more explicitly.

9   In Medieval ages, there was a saying in German cities: "Stadtluft macht frei," meaning that in cities people were no longer enslaved (although they remained so in the countryside).

the urban planning of the nineteenth and early twentieth centuries directed its attentions with increasing conviction towards the problem of how industrialization and its concomitant decline in living conditions for the majority of the urban population could be counteracted. Belts of small, neatly arranged housing settlements, that were rural in appearance and surrounded the city, were intended to contribute to reducing this problem—the concept worked only for the wealthy who could afford to live in the "garden cities." Another proposal was "strip cities," which were long, narrow strips of urban configurations along a high-capacity traffic artery. In such structures, open land was not far from any one point and always within easy access.

Only slowly did the negative judgment passed on the city once again dissipate from public discourse. In 1908, the artist and architect August Endell published the book with the programmatic title *Die Schönheit der grossen Stadt* (The Beauty of the Metropolis). Endell countered the omnipresent tendency to seek refuge in the past, which the contemporary city seems to demand. He propounded instead an orientation towards the here and now, which is all that the human being has the power to configure. The city is the "most obvious and perhaps most inherent fruit" (Endell 1908, 20) of modern life, whose apparent inadequacies (alienation from the earth, plants and animals) could be compensated by other pleasures.

As the title already implies, "beauty" is the characteristic that Endell sought to attribute to the metropolis; and it is artists and poets who were the first to represent this quality. For their pains, they were censured and heaped with moral approbation (ibid., 34). Endell came to their defense and began by listing the beautiful features of the city. In the process, the architect and future director of the Federal Academy for Art and Decorative Arts in Breslau (Staatliche Akademie der Kunst und Kunstgewerbe) made the most astonishing assertions by titling his chapters "The City as Nature" or "The City as Landscape," and finally, "The Landscape Beauty of the City." The weather in the city, the light, the fog—all of these things transform the city just as they do the landscape beyond. Endell's descriptions lose themselves in details and observations that enable the city to appear in the guise of the classical landscape. This is reflected in the extent to which the author was carried away with observations taken from an artistic perspective: squares, streets' trajectories, and the people in them, river beds, bridges, street cafes—despite any unappealing features, they all offer him considerable visual material to support their positive evaluation (ibid., 47).

Seen from today's perspective, it is not only Endell's plea for a positive view of the city and the parallels he draws between city and landscape that are interesting: the radical reorientation, allowing the city to be seen as a productive factor for the positive evaluation of our surroundings and our lives, is equally interesting.

The city may still have seemed to Endell to be a "horrible heap of stone" and "hopelessly ugly" (ibid., 48), but an artistic perspective helps him to discover the city's nature and landscape—in other words, its *beauty*. Early on, Endell indicates that our relationship to the environment is (also) a *problem of perception*. From this point of view, the dualism of city and landscape is at least partially sidelined. Endell is thus the direct predecessor of this book. And without the total perspective that he postulated—both in terms of scale and in the integration of different topographies—the concept of the "cityscape" or "Stadtlandschaft," which is so ubiquitous today, would not even be thinkable.

Endell's text cannot belie the fact that the strict differentiation between city and landscape persisted for most of the twentieth century. This is evident in the recommendations made by the urban planners surrounding Hans Scharoun who, confronted with the tabula rasa of postwar Berlin's city center, developed their own ideas about what they described with the neologism "Citylandscape" (Stadtlandschaft).

> The Citylandscape is a formal principle for the city planner, particularly in the effort to gain control over a large-scale settlement. It permits the expression of clear and appropriately measured subdivisions of scaleless, incomprehensible entities, as well as the ordering of these portions in relation to one another, just as woods, meadow, mountain and lake harmonize in a beautiful landscape. (Scharoun 2005, 40)

This concept of Citylandscape, clearly akin to Georg Simmel's ideas of landscape (described below), but itself hybrid, apparently suggests greater proximity between the two poles of the landscape debate. It is, however, only applied to a city in which the functions of "work," "living," and "green" remain sharply demarcated from one another.

Scharoun's perspective is that of a city planner: he does not relinquish the hierarchy of city and landscape in his proposal at the expense of the former. Nonetheless, the valuation of the metropolis appears to be based on solid criteria, and the Rousseauean understanding of the city as un-nature fractured. Both city and landscape are understood as mutually determined positive spaces. It should also not be forgotten: the concept of the Citylandscape has, in the process, finally been assimilated into the discussion about the planning of both larger urban *and* landscape spaces.

The use of a word such as Citylandscape in the planning of Berlin after World War II proves that the boundaries between the two poles had already become porous in terms of ways of thinking and, most particularly, as regards perception, even before J. B. Jackson's work. Nevertheless, in these early attempts, the separation between them remains sharply drawn, at least in design (and the fundamental attitude towards nature remains unchanged). This explains, for example, why the social discourse on tourism is still primarily influenced by the idea of a holistic and virtually eternal nature.—[10]

10 Concepts of landscape are inert, as a study (albeit somewhat dated) by the geographer Gerhard Hard demonstrates, relative to a daily understanding of the concept of landscape (see Hard 1970). He notes that in daily usage—and therefore, that which is most influential in society—the relationship to landscape still bears the mark of an ideal landscape image, even 200 years after industrialization. Nothing, according to Hard, disturbs and destroys the landscape in the eye of the viewer more than industrial buildings, industrial infrastructure, and the (modern big) city (1970, 71). The results of Hard's study remain valid in an everyday framework (if with certain limitations relative to the reception of landscape images in art): in the everyday life of society, we are more likely to encounter "ideal images" of the landscape, which are quite remote from the built, humanly colonized landscape of reality. One particular change has evolved primarily through art: in addition to the now-famous film *Koyaanisqatsi* (Godfrey Reggio, USA 1983), for example, European photographers including Margherita Spilutini, Walter Niedermayr, Nicholas Faure and, in their photographic series on agglomerations, the artist duo Fischli/Weiss have transformed the way we perceive the contemporary landscape over the past decades. Through their work, the integration, or even naturalization (Smith 1991, 65) of technical constructions in the landscape has entered general consciousness. Unlike the accusatory images of the ecological movement of the nineteen-seventies and nineteen-eighties, contemporary shots of →

"Landscape Three": The Dynamic Landscape

The majority of landscape theoreticians in the past two decades have followed Jackson's premise, that landscape has become dynamic and spatial. For him, man's apparent (but certainly also provisional) conquest of nature in the last quarter of the twentieth century made clear that the role of the landscape architect is to divorce himself from the obsolete aesthetic ideal of "Landscape Two" and to achieve "making mobility orderly and beautiful " (Jackson 1984, 155) the dynamic of "Landscape Three", as it originates in human action. He succeeded in pointing out the inseparable intertwining of nature and artifacts, and dealt with it appropriately. From the point of view of landscape architecture, his great achievement is to have shifted in the focus of discussion from urbanity to the *landscape-ness* of the new forms of our environment. This is a shift in perspective, which is of inestimable significance as regards our understanding of ourselves and the development of landscape architecture.

The transition from "Landscape Two" to "Landscape Three" marks two parameters that Martin Prominski summarized in 2004: the concept of an immutable, almost eternal arcadia is lost within the dynamic of *constant transformation.* This means that the understanding of Landscape Three is not based inherently on the return to this lost ideal condition—and thus to virtually timeless landscape—but rather, emphasizes explicitly the metamorphosis of topography and the human agent's role in its ongoing transformation. The *constant transformation* of the landscape is triggered by small-scale and short-term functional and ownership interests (Jackson 1984, 151 and 154). Rather than a global, distanced view, to local contextualization is called for to comprehend it. Its analysis must account for the social factors that also stipulate the associated spatial situation in its smallest detail. Among these are the historical development of the place, its societal significance, and the political, social, or economic pressure applied to it.

The *dynamic fabric of man-made spaces*, as Prominski paraphrases J.B. Jackson (Prominski 2004, 60), also overcomes the polarity of city and landscape. Rather than the opposition between manmade and (supposedly) natural space, Landscape Three affords the insight that there is no natural landscape space on the planet that has been spared from human contact and reconfiguration. By means of *the sublation of the polarity of city and country*, the persistently common distinction in everyday life between natural and artificial landscape becomes largely obsolete. Thus, the city can also be described as a form of landscape—an approach that had already made itself known centuries ago in painting, but has only become presentable in landscape theory in the recent past. For the purposes of analysis, this means not only that the "open" landscape must be treated as an artifact, but also that urban territories must be included in the considerations of landscape theory and landscape architecture. This has a significant effect on serious considerations of landscape: as human artifacts, all aforementioned forms of our everyday environment indicate *societal means of action*, which have left their traces and imprints on the form assumed by the landscape.

Immersion in the Dynamic Landscape

In a number of daily situations, most people are made aware of the fact that the human being does not move through his environment as a machine for seeing and hearing, and that he orients himself not only on the basis of spatial configurations, but is also affected by light, color, atmosphere, and mood. It was, however, not always easy for science to integrate its knowledge of the contingencies of spatial experience into its thinking. As of 1963, Otto Friedrich Bollnow could find only very few

41

11 Bollnow quotes Dürckheim, Graf Karlfried von: Untersuchungen zum gelebten Raum. In: *Neue Psychologische Studien, Vol. 6.* München 1932; Straus, Erwin: Die Formen des Räumlichen. In: *Der Nervenarzt*, 1930; Binswanger, Ludwig: *Über Ideenflucht.* Zürich 1933. All these texts "did not extend beyond the more narrow field of philosophy and seem to have been quickly forgotten outside of medical circles" (Bollnow, 1963, 14). He mentions, as philosophical predecessors, Minkowski, Eugène: *Le temps vécu.* Paris 1933. Cassirer, Ernst: *Philosophie der symbolischen Formen.* Berlin 1923–29; Lassen, H. *Beiträge zu einer Phänomenologie und Psychologie der Anschauung.* Würzburg 1939 and Bachelard, Gaston: *La poétique de l'espace.* Paris 1957 (The Poetics of Space, 1958).

12 A comprehensive sociological examination of the concept of space upon which Vöckler's work is based can be found in Martina Löw's book *Raumsoziologie* (2001). She differentiates between an absolute "concept of enclosed space" and a "relational" concept of space, which understands space as a dynamic system constituted by the "locational relationships" among bodies. The body of the viewer is, in this concept, understood to be the privileged body. Within the relational understanding of space, the activities of daily negotiation are tantamount to the production of space. Other authors who propound positions on subjective landscape construction, which are related to the psychoscape in broader terms include Franzen (2000) and Böhme (1989, 1995).

precedents for his concept of space in *Mensch und Raum* (*Human Space*), which postulated *lived space* (gelebter Raum) as a research counterpoint to the abstract spatial concept common in math and physics.——[11]

More recent studies on the subject of the city have taken up the topic of lived space and pursued it further. Kai Vöckler, with his concept of the *Psychoscape,* seems to belong more to the category of imagination, which so worried Bollnow.——[12] He works toward identifying a modality of perception which "permits a new manner of experiencing reality" (Vöckler 1998, 277) and builds upon the work of Georg Simmel, who had highlighted the role of *mood* for the constitution of landscape as early as 1913. Vöckler, paraphrasing Simmel, describes landscape "as a mental construct that lives only by means of the 'unifying power of the soul'" (Vöckler 1998, 278).

From this position, it is possible to deduce that "in fact [...] innermost nature [is] aesthetically *experienced* in the image of landscape" (ibid., 278), a feature employed in advertising when it senses a positive potential for identifying its products with landscape. Vöckler offers the example of a cigarette advertisement: "[...] the atmosphere can be inhaled, internalized by consuming the cigarette. In this way, smoking a cigarette today is also a landscape experience" (ibid., 279).

The transposition of the aesthetic landscape experience into the human "soul" conversely means that the subjective internal experience of it also plays a role: "Psychic dispositions" have "an essential influence on every aesthetic experience" (ibid., 281). The ability to pass judgment upon, for example, the "generic city" (Koolhaas 1995) is equally influenced by the constant transformation of the physical city, and by that which the subject projects onto it. A person in the best possible mood can find something positive even in the most inhospitable environment. The evaluation of the landscape arises from a complex interpolation between the real topography, the aesthetic sensitivity of the perceiving subject, and his psychic disposition. In other words, we no longer stand before the landscape as an image, but rather, within it. It is no longer seeing that is the sole component of the aesthetic experience, but rather, the entire experience. This concept is particularly interesting in the subsequent consideration of visual representation of landscape in film, in which I address cinema's immersive qualities.

When describing the aesthetic experience of the immersive landscape, traditional aesthetics must be reconsidered. The traditional approach is, as Gernot Böhme notes, a "theory of the art work [...] initially only an aesthetic of judgment and valuation, and finally, in a broader sense, art criticism" (Böhme 1995, 7). Traditional aesthetics is not suited to insights into the human being's daily experience and impressions (and increasingly, into current developments in art), as is necessitated by the affinity for landscape already described.

Böhme approaches aesthetics via ecology, rather than art, and in the process he points out the problem of corporeality: perception that was traditionally a *sight*-based perception is understood from this other perspective as a comprehensive sensation that helps to describe the whole corporeal sensual capacity. Aesthetics returns to being *aisthesis*, the name for the entire spectrum of perceptual theory in Greek philosophy. The primary subjects of this general theory of perception "are not the things that one perceives, but rather that which one feels through perception" (ibid., 15). Thus, the central concept of a new aesthetic has been found: the *atmosphere*. This particular medium of transmission between subject and object is what Böhme attempts to define and to tame in his work, an ambition that naturally entangles him in a discourse suffused with the contingency of the subjective and the individual: his new aesthetic "is concerned with the relationship between contextual spatial qualities and human well-being" (ibid., 22).

It is not by chance that one finds in Böhme's formulations the echoes of both word fragments embedded in the term "psychoscape"—although unfortunately, their order is reversed.—[13]

13 A discussion related to the ecological approach Böhme takes to considering the landscape can also be found in, among other places, the concept of *Lebensraum* (lived space) in Franz Xavier Baier (Baier 1996). It would also be appropriate to point to the way these thoughts align with the understanding of landscape in the works of C.C.L. Hirschfeld, for whom work on a garden was without doubt the creation of an atmosphere using consciously applied means (Hirschfeld 1776).

In connection with my work, what is interesting about Böhme's concept is, of course, the move away from a descriptive framework for aesthetics based upon the aesthetic structure offered by the traditional pictorial concept and instead, his orientation towards a spatial definition of its goals. In the wake of this reorientation, landscape can no longer be described in visual, aesthetic terms alone, but rather as an *immersive*, experiential, sensual, corporeal phenomenon. Böhme's analysis is true of those elements that can be made responsible for the creation of spatial atmospheres and therefore rests upon categories that are immensely interesting for landscape theory: he examines nature above all as the source of aesthetic *experience* and inquires into the reasons why a human being would qualify that experience "as beautiful, sublime [...] as jolly, melancholy, as serious, sweet, gruesome, light-hearted" (ibid., 179).

According to the concept of *aisthesis*, things are not only assigned a certain expanse and a defined volume in space. Instead, they simultaneously emerge from themselves and *have effect spatially* beyond their expanse by asserting their presence in their surroundings to a greater or lesser extent. In this way, they trigger affects in the corporeally constituted human being. To name those qualities of things that contribute to the creation of an atmosphere, Böhme introduces the concept *ektasis* into the discussion: this designates the quasi spatial characteristics of things that "articulate [the] spheres of their presence," and in turn "are sensed in corporeal presence by human beings" (ibid., 34).

The second important insight gleaned from Böhme's work relates to the role of language and of the image. The dominance of language, which forms the traditional aesthetics of judgment, recedes in the new aesthetic in favor of expressive forms, which may be able to communicate corporeal experience better than speech and writing. Thus, Böhme's work offers valuable points of corroboration for the consideration of film. Inasmuch as film, as no one would deny, communicates *atmosphere*, it also expresses the *ekstasis of space*, just as the human being can perceive it corporeally and sensually.

The spatial *immersion* of the human being in the landscape thus completes a shift in which the landscape constitutes the sphere of the subject and his *experience*. The spatial concepts that apply to this condition focus on the experiential qualities of lived reality, in place of the geometric determination of spatial positions. These qualities are open to interpretation, both at the level of the subject and at the level of societal attributions of meaning. A true understanding of the dynamic landscape is based on the condition that the analysis allows for individual experience of and social discourse about a landscape, and works through its insights interpretatively and reflexively.

The Dynamic Landscape: Attempt at a Definition

The definition of the dynamic landscape also includes the *immersion* of the human being in his environment, in addition to the *sublation of the polarity between city and country* and *constant transformation*. The aesthetic of the relationship between man and landscape has liberated itself from the strict separation of viewing subject and viewed landscape object, in which the idea of an object confronts the human being as a unified entity. Georg Simmel held this characteristic to be fundamental for the perception of the landscape:

> To conceive of a piece of ground and what is on it as a landscape, means that one now conceives of a segment of nature itself as a separate unity, which estranges it from the concept of nature. (Simmel 2007, 22)

No longer merely an aesthetic and moral counterpart, the dynamic landscape is, according to this definition, to be understood as a *concretely inhabited space pertaining to everyday life*, and a place of social interaction and experience, that needs to be reclaimed.

To speak about the landscape thus means to establish a positive relationship to the social space of the lived environment. Contrary to the usage of such terms as "surroundings" or "environment," however, it implies aesthetic demands that—to speak in the language of phenomenology—facilitate a positive *corporeal* experience. The visual is the kingpin in defining the dynamic landscape, but unlike the case of the aesthetic landscape, its dominance is relative. The analyses of the filmic translation of the landscape in the second part of this work therefore consider not only the image of the landscape, but also the "invisible" qualities of the lived environment, which significantly influence our daily interaction with landscape.

Methods of Contextualization and Interpretation

The historian Carlo Ginzburg focuses on the problem of the traditional scientific paradigm of epistemology, which attempted to set itself and its conclusions apart from society's influence. The problem of the humanities and social sciences is their original task, formulated by Galileo Galilei, of serving as helpmates to the deciphering of "the language of the universe," which can only be accomplished by the natural sciences. For Galilei, the "letters" of which this language was comprised were "triangle, circle, and other geometric figures," not, for example, smells, tastes, or sounds.—[14] In many branches of science that fulfill a direct societal function—by which Ginzburg means in particular medicine, psychoanalysis, history and criminal justice—it is not so easy to eliminate the *individual* for the benefit of the general, as would have to be the case in order to conform to Galiliei's dictum. Even during

14 Galileo Galilei as quoted by Ginzburg (1989, 108).

his lifetime, it was evident that the "real obstacle to the application of the Galileian paradigm was the centrality of the individual element in some disciplines. The more that individual traits were considered pertinent, the more the possibility of attaining exact scientific knowledge diminished" (Ginzburg 1989, 111).

In order to deal with what is unavoidable—namely the individual and local knowledge based upon the "concreteness of experience"—so as to achieve a reliable epistemology within this context, Ginzburg proposes an alternative epistemological model. He calls it the "paradigm of clues." The "evidentiary method of clues" is "unconditionally" bound to the concrete, and thus, to the complex web of social and individual processes. Quantification is usually no more than a support function here, so that a "remainder of doubt" within the epistemological process is never entirely eliminated, according to positivist standards (ibid., 104). These clue-based methods do not work quantitatively, measuring or proving in a strict sense, as do the positive sciences, but rather qualitatively. Like a doctor who focuses not on the illness itself, but rather on its symptoms; like a criminal inspector who focuses not on the crime, but rather on the clues it leaves behind, so is every science that is based upon diagnosis— in other words, on the classification of a phenomenon (or a group of phenomena) within a category—bound necessarily to work with clues. It must furthermore understand these clues in relation to their context. The interpretive dimension of this epistemology is anchored within the person or persons who evaluate the clues. In most cases, this approach is sanctioned by society ("socially robust") because the diagnoses it produces are verified or falsified by reality.

Reading Clues: The Landscape as a Medium

The Swiss art historian André Corboz describes landscapes as a "palimpsest," meaning a surface that is repeatedly erased (although never completely) and rewritten anew (2001, 1983). Considered in this way, it is easy to transpose the paradigm of clues onto the landscape. The clues that can be read here point to different land uses. The geographer Gerhard Hard has followed this process exactly. In his botanical study *Spuren und Spurenleser* (Clues and their Readers), he explains the clues that he finds in vegetation, as artifacts that indicate the intentional and unintentional activities of human beings (1995, 117).

> The traces of nature are not merely facts of the natural sciences, but rather, they indicate something other than just themselves. In other words, they are (also and above all) *clues*. (ibid., 38)

Botany, as Hard practices it, is actually a ratiocination of social phenomena. It includes, implicitly or explicitly, that which human beings have contributed through the most varied forms of action. Only by recognizing the reasons behind the current form of a landscape can the pure act of looking at signs amount to an actual iconography or icono-logical interpretation. Signs become clues, according to Hard, at the moment when someone recognizes and beholds them as being signs; the reader of clues is responsible for the existence of signs (ibid., 63). Thus, it is the initial job of the reader of clues to decide which ones must and may be understood to be signs. He establishes the framework of interpretation by himself and thus becomes the active producer of his interpretations.

Understanding and Communicating through Narratives

It is worth noting that the moment Hard attributes meaning to a clue, when it departs from the strictly observatory mode and enables observations to lead to the act of interpretation, is also the moment the term "the narrative" comes into view. In an anecdotal example, in which a previously closed decorative lawn in a city park is transformed into an "accessible lawn" crossed by paths,

Hard moves seamlessly from the newly created accessible lawn to urban politics (1989). Along the way, he is able to tell a short story that introduces the place in the context of its genesis (and eventually, its further development as well). However, it is not only by means of an analysis of clues in the landscape, but also through their interpretation as *signs* that Hard arrives at *meanings*. He is able to rescue clues from the subtexts that intentional and unintentional human action has left behind at a place.

The "narrative explanation," as Hard calls the reading of clues, does not indicate a final state or active transaction, but rather the transformation of the landscape. This transformation is characterized by the interrelation of the two conditions, before and after, by means of an "appropriate description" or a "true story" (1995, 74). Narration thus becomes a way of reading clues by integrating facts and precise observations in a plausible overall form; it is a model that thereby enables the primary role of understanding and communicating the historical and social development of a landscape.

> The world of the reader of clues is not comprised of objects, as is the world of the everyday person, but rather of clues. The reader of clues creates a world from clues and, in the process, a world of narratives. As D'Haenens writes: Pas de traces, pas d'histoires; and one should really add: Pas d'histoires, pas d'histoire. (ibid., 70)——[15]

15 Here, Hard paraphrases Théorie de la trace (1984) by the Belgian historian Albert D'Haenens.

Gerhard Hard is not the only landscape scholar who focused on the reading of clues. André Corboz takes a similar approach when he speaks of landscape as a "palimpsest" that retains the traces of the various stages of its development over time. On the basis of these "clues [...] which remain of the territorial processes of the past" (Corboz 1983, 163), historical layers can be reconstructed and a long-term dimension can be reattributed to the landscape. The contemporary state of a territory is an invitation, if not a mandate, to read its clues and to see it "as the product of a very tedious and slow layering process, which one should know about before intervening" (ibid., 163).

In the cases of both Hard and Corboz, the reading of clues integrates physical material phenomena, as the carriers of meaning, into a process of transformation, and thereby into a narrative. In this way, the processes and actions through which contemporary topography was formed can be retrospectively reconstructed. The reader of clues is, in other words, a researcher within a complex science, in which historical developments must be represented independently of societal realities. To this end, plausible and contextualizing narratives are particularly appropriate.

The basis for the complex science of the dynamic landscape is thus the interpretation of topography as a semiotic system, which must be read and interpreted. In order to understand the current form of a landscape, readers of clues treat these as elements of a societal reality, which is formed by social practices. In a word, readers of clues approach the dynamic landscape as a *medium*. This leads to the medially communicated landscape, which is the topic of the second part of this book. The question as to which forms the filmic "narratives" of the landscape can take, and what role is played by the writing of subtexts, particularly in terms of what it offers for the artistic treatment of landscape, will be discussed using examples.

As an ethnographer, Clifford Geertz was faced with the semiotic problem of facilitating the description and evaluation of those processes, which unfold within a complex societal and cultural web of relations. He points to the fact that a description without interpretation is impossible within complex semiotic systems. As the interpreter of phenomena, the human being is himself enmeshed within them.

In the same way as Hard and Corboz in relation to the landscape, Geertz also makes use of terminologies and ways of thinking borrowed from semiotics when, confronted with foreign (and his own) cultures, he defines "culture" as a system of signs. And like these other writers, he also wants to use his observations and descriptions in order to reach a point where specific societal meanings can be attributed to specific actions:

> The concept of culture I espouse, and whose utility the essays below attempt to demonstrate, is essentially a semiotic one. Believing, with Max Weber, that man is an animal suspended in webs of significance he himself has spun, I take culture to be those webs, and the analysis of it to be therefore not an experimental science in search of law but an interpretive one in search of meaning. It is explication I am after, construing social expressions on their surface enigmatical. But this pronouncement, a doctrine in a clause, demands itself some explication. (Geertz 1973, 5)

To understand what a thinking human does is such a "kind of intellectual effort" and an "elaborate venture", according to Geertz (ibid., 6). The "intellectual effort" comprises taking into account the role and predisposition of the describing author, who himself is deeply interwoven into the culture's web of meaning. It is unavoidable that subjective, culturally encoded perspectives seep into any description. His recommendation for dealing with the contingency of this situation is the method of the *thick description*—[16]: arbitrary and often entirely fortuitous decisions become relevant if the position of the describing author is also reflected in the description. Transparency is the thick description's most important prerequisite. In order to understand and to be able to locate action within an observed cultural (and therefore semiotic) system, it is not enough to assume a purely phenomenological approach and method. Descriptions of cultural systems are already delivered in daily life in an interpreted form. In other words, they are "thick" and often assume a narrative form, so as to reflect the complexity of events:

16 See Geertz (1987/1973). For the concept of the "thick description," Geertz relies on the work of the philosopher Gilbert Ryle, who developed the concept in two essays ("Thinking and Reflecting," 1967 and "Thinking of Thoughts," 1971).

> Right down at the factual base, the hard rock, insofar as there is any, of the whole enterprise, we are already explicating: and worse, explicating explications. (Geertz 2000, 9)

In addition to the necessity of considering the interwoven nature of the person who is both immersed in the dynamic landscape and interpreting it from this standpoint, there is a second reason why Clifford Geertz's concept of the *thick description* seems appropriate as regards the rapprochement towards the dynamic landscape described in this book: this rapprochement occurs with the help of its *visual representation in film*. In other words, it occurs by means of sources, which make landscape accessible as an *already interpreted* but fundamentally *descriptive* narration. A (successful) film can thus already be understood as a thick description (for example, of a landscape).

In the quotation above from Geertz, I recognize my own position as a scholar who analyzes landscape by means of films (in other words, with explications of explications) and who attempts to "snatch from a fading moment" (1987, 30) the discourse that is taking place.

Working with Images

The Role of the Image in Landscape Architecture:
Speaking and Thinking about and in Images

The above overview of current landscape theory argues
that the image, as the bearer of information about
the landscape, has lost meaning, because a portion of
its representational role has shifted to other forms of
communication (for example, "narrative descriptions").
Nonetheless, *one thing* remains unchanged in practice:
any attempt to consider landscape involves images.
Furthermore, images are used when something is to be
communicated that cannot be easily phrased in words.
They can to a large extent replace the verbal form, for
example, if specific spatial qualities are to be developed:
to capture a spatial atmosphere in words is difficult, but
in images, it is incomparably easier to approximate the
quality of an experience. Images thus represent a fundamental communicative prerequisite to the design process.
Landscape architects use them not only in their work
process, but also often *think* in visual form. Without
images, the design of a landscape is unthinkable, because
without them there is no landscape, only environment
(Corner 1999, 153). The significance of the image in the era
of the dynamic landscape is, even if not entirely unchal-
lenged, at least still eminent.

Nonetheless, the possibility to work with images in landscape architecture is in crisis. It was James Corner, among others, who repeatedly diagnosed the fact that there is a defect in the contemporary practice of landscape architecture. Its pictorial culture has not kept pace with the changed visual culture of a society characterized by an increased density of visual information. Corner also identifies the crisis within the theory and traces it back to the contemporary theoretical approach, in which human experience and perception—as well as the interpretative power of such cultural products as literature, painting, music and architecture—have been largely reduced. One way he sees of overcoming the dilemma is a reintegration of poetic values, so as to redirect landscape architecture from its technological trajectories back to a path that is relevant to lived experience (Corner 2002). Corner emphasizes that images are the bearers of these values.

The landscape architect and theoretician Christophe Girot goes so far as to speak of the loss of imagination as the factor that hampers the work in his discipline:

> It is surprising to find, in an age where pictures are vibrant and moving all around us, that landscape architecture is experiencing an extraordinary loss of imageability. This can be plainly explained by the fact that we are now working and living in the absence of visual references that are congruent with today's environment. When looking at the mangle of unmentionable landscapes with no proper form or name that clutter our urban peripheries, our visual references are misplaced and lost. (Girot 2002, 49)

Thomas Sieverts, in his now-famous book *Cities without Cities: an Interpretation of the Zwischenstadt* (2003), shifts the problem to the societal acceptance of the new. Sieverts states that the problems of new urban forms cannot be alleviated using classical urbanistic means, instead, a tentative solution would have to start with the inhabitants themselves. In large portions of society, a contradictory simultaneity dominates between the new landscape, media-visual societal reality, and the static, aesthetic understanding of the landscape. Societal considerations can only be mitigated slowly, through the creation of role models. Sieverts therefore suggests a search for new dominant images, in order to make new forms of the city legible and acceptable. The difficulty of contemporary landscape practice thus comprises not only the development of adequate images in design and theory. The second challenge is to mobilize new understandings that counteract landscape myths deeply engraved into societal structures.

The task is to create a new congruency between the professional understanding of landscape, the dynamic imagistic world of the twentieth and twenty-first centuries, and a new everyday understanding of landscape. Only after this has been achieved will it be possible, as J. B. Jackson demanded, "to make orderly and beautiful" the dynamics of landscape transformation.

Landscape architecture has begun to tap into this dynamic: in professional circles, the way landscape is dealt with has been reconsidered reluctantly for some time. In some cases, one can establish that the images and concepts underpinning current design display a new quality, and take a dynamic approach as their orientation. Examples of this shift can be found, among other works, in Richard Haag's *Gas Works Park* in Seattle (1975), the transformation of a smelting plant in the *Landscape Park Nord* in Duisburg by Peter Latz and Partners (1994), or the Dutch pavilion at the Hanover World Fair by the architects of M V R D V (2000), which attracted notice. These projects testify to the application of a new understanding of how to deal with the landscape; but a new, comprehensive culture of images in landscape architecture is as yet only just beginning to take shape.

Eidetic Images

For two decades, James Corner has concerned himself with the question of landscape representation within and for design in landscape architecture. As the representative of an artistic, creative profession, he vehemently opposes the scientific, technical view of traditional landscape architecture and its logic of objectification. As a designer, he also cannot identify a great deal with the tradition of the "scenic landscape", since these representations overlook the "ideological, estranging, and aestheticizing effects of detaching the subject from the complex realities of participating in the world" (Corner 1999, 156). Distance and separation, the *loss of proximity*, is the ineluctable position of the human being in relation to the aesthetic landscape.

According to Corner, in an ideal case, (architectural) drawings should communicate "metaphorically," not as the "notational" or "projective" directives for action intended for the job foreman executing a project. Such images suggest landscape qualities, without immediately solidifying them. They do not attempt to show the visible world as it is (or will be), but rather to translate *experiential qualities* into the medium of drawing. They form a system that reveals the performative dimensions of a landscape project, avoiding reduction and immediacy in favor of interpretative density. Corner describes this kind of representation in comparison to the distanced view of the aesthetic landscape as follows:

> The emphasis here shifts from object appearances to processes of formation, dynamics of occupancy, and the poetics of becoming. While these processes may be imaged, they are not necessarily susceptible to picturing. As with reading a book or listening to music, the shaping of images occurs mentally [...]. A move away from ameliorative and scenographic *designs* toward more productive, engendering *strategies* necessitates a parallel shift from appearances and meanings to more prosaic concerns for how things work, what they do, how they interact, and what agency of effects they might exercise over time. (Corner 1999, 159)——[17]

17 By differentiating between "image" and "picture," Corner refers to W.J.T. Mitchell's Picture Theory, in which he uses the concept "picture" to describe wholly visual representations ("to picture or depict") and "image" to describe a broader send of iconicity ("to image or imagine").

The inclusion of qualities relating to the peopled, lived-in landscape that cannot be easily subsumed pictorially demands images that draw not only on the visual, but also on the mental side of their construction. Corner calls this kind of representation an "eidetic image," a concept that he takes from W.J.T. Mitchell (ibid., 161).—[18] The term does not signify the visual, representation of a future landscape; rather, the eidetic image communicates to the viewer the idea of the lived-world qualities of a planned landscape. According to Corner, an image such as this is far more productive than the traditional visualizations used in design disciplines, such as sectioning and planning, because it not only projects the future, but also demonstrates how a planned landscape will *affect human beings*. In other words, it is not enough to simply represent topographic qualities, but it is also necessary to link them to other aspects, which shape the landscape as well as our assessment of them. Rather than showing a landscape simply in an arbitrary present or future condition, it simultaneously *interprets* that condition relative to its context. Eidetic operations, inasmuch as they are techniques of landscape architecture for the representation and construction of new landscapes, comprise numerous components that include the visual, the auditory, the cognitive, and the intuitive.

Corner's quest for performative representational forms for landscape architecture focuses on an exemplary method for visualizing the complexity of the dynamic landscape. It seems nonetheless dubious to me whether "eidetic images" are in fact appropriate to the representation of precisely the performative components of landscape. They mostly visualize precisely quantifiable data regarding the behavioral patterns of entire societies. They can make social behavior, economic value, topographic classifications, or agrarian uses, accessible to both theory and practice, which can then work with them. However, the translation of experiential qualities—as they are expressed and communicated individually and in diffuse concepts—seems beyond their capacity.

18 Mitchell, W.J.T. *Iconology: Image, Text, Ideology.* Chicago 1986, p. 10.

With the analysis of film in subsequent chapters, another method will be presented that may be able to translate the understanding of the dynamic landscape into images. To this end, it is helpful to summarize the insights of this work thus far, and to formulate a catalogue criteria for an adequate form of representation. Three working hypotheses will accompany the argumentation. The catalogue of criteria and hypotheses serve as the basis for the discussion of the filmic dispositive in the third chapter.

Three Primary Factors of the "Dynamic" Image of the Landscape

One terminological note in advance: in order to keep matters simpler, I will call the visual representation I am pursuing the "dynamic image," in analogy to the dynamic landscape. In a book on film, however, it would be more appropriate to use the plural form since film, as is well known, usually operates with twenty-four or twenty-five images per second, but using the plural form can be quite tiring, and so I have decided in favor of the singular form.

A second note: with the word "image," I am designating a conceptual field that extends beyond visual representation and includes "internal" or "eidetic" images. This ambivalence is the source of both an inspiring proliferation of meaning, as well as a blurriness, which undermines linguistic precision. The description of the dynamic landscape is also marked by this ambivalence, since "landscape image" can also often be understood to mean the (societal) understanding of landscape, or, in other words, the *internal image* that a society *makes* for itself of the landscape. Representations are also always reconfigured interpretatively by internal images, as I have already maintained. I use the term image in the word's double meaning, to denote a mental concept in which visual representation and internal image work together. In order to distinguish between the two meanings, I use the terms "depiction" ("Abbild") or "representation" (which may also include the soundtrack of a film) to signify the purely visual representation of a landscape.

In the introductory outline of the concept of the dynamic landscape, three primary factors emerged, which are key to this new understanding: *sublation of the polarity between city and country, constant transformation*, and *immersion*. If transposed onto the culture of images, they place the following demands on the dynamic image: The elimination of the dichotomy between city and surrounding land means that the concept (and depictions) include not only "open" landscape, often also described as "green," but also manmade spaces with landscape qualities. In other words: *the image of an urban, built environment is also a landscape image*. It becomes landscape-like, for example, through the scale of what is represented.

The second factor of the dynamic landscape is *constant transformation*. This has material and mental components. In relation to its representation, different aspects become important in reflecting the perception of transformation and also a transforming perception.

The material components are comparatively obvious, since the dynamic landscape is conceived as process: by means of both human intervention and the natural process of growth and seasonal and life cycles, the landscape transforms itself continuously. Every gardener knows this with regard to what he has planted. The second demand placed on the image of the dynamic landscape is therefore that of *representing time*, without which the processuality of perception and topography cannot be depicted.

The perceiving subject's own movement is the reason for the transforming perception. Driving at high speeds, in particular, has created a qualitatively new mode of landscape perception. The expansion of private and public transportation, with its ever increasing velocity, has changed this mode of perception to the extent that an "end of the foreground" can be postulated (Schivelbusch 1977, 61): the space closest to the traveler disappears almost entirely from his perception, owing to the high speeds at which he shoots by.

High-speed travel also has the consequence that the human being is able to perceive distant spaces in relative temporal proximity, which produces a kind of overview or total view that was not possible earlier. Air travel offers this new perceptual quality to an even more extreme extent: once distant cities move into the temporal distance (and experience) of a morning commute. In addition, literal overviews are afforded from an aerial perspective. Le Corbusier wrote enthusiastically about the advantages of the aerial perspective in 1935. His delight dates to a time when air travel became a reality for human beings and reveals the degree of visual "shock" this new experience represented for his contemporaries. The overview represents a new pattern of perception: in lieu of concentration upon things close at hand within one's lived space, what emerges is the distanced gaze of an analytic subject, who, like Le Corbusier from the airplane or Wolfgang Schivelbusch from the train window, apprehends the abstract beauty and defects of the landscape on a large scale. *One's own bodily movement* as a factor of perception is an unconditional component of the representation of the dynamic landscape.

Beyond the growth of the natural environment and the varied forms of motion within the landscape, however, the concept of constant transformation also includes mental aspects. This first becomes clear if landscape is viewed as a semiotic system that is actualized and completed in society or in the mind of the viewer: the dynamic landscape cannot simply be comprehended as a topography of some visual form or other, but must be examined as a set of contextual phenomena, which have social meaning (historical, political or economic in origin). Only then can a place be understood in all its complexity. This means that for the adequate visual representation of landscape, both its image and its *context* are of interest, in order to reach a complex understanding of it. This context, which is reflected materially in countless traces left on the landscape, is often related in our society in the form of narratives. The *summarizing* of these narratives is a further precondition for the representation of a transforming landscape, in order to understand its *societal position*.

The third factor, finally, is the immersion of the human being. Unlike the aesthetic landscape, the dynamic landscape engages us as tangible *space*, which we, as active producers of our perceptions, internalize using the entire spectrum of our capacity for bodily experience. The immersion in the landscape replaces the aesthetically distanced gaze with a phenomenologically comprehensive, corporeal aesthetic. An adequate representation of the dynamic landscape must therefore suggest the *quality of experience* that the real space offers. It reflects the subjective and interpretive components of communication of the environment and makes the representation thus more transparent.

Secondary Communication of the Landscape

As a peripheral remark in her book *Die vierte Natur* (The Fourth Nature), Brigitte Franzen formulates a fundamental thought on our relationship to nature. This thought carries an explosive potential for the consideration of the image's function in contemporary landscape culture. In it, the relation to nature has become synonymous with the relationship of society to a landscape:

> The extent to which the perception of nature nonetheless functions especially as a way of looking at nature and thus does not require a space (of nature), or to which it can be constructed secondarily by means of communications media (image, photograph, film, television and cyberspace), would be equally dubious. (Franzen 2000, 20)

The discussion of speed demonstrates that the experience of landscape has in a certain way dissolved its ties to the real landscape, which is increasingly experienced through the window as a passing visual impression, with an equally muted background soundtrack. In comparison to the direct corporeal experience of a strolling pedestrian or of Goethe riding in his coach,—[19] the experience of the landscape from a swiftly-moving vehicle is, in a certain sense, already a mediated one. If containment in a train compartment reduces the passenger's contact with the landscape to a minimum, then the coincident viewing of distant landscapes, temporally compressed via rapid travel, has simultaneously enriched our experience of landscape. Seeing while traveling by vehicle has become a dominant mode of our landscape perception, as I have demonstrated elsewhere by means of a small calculation exercise (Truniger 2001, 17): assuming the per capita distance traveled over land in Switzerland—as reported in 2005— of 15,700 kilometers, it can be supposed that travel at high speeds is among the likeliest forms of direct daily experience with the landscape for the majority of people (or at least, for Swiss people). The most common daily perception of our environment seems to be a distanced and disembodied one.

Similar to the train, which initiated the new mode of seeing in the nineteenth century, two other inventions from that same century have fundamentally transformed our perception of landscape: photography and film. As with photography a half-century earlier, the early days of film saw countless cameramen trailing through the landscape in the service of such pioneers as Edison, Skladanowsky, or the Lumière Brothers, to film small scenes of everyday life and the landscape in which it was embedded. Over the course of the years, views of the most remote areas of the world were disseminated by film and photography around the globe. For the first time in history, the simple person who had never left his hometown experienced distant lands, not in words and

19 Goethe describes the experience of the landscape seen from a coach in the diary of his Swiss journey. Wolfgang Schivelbusch dedicates some introductory thoughts to that passage (1977, 51).

sparse painted or etched images alone, but rather, in the abundance of photographic prints, films, and narratives. This situation has become matter-of-fact today: the whole world can be accessed via films and photographs. It would be inaccurate not to accept these media-based sources as anything less than an essential factor affecting our relationship to the landscape. Every visit to a strange (or even known) region is tantamount to the pursuit of places that we already know from images and films before our departure. For generations now, our relationship to landscape has been based to a significant extent upon visual knowledge of the world provided by photographic media.

If photography revolutionized mankind's knowledge about the world's form, then it was the filmic representation of foreign places that introduced a decisive new quality: cinema not only produces visual knowledge, but also has simultaneously an inherent immersive quality, which was significantly more deeply felt at the inception of the film than it is today.

    If our relationship to landscape today is largely communicated through media, and if film fosters the immersion of the viewer in its fictional (or documentary) representation by means of its very disposition, then it is the appropriate form of communication for the dynamic landscape. I would like to formulate the synthesis of the two conditions as a working hypothesis: in film, the viewer not only perceives the landscape visually and aurally, but *actually experiences* it in a transformed state. Film facilitates a *secondary experience* of landscape.

At least in research on attention restoration, experiments have proven that this hypothesis is not utterly unfounded (Berto 2005; Berman 2008).—[20] But it will nonetheless provoke dissent: for the "walking artist" Hamish Fulton, for example, there is no work of art that can convey the experience of walking or hiking (Fulton 2001, 8). This experience comprises not only seeing and hearing, but also physical

[20] The psychologists Marc Berman et al. demonstrated that looking at landscape photographs has a similar effect on the reinstatement of attention as a circa fifty-minute walk in the Ann Arbor arboretum. The capacity of the experiment's subjects was measurably increased in both cases, whereas an equally long walk in an urban environment or exposure to photographs of an urban environment did not contribute to any significant difference (Berman 2008).

exertion, bodily exhaustion, exposure to the elements, and the inhaling of air and its fragrances of civilization and nature.

The concept of a *secondary experience* relative to film must be more precisely defined: it cannot be understood as the literal translation of landscape experience, but rather as the capacity of the cinema to connect memories to experience, through which a real landscape experience can be approximated for the moviegoer in his theater seat. In this way, filmic perception differs significantly from static forms of landscape representation. It is elevated above the level of perception to that of actual experience. It is thus entirely possible to agree with Hamish Fulton that the secondary communication of the dynamic landscape cannot ontologically replace the primary experience of nature. Nonetheless, the two appear to have important effects in common: revitalization, comfort, and the conveyance of an almost transcendental feeling of beauty.

Based upon this consideration, the benefits of a landscape film analysis should be reevaluated. It does not merely entail the quest for new working means to be used in the design and theory of the landscape. It also lays a foundation for new societal practices for the perception and consumption of landscape in an urban society that is estranged from nature and that has become accustomed to a life with surrogates. In a world where experiences of landscape and nature are largely conveyed secondarily, film appears to be the medium of choice for the "aesthetic presencing" (Ritter 1990) of the dynamic landscape.

Filmic Landscape Communication

Immersion: The Emotional Presence of the Moving Image

Cinema has created a new relationship with the world. It evokes past events in such a way that they feel like the present. We have learned to integrate filmic representations of the world into our own lives. As Walter Benjamin would say, we have become used to the mediated communication of knowledge about our world (1977, 41). The extent to which this is true sometimes makes it seem as real to us as a primary experience we have had while traveling. The most famous places in the world evoke a sense of *déjà-vu* in first time visitors, because they have seen them in countless films to the point where they were assimilated into memory. We travel to the South Seas on the trail of James Bond, to New York with images from films like *The French Connection, Spiderman,* or *The Naked City* in our heads, to Los Angeles in search of the locales from *Melrose Place,* and to the Alps with memories of Swiss folklore films or Bollywood dance scenes.

Many explanations have been offered for the participation of the viewer in the action on screen. Benjamin (1986) called the capacity of the human being to imitate animate and inanimate material the "mimetic faculty." The presence of actors, who are the primary figures of identification for the film audience, can inspire "somatic empathy," as Christine Noll Brinckmann (1999) points out. However, a consideration of landscape film, which usually dispenses with character-driven action, requires a more general explanation of the viewer's immersion in the action on screen.

It is important to ask whether a new form of sensual experience of the world has been generated concurrent to the new relationship to the world, which the cinema has introduced.

I think so. The connection of evocative images and the recollection of things actually experienced generate a secondary landscape experience, whose object is only present medially; nonetheless, the actual experiential quality is real. This proposition will be expounded in the following section.

The Experiential Qualities of Photography and Film

In her famous book, *On Photography*, Susan Sontag characterized "modern society" by virtue of its relationship to the image:

> [...] a society becomes "modern" when one of its chief activities is producing and consuming images, when images that have extraordinary powers to determine our demands upon reality and are themselves coveted *substitutes for firsthand experience* become indispensible to the health of the economy, the stability of the polity and the pursuit of private happiness. (2005, 119)—[21]

21 Italics by the author.

Sontag's analysis goes deeper than citing the omnipresence of images in the world: she defines the image as a *surrogate experience*—as a "potent means for turning the tables on reality—for turning it into a shadow" (ibid., 141).

Despite its true-to-life depictions, photographic technology alone was not initially able to adequately produce the feeling of immediate presence. Only when photography became serial in the form of film did it produce the potential to instill in the viewer the illusion of being present amidst what was being shown.

In photography, the viewer primarily perceives a moment in the past. The photographic image shows, as Roland Barthes observed, a "this-has-been" (Barthes 1981); in other words, it depicts without dissembling a scene that *was* seen exactly so at a specific moment in time from the specific perspective of the camera. When the photograph is viewed, however, this moment in time is always in the past. Even digital photography, whose manipulability rocked the ontological status of images as witnesses to a *"necessarily real thing which has been placed before the lens"* (ibid., 76), has still not entirely overcome the nimbus of the past, despite the second-by-second production of images.

Unlike photography, film makes action *present* by means of motion. There is no question that the original experience of this action (more or less what was experienced by the camera man) is past, but in the viewer's experience of the film, it is made current and given the capacity to evoke a new sensual perception, which conforms more or less to the original. Soon after the first films were screened, photography—as the carrier of images from all around the world—was faced with competition. The public convened in Varietés, where they enjoyed small scenes, which, at best, were staged as realistically as possible by decorating the theater. In *Hale's Tours*, for example, travel films made aboard a train ("phantom rides") were enacted by dressing up the theater to look like the interior of a train, including a conductor who punched tickets, thus creating a simulation of the spatial-atmospheric experience.—[22]

Although photography is also credited with a certain quality of preserving experience—Sontag, for example, says that, "photographs really are experience captured, and the camera is the ideal arm of consciousness in its acquisitive mood" (2005, 2)—it cannot be overlooked that at the beginning of the twentieth century, film began to overtake photography as the primary information medium about the world. This probably occurred because cinema

[22] See Raymond Fielding (2008/1968–69) and Tom Gunning (1990/1986). Gunning quotes the article "American Vitagraph: 1897–1901" by Charles Musser, which was published in *Cinema Journal* (Vol. 22, no. 3, Spring 1983, pp. 4–46).

proved better at satisfying the desire of the visual tourist for an experience than the practice of still photography, bound as it was to the past.

Phenomenology of Film

Repeatedly in the history of film, notice has been taken of the realism of filmic representation, which can capture life and movement and transport it to the movie house. In his essay "L'évolution du language cinématographique", the film theoretician André Bazin, a passionate defender of filmic realism, pointed out the discrepancy between ambition and reality as it has formed cinema since it began: black and white film, the absence of sound until 1927, the fragmenting effect of editing single shots, the limits of the image's frame and the significant fuzziness resulting from inadequate focal depth (2004). Nonetheless, despite the limitations of filmic representation vis-à-vis real seeing, which were only partially overcome over time, film was and remains able to produce its own form of reality. The Hungarian film theoretician and dramatist Béla Balázs describes film as the medium of an imminent visual culture, which can (once again) take over from conceptual culture and allow the *legible* spirit to become *visible*. The art of printing books had, as Balázs so pointedly formulated it, "gradually rendered the human face illegible over time" and forced "the other forms of communication" into the background (Balázs 2010, 9).

Balázs was, perhaps, the first phenomenologist of film theory. He did not, however, defend the fidelity of human perception, but instead the poetic transposition undergone by the soul of human beings and means by which film would give culture a new visual dimension and lend humans a new face. Film's expressive qualities would help mankind "[relearn] the long-forgotten language of gestures and facial expressions. This language is not the substitute for words characteristic of the sign language of the deaf and dumb, but the visual corollary of human souls immediately made flesh. *Man will become visible once again*" (ibid., 10).

This potential for artistic retransfiguration—the *stylization of nature*—is for Balázs nowhere more evident than in the image of the landscape (ibid., 52):

> Not every piece of land is a landscape. Objective, natural nature cannot be so termed. Landscape is a physiognomy, a face that all at once, at a particular spot, gazes out at us, as if emerging from the chaotic lines of a picture puzzle. A face of a particular place with a very definite, if also indefinite, expression of feeling, with an evident, if also incomprehensible, meaning [...].
>
> To discover, frame and emphasize this physiognomy from nature's puzzle picture is the aim of a stylizing art. The setting up of the apparatus, the choice of motifs and lighting, or the use of artificial lighting is the form adopted by the intervention of human beings in objective nature to create the indispensable subjective relation to nature. For art, it is only the animation of nature by the human spirit that counts. But the only things to be animated are those that express a meaning, and a human meaning in particular. (ibid., 53)

That which Balázs calls "the animation" in this passage is explained in another section. The "spirit of the whole," which the film director is responsible for capturing, expresses itself in the "mood." This effect is, as is well known, a characteristic relating to the subject and must first be objectified before it can be communicated:

> Like the mood of a landscape, the mood of an event can often be captured in close-ups of its smallest details [...]. A close-up of such moments makes it possible to convey a subjective image of the world and, notwithstanding the objectivity of the photographic apparatus, to depict the world as colored by a temperament, illuminated by a feeling. This is a projected lyricism, a lyricism made objective. (ibid., 44)

The close-up, which in essence allows the expansion of a film's field of vision, does not represent the pure human gaze, but rather an artistically interpreted "image" of the landscape, which with the mood (the soul) allows the meaning (the sense) of a place to be expressed. In this way,

Balázs claims for film the status of a means with which to translate the experience of landscape into a generalizable and accessible form.

From today's perspective, it no longer seems relevant to reduce the experiential quality of film to a single characteristic of cinematography. Balázs' vocabulary has gone out of fashion. Nonetheless, his work is an early example of the kind of thinking that points in the direction I took in the preceding chapter, in search of the representation of the dynamic landscape; what is at stake here is not merely the pure, visual aesthetic of film, but rather a more broadly understood, bodily gaze that contextualizes these phenomena. At the same time, it interprets them as the bearer of meaning; it takes into account not only what is visible in the landscape, but also the atmospheric, which can be made intersubjectively accessible by means of film.

The Kinesthetic Subject

Vivian Sobchack's work beginning in the nineteen-nineties also approaches the filmic experience with the assistance of phenomenological philosophy, and describes the human body and its experience as an active organ of filmic comprehension. Sobchack attributes to Maurice Merleau-Ponty's existential phenomenology the capacity,

> not [...] to exercise transcendental phenomenology's capacity for describing "essences" or demonstrating "universal" structures, but rather [...] to cry out my *inherent qualification* of the world of essences and universals, to allow for my *existential particularity* in a world I engage and share with others (Sobchack 1992, XV)—[23]

23 Italics in original.

Using the example of the film *The Piano* by Jane Campion (AUS 1993), Sobchack describes what she means by the physically inherent capacity of every human being to understand the world *as a body*. The opening shot shows blurry images in the first frames, taken at a range far too close to be in focus. In the following shots—filmed against

such strong light that they are still hardly recognizable—
they prove to be the primary character's (Ada) fingers and
hands seen from her perspective. Only in the third shot is
the situation made clear for the viewer: it shows a young
woman with her hands in front of her face from the reverse.
Sobchack describes her first impressions of the film:

> Despite my "almost blindness," the "unrecognizable blur," and
> resistance of the image to my eyes, *my fingers knew what I was
> looking at*—and this *before* the objective reverse shot that followed
> to put those fingers in their proper place (that is, to put them where
> they could be seen objectively rather than subjectively "looked
> through") [...]. From the first (although I didn't consciously know it
> until the second shot), my fingers *comprehended* that image, *grasped*
> it with a nearly imperceptible tingle of attention and anticipation
> and, offscreen, "felt themselves" as a potentiality in the subjective
> and fleshy situation figured onscreen. (ibid., 63).——24

24 Italics in original.

Already inherent in his existence as a physical being, the
film viewer has the capacity to understand the world *as a
body*. This understanding is not located in the cognitive
center, but instead can trigger a response at the subconscious level. A virtually unconscious understanding is
possible because the world and the human being share
a common material basis. Sobchack therefore does not use
the verb "to understand," but instead, "to comprehend"
and "to grasp"—words whose complex of meanings already
carry materiality within them etymologically. The affinity
of the common material existence to the filmic representation and its viewer is what Sobchack calls "the address of
the eye." For her, film is not only experienced by the eye
(she does not single out the sense of hearing), but instead
by the entire corporeal existence, influenced by the history
and the incarnate knowledge of the cultured senses:

> We are in some carnal modality able to touch and be touched by the
> substance and texture of images; to feel a visual atmosphere envelop
> us; to experience weight, suffocation and the need for air; to take
> flight in kinetic exhilaration and freedom even as we are relatively
> bound to our theater seats; to be knocked backward by a sound; to
> sometimes even smell and taste the world we see on the screen. (ibid., 65)

The consciousness of these "other forms in which our bodies produce meaning" is, nonetheless, so suppressed in normative terms by the hierarchy of senses and the primacy of seeing that the assertion of a prereflexive corporeal comprehension seems extraordinary today.

According to Sobchack, the body possesses the power to function simultaneously *literally* and *figuratively*. In other words, it can feel things that are expressed directly by its sensual organs, but it can also comprehend things that it only experiences indirectly (through media). Sobchack calls this subversive body of filmic experience the "kinesthetic subject," a concept that transposes two medical terms onto the physical condition of film viewing: *synesthesia* and *coenaesthesia*. The former, and more common of the two concepts, describes the ability to connect sensual stimuli across more than one sense—for example, not only to hear music but also to see it. The latter denotes, among others, the condition in newborns, which does not differentiate between self and world, nor among single sensual impressions, but rather perceives everything simultaneously and with equal intensity as an undifferentiated whole. In the kinesthetic body, the strict division between subject and object is sublated when the situation on the screen—for example, the preparation of food—not only makes the viewer's mouth water but also evokes memories, which recall the smell of a kitchen or the taste of fruit. Through the act of *seeing* the activity in the kitchen or how a dish is eaten, the viewer *knows* how the kitchen *smells* and how the dish *tastes*.

Sobchack offers a second reason for the immediacy of understanding experienced corporally by the movie viewer: the medium communicates with "lived modes" of perspectival and sensual experience, among which the most dominant are seeing, hearing, and the perception of movement (ibid., 74). In the apparent separation between body and sensual impressions, these modes are responsible for creating the feeling, which is experienced even more strongly in the cinema: that subjective/bodily and objective/visual (or, expressed in other terms, felt and rationally apprehended) impressions can influence each other in daily life. Cinema lives, in this sense, off the ambivalence of its structure, which simultaneously denies bodily participation while also enforcing sensual/perceptual immersion in the bodily address of its action, and thus exploits a fundamental (but not consciously perceived) uncertainty within the viewer's body.

The components of sensuality in relation to perception are made even more obvious in the work of the philosopher Merleau-Ponty, upon whose phenomenology Vivian Sobchack draws. Sensation is for Merleau-Ponty the product of the way "the senses communicate with each other" (2002, 262). The special form of synesthesia draws upon a level, which, as in the case of coenaesthetic perception, predates the separation of the senses. The communication of the senses cannot, for Merleau-Ponty, be explained by virtue of facts derived from cerebral physiology, for example, "by excitations ordinarily restricted to the region of the brain that become "capable of playing a part outside these limits" (ibid., 266). In order to do justice to the aesthetic experience, the dominant thinking and above all, the conceptual definition of sensation (which wants to speak clearly on behalf of every sensual perception: seeing in the visual, hearing in the sonic) must be fundamentally challenged. Our preferred model of thought to address how sensation comes into existence is shattered by synesthesia's perceptual modes:

> "For the subject does not say only that he has the sensation both of a sound and a color: it is the sound itself that he sees where colors are formed" (ibid.).

Merleau-Ponty postulates that synesthesia exists as an evident part of our daily perception, in a version that is hardly even noticed any more: the body and its "memories" form a resonance chamber for sensual stimuli, which invoke complex reactions and sensations. His examples make clear, however, that identification is not limited to *bodies* on screen. Even the observation of inanimate material such as a twig, water or fabric can lead to the recollection of corporeal knowledge and thus significantly influence the manner in which we experience landscape in the cinema:

> The form of a fold in linen or cotton shows us the resilience or dryness of the fiber, the coldness or warmth of the material. Furthermore, the movement of visible objects is not the mere transference from place to place of colored patches which, in the visual field, correspond to those objects. In the jerk of the twig from which a bird has just flown, we read its flexibility or elasticity, and it is thus that a branch of an apple-tree or a birch are immediately distinguishable. One sees the weight of a block of cast iron which sinks in the sand, the fluidity of water and the viscosity of syrup. In the same way, I hear the hardness and unevenness of cobbles in the rattle of a carriage. (ibid., 267)

The Haptic

Another term for the quasi-material impression that cinema can invoke in a viewer is used by the film scholars Laura U. Marks and Giuliana Bruno (Marks 1999, 2002; Bruno 2002).

Marks distinguishes between *optical visuality* and *haptical visuality*. Both usually operate simultaneously when watching a movie (Marks 2002, 2). The act of seeing is, for her, a "dialectical movement" between only visual and bodily, multisensorial perception. She borrows her central concept, the *haptic* of the cinematic image, as well as the distinction between optical and haptic visuality, from the art historian Aloïs Riegl and the film theoretician Antonia Lant, who was the first to consider Riegl's work in relation to contemporary film theory.—25

25 Riegl's relevant texts are *Stilfragen* (1893) and *Die spätrömische Kunstindustrie nach den Funden in Österreich*, 2 volumes, Vienna (1927). For Antonia Lant's consideration of Riegl's work, see Lant (1995). Before Lant, Walter Benjamin had already considered Riegl's work (1997/1936).

Marks develops her theory of the haptic mostly using video, and finds the source of its tactile qualities primarily in those moments when the image is characterized by disturbances, lack of focus, and reduced visibility in relation to the image of reality. To produce images of the world that approximate reality, the ideology of the medium is broken for a short time in these moments and the viewer loses the sense of control over the image. The "gap" that is generated can be leveraged to question the way realistic visuality is offered in the moving images. The concept of the haptic thus relies on special moments of cinematographic representation. These are disruptions in the filmic illusion, which mainly affect the texture of the image. The viewer's figurative reaction seems here to be limited to the realm of visual representation alone—an observation that was also made in a somewhat milder form in the case of Sobchack's example from Campion's *The Piano*. Marks' argumentation about the haptic quality of the video image is complete and convincing in itself, but it also suggests that the tactile perception of video occurs hierarchically after the primary optic perception—in other words, it is only operable where non-infringed seeing is no longer possible.

By contrast, Giuliana Bruno develops her concept of the haptic from her studies of the relationship between film and architecture. In her comprehensive work, *Atlas of Emotions*, she accomplishes a "Cartography of the Subjective" (Bruno 2002). Intended here is a compendium of those experiential qualities of architecture and film that decisively imprint themselves on our relationship to the world, but are usually omitted from scholarly studies because they are difficult to generalize.

The haptic, as Bruno defines it, is an emotional quality of space, which film shares with architecture. It is accessed initially by motion,—[26] because it is through motion that architecture and film produce meaning. She quotes the essay "Film and Architecture" by Sergei Eisenstein, in which the author points out the close connection of the two art forms in their capacity to create embodied spaces. Eisenstein claims that the sequence

26 Bruno writes "*emotions*" (2002, 64).

through the Acropolis is a prototypical situation for film (Eisenstein 1989). Both walking and seeing are, in a film, bodily actions: it is not only in an architectural ensemble that the human being is involved as a perambulating body. In film, too, the human is conceived to a certain extent in the same way. Using a play on words, Bruno closes in on her definition of the haptic in film: she relates the haptic to habitation, and thereby places filmic experience in direct proximity to the material basis upon which the human being lives and moves: "One lives a film as one lives the space that one inhabits: as an everyday passage, tangibly" (Bruno 2002, 65). For her, the haptic nature of a film is thus a reason for the feedback through which cinema conveys, to the immobilized body of the film viewer, the corporeal-spatial qualities of space as it is lived and used every day.

The Double Presence of the Body in the Cinema
as the Basis of Secondary Experience

The haptic medium of film is located firmly within the ambivalence of corporeality and subjectivity, which in everyday life unifies the sensual perception of the present with the fixed experience of what has already been lived. The transposition of sensual information from one canal to the other, as Maurice Merleau-Ponty postulates it with the idea of the synesthetic communication of the senses, or the power of our cognitive system to combine literal and figurative experience, allows us to "experience" the composites of the direct experience of watching a film and the corporeality of stored information. In this situation, consciousness of direct experience versus transposed sensation shifts towards the uncanny, and the *senses begin to communicate.*

The film viewer experiences an ambivalence, which is fundamentally of his own making: he sits, entirely motion-less, sandwiched between other viewers in a dark room, and stares rigidly ahead. He sees himself transported immediately into the film, but he does not entirely *lose* himself in watching. He knows at all times that his situation in the movie theater is contrived, but he can only remain conscious of this fact by force of will as he struggles against immersion in the filmic action. Thus, it cannot be contended that the double presence as body and as kinesthetic subject in the narrative space of the cinema is entirely dissolved to the benefit of the latter. The viewer is always aware of the double overlay of his situation to varying degrees of clarity. He also knows that the action, which unfolds in front of him and in which he feels himself transported, is not his own experience:

> Watching the film we can see the seeing as well as the seen, hear the hearing as well as the heard, and feel the movement as well as we see the moved. (Sobchack 1992, 10)

Of course the experiences of the viewer in the movie theater do not correspond directly to those in real space. He does not taste salt on his tongue when he watches a film of people at a dinner party consume oysters and does not have his life threatened in a shoot-out on screen, no more than he confuses the life endangerment of a mountain climber hanging tenuously between two carabineers with his own. He does not believe that he himself is standing on the grass when he watches soccer on the screen—but under the table his foot kicks along with the action. Nonetheless, the centering of the (decentralized) gaze offered in film occurs successfully; nonetheless, the immersion in the film's action is successful.

The experience that film shares with reality is not an actual sensorial one, but rather the *experience of an emotion*. IIt is not the bodily experience, which is identical, but rather the mixture of memory and emotion that the film's presentation unleashes figuratively. By means of the communication of the senses, connections are made in the cinema, which simulate real sensorial experience. At least, as a "thick" emotional experience, the cinematic experience is as real as the joy that overcomes the hiker on seeing his first rare plant.

Balázs was already of the opinion that film as a "medium of direct, embodied experience" was able to communicate subjective experience intersubjectively. In the words of Vivian Sobchack,

> As a communicative system, then, what is called the "film experience" uniquely opens up and exposes the inhabited space of direct experience as a condition of singular embodiment and makes it accessible and visible to more than the single consciousness who lives it. (1992, 9)

The projected film allows the viewer to re-experience the nature and landscape presented, if not of course physically, then in fact emotionally. Film thus conveys not only images of the landscape, but can also release the emotions relating to bodily presence and thus provide a more thick experience than static images may. In short, this means that, since the early twentieth century, cinema offers human beings the experience of landscapes, which they have never physically visited.

The question that remains is, of course, what is nature's function? The train of thought just described suggests that, as Rolf Sieferle has proven (1997), it not only relinquishes its position as the differentiating characteristic between various landscape types, but also its unconditionality as the primary experience of landscape it once offered for satisfying that particular desire for nature that has accompanied Western man at least since the Age of Enlightenment. The direct experience of nature for the purpose of recreation has today been marginalized by secondary experience in the form of artificial gardens or moving image media. Among the former are the gardens and landscape designs such as those by Martha Schwarz— who is famous for the Splice Garden at the Whitehead Institute in Cambridge, in which all the plants were replaced by their plastic replicas—or the reconfiguration of the former Thyssen mine into the Landscape Park

Duisburg-North by Peter Latz and Partner, in which the substance of the mining complex was retained and remade into an industrial park. The other form of secondary landscape experience is the subject of this book.

Motion and its Duration

As proven by the work of Sobchack and Bruno, motion on the film screen has consequences for the evaluation of the filmic image. Even Noël Burch, who cannot be accused of phenomenological thinking with regard to film described lateral camera movement as one of the primary guarantees for making the filmic image present, since it provided "tangible proof of the three-dimensionality of 'haptic' space" (1990, 181).

In contrast, Walter Benjamin offered another explanation: the viewing of a film lacks contemplation. While photography or painting allow the viewer ample time to lose himself in the image and to surrender to his "sequence of associations," this flow is controlled in film by the montage. Film exchanges its potentially nostalgic roots in favor of dynamic qualities.

The extent to which modes of reception related to the quickly moving image were still a cultural transformation for Benjamin and his contemporaries in the first half of the twentieth century can be estimated in relation to a conclusion drawn by Georges Duhamel: "I can no longer think what I want to think. The moving images have located themselves in place of my thoughts."—[27]

Duration is closely linked to motion, since every motion can only be appropriately apprehended by virtue of its duration. If an image in a film is entirely stopped (frozen), it regains the presence of a duration, which can unfold to a greater or lesser degree according to the length of a shot.—[28] One such special type of deceleration—stationary, excessively long shots from a tripod—emphasizes duration, understood as the

27 Georges Duhamel: *Scènes de la vie future*. Paris 1930. p. 52. Quoted by Benjamin in his first edition of the essay (1936, 39).

28 See Mulvey (2006).

presence of time's passage. Motion within the frame and its duration mutually structure each other. The human being regains a partial control over time, which he generally loses in the cinema, and images cease to assert themselves "in place of thoughts." Thinking resumes and the viewer soon begins, as in photography, to interpret the image contemplatively. The parameters of landscape experience derived from virtual and associative sources thus begin to mix more pronouncedly than they do in the normal filmic flow. As a consequence, the consciousness of one's own act of seeing develops. This can be observed in the most recent films by James Benning, which I discuss in the seventh chapter of this book.

Everything is Animate, Everything is in Motion

For the representation of the dynamic landscape, the medium's temporality offers the possibility of directly or indirectly depicting temporal processes. The following examples may sound banal from the standpoint of film, but for landscape architecture and theory—which I consider to be the "practice" to which the pragmatic treatment of film described here is directed—they deal with those aspects of film which have the capacity to represent constant transformation, a central requirement within the depiction of the dynamic landscape.

The growth of plants, upon which most landscape design is based, is certainly the most significant process of constant transformation. That which photography can only represent in a series of images, is inherent in film: to show transformation directly in real time, to show it as observed over time in a montage sequence, or to show the structure of very slow transformation in time lapse. The representation thus loses the original temporal dimension, but maintains reciprocally the overview of a process that is expanded over time. Like things seen from a bird's eye view, details disappear in favor of a clearly pronounced, superordinate structure. Thus, the seasonal changes in color and foliage growth can be represented in film as a continuous process, if with increased speed; the different water levels of the sea at low and high tide, or a mountain river during summer drought and snowmelt season, when shown in temporal proximity, make visible the fundamental landscape transformations arising from these natural processes. Accelerating techniques create a helpful abstraction, which assists in the understanding of the essential nature behind these transformative processes.

Processes with shorter cycles can be represented directly in film: their own dynamics, for example, continuously create new perspectives and spatial relations. As the human being moves through it, he accesses the landscape bit by bit as a spatial sequence: the relationship of objects to each other and to the viewer changes constantly, representing a permanent triangulation by means of the sense of sight. Motion is a spatially generative activity, without which larger (landscape) spaces cannot be understood in relation to one another.

Thus, the filmic representation of constant transformation in the dynamic landscape has clear advantages over static pictorial media because, on the one hand, it lends presence to the reception of a photographic image and therefore the character of an experience. On the other hand, motion can pervade the landscape as a space. Time can be reflected in abstract or realistic forms; it creates an important second frame of reference for the landscape experience.

Filmic Montage

Another central aspect of filmic representation is montage. Also a function of film's temporal structure, it creates its own form of motion, which does not express itself as continuous transformation, but rather as moving abruptly among different points of view (and temporal planes). It is montage that makes filmic perception fundamentally distinct from everyday human vision: suddenly, an image is disrupted, only to be momentarily replaced by another, as if the viewer had been moved to another place—but in a fraction of a second!

The degree to which this mode of seeing seems real, despite the fact that it is impossible for the human being to be transported in an instant from his location, or to make leaps that take him to the other side of the globe, reflects the extent to which filmic montage has trans-formed the way in which we see our world. I would briefly like to swap cause and effect around for the purpose of the following considerations, and not ask in what way(s) film can depict landscape, but rather how landscape's depiction in film has changed our capacity to perceive (and therefore understand) the landscape.

Above all, filmic representation of transformation in the dynamic landscape seems to me to be influenced by two functions of montage. In today's media society, one is familiar with them even as a child, to the point of internalization: perception of continuity above and beyond interruptions and fragments, and the production of complex meaning from a combination of the most varied visual and acoustic information.

Montage as a Model of Perceiving Fragmentary Landscapes

Fragmentation, resulting from the urbanization of ever-greater swaths of Europe, has become an important catch phrase. Landscape was radically transformed in the twen-tieth century, and the concept of the periphery emerged to designate the new urbanized territories between old centers. Once sharply drawn boundaries between city and landscape became blurred, urban structures flooded their surroundings to such a great extent that the edges of cities began to touch and in some places formed an utterly heterogeneous and continuous, but seemingly incoherent area of settlement. Neither city nor landscape, this new "cultural landscape" is an in-between, characterized by disparate functions and by discontinuities that resist homogenizing perception and precise nomenclature. Thomas Sieverts has appropriately called this new settlement form "Zwischenstadt" (2003).

One becomes particularly aware of the heterogeneity of this situation when in motion. The quick, abrupt switch between areas with the most diverse topography and architecture is typical of the traveler's perception of this new landscape. A residential neighborhood follows immediately upon an industrial zone, and a rather arbitrarily configured green space is located directly next to the drive-in belonging to the fast-food chain McDonald's. The German urbanist Kai Vöckler describes the scene as follows:

> The periphery is, to borrow a metaphor from Cedric Price, "scrambled eggs." It does without everything that was constitutive for the traditional perception of landscape. The disparate, distracted and transitory qualities particular to it do not configure themselves into an image, and cannot be understood as a whole. That which is repetitive and homogenous in its image makes it "faceless." (1998, 80)

The impossibility diagnosed here of forming an image of this "landscape without qualities," which would allow it to be understood coherently, refers to the tradition of landscape planning and urbanism in which the development of larger areas was structured with reference to guiding principles (Leitbilder). And although the concept of the Leitbild only aims for visual representation in a metaphorical sense, the fact is that in the architectural disciplines, it most of the time actually is interpreted with images; in terms of both society and the profession, images are simply best suited to communicating landscape ideas.

The only constant attribute of the twentieth-century periphery, with its topographic ruptures, is its continuous and rapid transformation; it is not subject to the unifying strategy of a Leitbild. Its status is only ever temporary; its essence is the pace of its transformation, its complexity and multivalent forms, which can usually only be understood individually. In order to grasp this essence, typological ruptures must be bridged, continual transformation followed, and both the individual and multiple meaning of landscape spaces apprehended. It is all this that makes the periphery the quintessential dynamic landscape.

Seeing while Driving

The perception of the periphery varies according to its use: its "user" moves quickly, because he is usually motorized. Topographic ruptures appear to him in the accelerated sequences and perceptual modes of driving, while the specific, exceptionally fast-paced economy of concentration allows him no continuous attention at all. The person in the automobile experiences the landscape as subdivided, in perceptual portions, from which unusual sights stand out.

The path taken by those who know a place and can orient themselves on the basis of a few landmarks becomes a kind of narration of sequential visual events. For them, individual landmarks do not relate primarily to one another topographically, but rather are connected via the simple, overarching "narrative scheme" of the path taken, which is structured temporally. In other words, the driver of the car perceives the periphery in a sort of unified montage, consisting of temporally sequential fragments.—[29] Today, as the mobile human being perceives the landscape, in most cases from the car or train window, this is true not only of the periphery, but of all regions accessed by transportation infrastructure.

An affinity between everyday seeing and filmic montage emerges: montage, like the experience of seeing at high speeds, can be described equally as the production of consistent meaning from a temporally distinct sequence of fragments.

As is well known, the unruptured impression of action in the cinema arises not (only) from the minute reconstruction of events in real time, but rather, for the most

29 Stephen Carr and Dale Schissler, in their study *The City as Trip* (1969), used the example of two stretches along two highways leading to Boston to illustrate how different types of viewers (driver, passenger, and commuter) recall the two stretches. They came to the conclusion that as early as the first trip, a set of landmarks were noticed and recalled. A change in these landmarks did not occur over time, through habit. The study subjects' gaze fell primarily on visually apparent "landmarks" that, according to the study, led to a sequential order along the route, which served to recall the stretch. The particular elements along the route were recalled with large gaps in the intermediary spaces.

part, through their dissolution into a series of significant moments of action. Continuity editing, for which the classic Hollywood film became famous, is a prescriptive catalogue comprising individual shots into which action can be structurally dissolved, in order to create the illusion of spatial and temporal continuity for the viewer. Even lengthier courses of action can be made understandable, if one follows this system, by means of a limited number of shorter shots that show the lynchpins in the action; what lies in between is shortened by means of montage, but then reconstituted into a coherent and apparently uninterrupted set of occurrences in the viewer's head.

It is not necessary to preserve the precise temporal sequence, but the sequence of individual action must be followed. In continuity editing, larger time leaps are also possible, without significantly disturbing the impression of continuity. These leaps are, however, usually characterized by visual markers, such as fade-ins and fade-outs. These markers belong to the comprehensive system of filmic codes, the deciphering of which is practiced, often subconsciously, by the viewer acquainted with classic narrative cinematic forms. Conscious seeing and recognition of specific elements within this code—and that also means the perception of the actual ruptures in the filmic continuity—require a certain amount of exertion: this is the unaccustomed concentration demanded for structural seeing, rather than the "normal" content-based way of seeing. It is possible to make similar statements for ways of seeing the landscape, in which we often only consciously perceive the "strata of memory" (Schama 1995, 7) and the aspects we already know of a pattern, which is predetermined by societal or medial conventions.

Object Constancy

However, the impression of coherence that our cognitive system is able to generate, despite ruptures in perception, can still be traced back to a deeper plane of human vision.

Sight, as sensual apparatus, possesses a physiological idiosyncrasy that makes the physiology of perception into a process of constructing continuity from fragmentary individual moments: because the eye only delivers a truly focused image within a very limited area and also loses its ability to see fully after one to three seconds when it remains focused on one point, it is forced to make constant jumps, so-called saccades (Yarbus 1967, 1, 129). These swift movements of the eye are not sensed by the human perceptual apparatus, since the process of perception is repressed for the duration of the jump (ibid., 1, 144).

Even at the stage of visual perception, the human brain thus practices daily the reconstruction of total perception from fragments, by repressing gaps and drawing conclusions about the ongoing sequence of a perceived situation. It seems logical to compare film montage with saccadic perception as Edgar Morin has done:

> The mobility of the camera and the succession of partial shots on one center of interest bring into play a double perceptive process that goes from the fragmentary to the totality and from the multiplicity to the uniqueness of the object.
>
> Fragmentary visions converge in a global perception [...] The perception of a landscape or of a face, for example, is a partial and intermittent operation of discovery and decoding—we know that reading is a succession of visual leaps from fragment to fragment of words—from which a comes an overall vision. (2005, 122)

The precondition for global perception from fragmentary visions lies, for Morin, in the temporal sequencing of visual information for both everyday sight and film. This could also be phrased as the shifting of what is fragmentary on the temporal plane, while simultaneously retaining object constancy (*constance des objets*). The constancy of the situation, which is (normally) a given in reality, provides the basis for the viewer's expectation of coherence in a filmic sequence, so that he can also patch the cracks in the continuous view that is constantly undermined by cuts. In the example mentioned above of the drive through the urban periphery, object constancy is established through the temporal interval between beginning and end, in other words, through the journey itself, which the human being experiences as unitary.

The filmic montage code forms a system that allows for the impression of continual action to be created from a sequence of fragmentary views; this impression is not limited by spatial or temporal ruptures. The reason for this is the shift in primary interest: the film viewer does not foreground the visual continuity of his sight-based impression, but rather the object constancy—in other words, the logical integrity of the action or argument. I will refer below to the concept of the "overarching narrative." I will also use the concept "story", but use it in a broader sense than it has in the usual sense of narratological terminology. This is because my analysis deals mostly with films that do not have a classic plot carried out by people, as is primarily true for the cases for which the terms "narration" and "story" were developed. I also use the concept of "action" in a parallel manner, for developments that are not related to human actors.

Schematics learned through watching films and predetermined by culture, in combination with individual imagination, aim to organize fragmented medial content into a meaningful system, despite all contradictions. The human being bridges, in radical ways, ruptures in his perceptual or cognitive situation, in the interests of satisfying his expectations of coherence. This observation can be transposed to the example of the driver in the periphery. The perception of a route one travels with considerable speed is subject to cognitive substitution processes that are comparable to watching a film: the driver, like the film viewer, must find his way in a fragmented environment. Above, I have already suggested that the driver solves this problem by "inscribing a story" onto the route traveled daily, in order to internalize it individually. The overarching narrative can be simplistic, filled only with a sequence of singular perceptions (usually of landmarks), in temporal sequence, with large gaps among them. Nonetheless, this narrative will almost entirely displace a detailed perception of the route over time. The driver notices the pedestrian who coincidentally crosses the street, or the new paint color on a house, but in the overall perception of the route he recalls and which essentially determines his relationship to the space traversed, they only play a role if they disturb or change permanently the flow of the overarching narrative.

The route taken therefore becomes a totality by virtue of its object constancy, in which single perceptions are positioned in a meaningful relationship. For the driver, gaps are filled because at all times he knows his position between two landmarks and therefore his position in relation to the entire route. He always knows at what point in the narrative of the route he is located. He can reconstruct the totality in his memory based upon the sequence of single perceptions, just as he can recite the plot of a film. It will seem complete to him despite the absence of whole stretches of roads, even though he knows that it contains gaps. By the same token, the moviegoer cares little whether he still remembers every shot after the film.

According to the study *The City as a Trip* (Carr and Schissler 1969), in which the perception of people traveling by car was studied, the overarching narrative of people with comparable visual preconditions is, interestingly enough, similar. Carr and Schissler discovered that the memory of the route traveled included the same landmarks for all the study's participants. Their results imply that individually acquired knowledge of a route is communicated intersubjectively by means of this significant consensus. As when watching a film, the perception of the fragmented (by driving fast) landscape has a basis that can be compared easily among most individuals. In both situations, individuality of experience and objectivity of the knowledge gained are apparently not mutually exclusive.

There is no doubt that the emptiness of the suburb
in Michelangelo Antonioni's film *L'eclisse* (Italy 1962)
reflects the emptiness in the relationship between the
protagonists. This conclusion is important for an understanding of the specific kind of filmic narration that
depicts much only through connotation. However: the
evaluation of the landscape is only peripheral to it.

It is equally correct that the reputation of the suburbs
worsened increasingly in the nineteen-sixties, because the
consequences of the functional separation that occurred
in the bedroom communities built after World War II had
begun to be palpable.—[30] The absence of street life in the
newly built neighborhoods gave the inhabitants the feeling
of being in the wrong place. *L'eclisse* refers not only to the
emotional void between people, but also to the urbanistic
development, without which Antonioni would have had to
find a different setting for his story. For the urbanistic
and landscape theoretical analysis of *L'eclisse*, its depiction of the "inhospitable" city (Mitscherlich 1965) as historical
document is more interesting than is the observation
about the situational parity between protagonists and
suburb—both conclusions are related, but their respective
foci are different.

30 Alexander Mitscherlich
(1965) coined the well-
known German expression
for these communities:
the "unwirtlichen Städte"
(inhospitable cities).

Landscape is often so prefigured by overarching narratives that its topographic form and wealth of historical
and social meanings are no longer really perceived. An
internal concept of any particular landscape, which has
worked its way from a societal consensus into the thinking
of the individual, draws a veil over what is actually
perceived and pushes contradictory factors past the
viewer's consciousness into a void. Even today, for example,
one can hardly expunge the thought that the Alps are
pristine, even though one knows (and sees!) that most of
the peaks are accessible via cable cars. Furthermore, one
encounters at each step through the karstic landscape not

only its use for herding, which has transformed the alpine meadows, but also the branching systems of hundreds of kilometer-long drainage canals and dammed lakes, not to mention military installations, that make the mountains essentially an industrial zone. The consciousness of what can actually be seen in a landscape requires an active confrontation with what is seen. It can often only be realized by turning away from myth-making narrations.

The second function of montage for the filmic representation of continuous transformation of the dynamic landscape is emphasized here: the production of complex meaning from a combination of the most varied visual and acoustic information—in other words, the production of (his)stories.

There are cases in which the perception of a landscape, as is the case with automobile travel, is mostly dependent upon an overarching narrative, which itself can be entirely independent of the actual perceptual situation, as Simon Schama has demonstrated in other situations (1995). In such cases, it is possible to find a new overarching narrative for the landscape to replace the old "official" reading, which exercises power through its corresponding appeal for society. Such a narrative can be introduced by film, among other means.

In this context, it is worth noting that *L'eclisse* embedded the suburb of the nineteen-sixties in a story that ties itself into the image of the city in a seemingly natural way, and thus becomes a determinative way of seeing it. The new narrative is inscribed onto the landscape and thus gives new form to our relationships to the place portrayed. Even more successful in this regard were John Ford's Westerns, which used powerful images to anchor the idea of the Midwest as the locus of white man's conquest. James Benning opposes this one-sided intellectual occupation by connecting counter-narratives to images with a potential for identification, similar to John Ford's (however, they are not as widely known). His reading of the Midwest, which I describe in my seventh chapter, can be understood as

directing perception and thus influencing landscape itself
as a medium.

The analysis of the dynamic landscape in the preceding
chapter underlined the importance of a contextualizing
point of view. The very image of the landscape that was
the central parameter of the aesthetic perspective has
lost relevance and has been replaced by a complex web
of information about the space we call landscape.

The film analyses suggested in this work consider—in
addition to the visual representation of landscape—additional factors that contextualize the image of landscape or
topography as part of a social system within a narrative.
They deviate substantially from the traditional manner
in which film deals with landscape: the focus is not on
the depiction of the landscape, although the landscape is
present in the images, but rather on the relation into which
landscape enters vis-à-vis other factors within the filmic
narrative. Film thus harbors a broad potential, which is
indispensible for the representation of the dynamic landscape as spatial construct: it deciphers its qualities as a
medium saturated with cultural information. The dynamic
landscape is not approached as an aesthetic object, but
rather as a medium of social processes. This understanding of landscape is largely independent of topography,
and is instead comprised of a web of societal relations. It
is a lived space that is identified through meanings and
structured geographically, topographically or typologically
by virtue of the filmic image. To capture it requires an
understanding of its shifting historical functions in the
society that produced its contemporary form, and of the
factors, through which the current value of a landscape
is determined.

For John Brinkerhoff Jackson, it was also clear that a
concept such as "place" cannot alone mean a topographic
locale in "landscape three," but must also include its
human inhabitants (1984, 155). Hence, its analysis deals

with relationships that lend a landscape meaning in a society, in other words, the effect that it has on the life and coexistence of its inhabitants. The analysis should therefore not only take into account a diachronic perspective on topography, but also the calibration of land price tendencies within global economic currents; the function of a landscape for the constitution of national consciousness; the reputation within the society of a specific region; and the myths in which it is shrouded. To no lesser extent should it consider the behavior and positive or negative reputations of the inhabitants who are identified with an area. There are infinite numbers of influences; their identification, evaluation, and calibration must be taken on case by case.

The conditions under which landscape is communicated come into focus. The meanings which society attributes to it, the content of communication about it, impress themselves on to real, material space (Lefebvre 1991, 1974; Bourdieu 1991, 1984, 1979). Materially and medially communicated landscapes are interlocked in a complex reciprocal relationship. The study of one is not complete without the study of the other.

[II]

Filmic Land Survey

Rüdiger Neumann: Learning to See Landscape

Seeing, just seeing, not rendering visible what is thought, but rendering what is seen thinkable. (Rüdiger Neumann)

Once in a while, there is heated debate about the question of the criteria by which landscape can in fact be judged. At these moments, one would like to argue with hard facts, to present numbers, diagrams, and visualizations that prove precisely which landscapes can be positively evaluated and which cannot. Economic and demographic analysis can succeed in reducing the complex system of relationships to selected qualifiable parameters for examination and in evidencing clearly single effects, usually social or economic development factors. However, as an *aesthetic* phenomenon, landscape is only understandable and describable within the framework of aesthetic discourse. This entails a competition among points of view, not measurable data. It is almost impossible to counter the accusations of argumentational arbitrariness coming from the natural sciences and, consequently, landscape architecture and landscape theory are at a disadvantage to the precise sciences. This unfortunate situation is known well enough from the humanities and culminates in the question of what can be granted the status of firm knowledge in these incxact forms of scholarship.

One possible reaction to the demand for relevant facts in the study of landscape can be seen in the tendency, present in the humanities (and also for example in art), to approximate the methods of the positivist sciences, rather than to emancipate oneself from them. This approach strives to create the signature of the scientific by applying a predetermined methodology. The motivation is largely two-fold: in order to gain credibility for their own results, or as an ironic commentary on the exacting way of working endemic to the positivist sciences.

In the history of film, too, there are multiple examples of a systematic approach to the representation of the landscape. For example, in *Inland Archiv* (CH 2003)—an installation video work by the Swiss artist Erich Busslinger—the author determined the places where he filmed through the arbitrary choice of postal codes. All in all, the archive includes several hundred one-minute-long shots. The collection comprises a pictorial section through the nation. The viewer gains a kind of overview from the kaleidoscopic juxtaposition of mostly mundane situations, all of which have one thing in common: they were filmed in Switzerland.

Another, if not the primary example, is the "structural film" (Sitney 1970, 1993), a genre of experimental film that devotes itself primarily to research into the formal aspects of filmmaking, and often moves between systematization and coincidence. In the late nineteen-sixties and, even more so, in the nineteen-seventies, landscape became one of the primary topics in experimental film. The most important films of this period—including the more than three-hour-long *La region centrale* by Michael Snow (CAN 1971), Chris Welsby's *Seven Days* (GB 1974), or Gary Beydler's *Hand Held Day* (USA 1974)—focus primarily on the technical preconditions of the filmic constellation for the depiction of landscape. Shooting and montage were generated by *a priori* rules that governed, for example, the choice of perspective or the camera movement, the moment of filming or the use of camera technique. A liaison with

classical traditions of landscape representation is only
secondarily important in these films.

The work of the Hamburg filmmaker Rüdiger Neumann,
although clearly indebted to the tradition of structural film,
distinguishes itself from the majority of "landscape films"
of this period in this respect: he was, from the start, as
interested in classical landscape depiction as he was in the
process of its production in film. This chapter concentrates
on his work and the development stages of his preoccupa-
tion with the image of the landscape and, in particular,
with the *aesthetic* of the landscape image in film.

Chance and Systematization

Rüdiger Neumann began his career as an independent
filmmaker with films that used a reductionist system to
satisfy a previously defined epistomological interest. In
the second half of the nineteen-seventies, he subjected the
production of images to a strict system, in order to ensure
a standardization of depiction and an independence from
the cameraman's aesthetic predilections. However, in the
course of his artistic development, Neumann distanced
himself increasingly from a preconceived experimental
structure. His subjectivity as author and observer of the
landscape gained increasing weight. By considering the
shifts in his work over the course of fifteen years, the
following will attempt to demonstrate the limits of objectiv-
izing the image of the landscape. Clear parallels can be
drawn between his work and the scholarly paradigm shift
towards transdisciplinary models of epistemology: from the
attempt to approximate the positivist tradition of science
to the development of an independent, free approach to the
landscape. At the same time, Neumann's work is, even if
unconsciously at the time, a witness to the shift from the
aesthetic to the dynamic understanding of landscape that
occurred simultaneously in landscape theory.

Zufalls-Stadt (GFR 1978)

Starting in 1975, Neumann set himself the goal of making a film about West Germany, which was intended as a series of postcards from that country for an artist colleague, Marcia Bronstein, who had immigrated to Germany from the US. Rather than concentrating on the tourist attractions, Neumann made it his task to film a portrait of "ordinary" Germany. The film was meant to capture how Germany looked at that time outside of the official images. Rüdiger Neumann describes it as follows:

> It all began with the fact that Marcia Bronstein came from the US to Hamburg as the girlfriend of my filmmaker friend Klaus Wyborny. I thought it would be interesting to have a pile of postcards for her from what was then the Federal Republic of Germany. It would have to show everything that postcards infrequently show, particularly the non-sightseeing sites, what is not generally known, the entirely everyday, whatever was not selected for visual or conceptual reasons, but instead, what became part of a sample through mathematical coincidence. I would then give Marcia Bronstein this collection of postcards when she asked me what Germany looked like. (Email to the author from May 15, 2005)

The resulting film *Zufalls-Stadt* (Chance City) marked the beginning of a fifteen-year-long, ongoing concern with the landscape as subject, which ended only in 1993 with *Stein/Licht* (Stone/Light).—[31]

As the title already implies, *Zufalls-Stadt* depicts ninety-eight places chosen by chance and organized according to statistical values. Neumann subdivided all the places in Germany, during his preparatory work, into groups with the same number of inhabitants, categorized according to demographic classes, which more or less correspond to what could be found on a geographic map. Thereafter, he determined the percentage of inhabitants in each respective class, as measured against the entire West German population. On this basis, Neumann attributed to each class the corresponding proportion of shots in the planned film. If,

31 In any case, *Zufalls-Stadt* is the first film that Neumann agreed to show at our meeting in December 2005. The work on his next project *Zufalls-Horizonte* (Horizons of Chance, 1980) began before the filming of *Zufalls-Stadt*. In 1977, he had completed his first version under the title *Zufalls-Topographie* (Topography of Chance), which he soon began to rework. The proceedings on this film are accounted for in Heim/Herzogenrath (1977). The locations of *Zufalls-Topografie* and *Zufalls-Horizonte* correspond to each other, even if not every location is evidenced in both films.

for example, 12% of all inhabitants of West Germany lived in cities with populations of between 50,000 and 100,000 at the time the film was planned, 12% of the shots in the finished film would represent cities of this size chosen by chance.

The choice of camera location in the cities was also decided by chance, inasmuch as Neumann chose two coordinates on a city map using a calculator. In small locations, there was, according to him, "only one possible location to film."—[32]

32 Rüdiger Neumann in conversation on December 2, 2005.

The sequence in which each location was filmed followed a determined pattern of twenty-four shots each. The camera was rotated 15° in a clockwise motion after each shot, and in the first shot, which is always due north, oriented horizontally. In the second shot, it is lowered 15°; in the third, it is again horizontal; in the fourth, raised 15°, and so on. In this way, Neumann filmed panoramas from a single, unmoved camera location. Strictly following this concept, each of these panoramas ends after the twenty-fourth shot, pointed to the sky; immediately thereafter, separated by a cut, another horizontal shot oriented north from the next location follows.

The length of the individual shots is different in each of the chance cities and also determined by a chance principle, which Neumann could no longer recall in 2005. He created a portrait of one hundred locations this way. In the finished film, they are organized demographically, with the first scenes taken in the smallest towns. At the midpoint of the film is a panorama from the Hamburg harbor, because Hamburg was then the most populous city in West Germany after Berlin, which Neumann excluded because of its isolated status. This panorama is shown not once but twice over the film's full duration, creating a caesura around which the locations are mirrored: from the most populated place, the film proceeds panorama by panorama from mid-size and small cities to scattered settlements, passing through the various forms of settlement back to the starting point. The second series of panoramas after the caesura was filmed at the same places, but not at the same time.

The Neumannian panoramas of the chance city have a very particular quality. On the one hand, they pan intermittently, not continuously. On the other, the view defines a sine curve between the extremes and middle values of the vertically tilted camera. This strangely nodding camera movement makes the horizon sway and the landscape glide by on the screen, so that the viewer's gaze is caught in an unaccustomed flow. Two levels of landscape representation are generated, two different visual strategies are open to the viewer: the *content-based* strategy tends to register the moment of the standstill and sums up the topography and aesthetic of the landscape representation; the *formal* strategy concentrates on the camera movement and the wave-like rhythm as part of a specifically filmic representation of landscape.

At first glance, these seem to be largely unspectacular places filmed at a single, arbitrary moment. The ratio between natural and built elements within the frame shifts in favor of the artificial and then back to the more natural.

A formal view focuses on the rhythm of the shots, so that a disruption in the consistency creates a sense of irritation: in one shot, Neumann seems to have made a mistake with the prior camera angle and the following image breaks the flow of the sine curve. The apparatus, which Neumann has placed on the camera, seems not to have functioned reliably in every case: a small piece of wire that carried a movable weight was supposed to "memorize" each respective camera position for the next shot. If the camera was angled down, the weight slid forward along the wire, where it remained in the next horizontal camera position as a physical reminder of the previous position. The fact that the camera may have been shaken as it was positioned apparently influenced this simple apparatus in a few cases, so that it kept a false memory.

While the up and down of the view is inevitably percep-
tible, it is more difficult to orientate oneself between the
individual images. The spatial relationship between two
consecutive shots in the panorama can only be created
through the identification of an element that can be seen
in the previous and following image. Every random point
within the *cadrage* travels from the right side of the frame
to the left within the three other frames, as it traces the
sine-curve movement of the camera in reverse. It is only
when the viewer can understand this movement that the
panoramic rotation of the camera is actually legible in
sequence. Orientation can nonetheless be slightly out of
kilter: if the cutting rate is less than circa half a second,
then it becomes increasingly impossible for the human
eye to receive the pictorial information of a frame with
sufficient precision to register the details. The points of
orientation, which led the eye from one image to the next
and enabled an understanding of the camera's movements,
are lost. Perception of a rotation gives way to a seemingly
unconnected sequence of images. At this point, both
strategies of seeing become obsolete: neither content-based
nor formal seeing still offers useful information. What
remains is a diffuse impression of demographic density.

Zufalls-Horizonte (GFR 1979/1980)

Neumann's next film *Zufalls-Horizonte* (Chance Horizons)
is quite similar in structure to *Zufalls-Stadt*. It is
conceived strictly according to mathematical chance.
Neumann used an HP pocket calculator with a chance
generator to choose the sites for his shoots. To do so,
he chose one hundred sheets from a full set of official
topographic surveys—the German equivalent of the US
Geological Survey at 1:25,000. He once again excluded
Berlin. In the second step, he used chance to select two
coordinates. As close as possible to the intersection of the
resulting lines, chosen through two chance operations,
he determined a shoot location.—[33] He then organized

33 Depending on the
nature of the terrain, the
precise determination of
the actual camera location
was not always easy, ac-
cording to Neumann in the
aforementioned conversa-
tion on December 2, 2005.
In each case, he got as
close as possible to the
cartographically precise
location. Furthermore, a
number of locations did not
correspond to the direc-
tions: in the completed film
Zufalls-Horizonte of 1980,
I counted eighty-nine locations, although one hun-
dred had been presumed.

the locations from south to north according to their geographic latitude and traveled for almost exactly a year (between March, 1979 and February, 1980) throughout West Germany to visit the one hundred camera locations one after the other from south to north.

The only times he deviated from the south-north sequence were because of the tight financial framework in which the film was created. He did not visit locations that were close to one another in the south-north direction in immediate sequence if they were far apart in the east-west direction, as the strictly formulated concept would have required. Instead, he first filmed locations that were slightly further north, but at a similar geographic longitude to those he had just visited.—[34] Thanks to this flexibility in the concept, Neumann could often visit more than two locations per day.

34 Rüdiger Neumann in the aforementioned conversation, December 2, 2005.

Zufalls-Horizonte shows not only geographic movement, but also temporal movement. While the first shots show a landscape still hibernating under winter snow, the light and seasons change as the film progresses. The film covers an entire year's cycle of vegetation and ends at the Baltic seashore—the most northerly point of the trip—again in winter.

The camera work at each location is also subject to a concept: once again, Neumann points his camera to the north and orients it horizontally. The following, again unmoving frames are each rotated 15° to the right respectively, without moving out of the horizontal. The last image of this intermittent panorama does not repeat the initial image, but rather according to the logical sequence of what would be expected from second-to-last images, it shows a slight shift before a complete return to the original camera position.

What population density was to *Zufalls-Stadt*, shot duration, which approximates a caesura, is to *Zufalls-Horizonte*. The first panorama is filmed with an extremely

low cutting rate: the shots are 6-5-4-3-4-5-6-5-4-3-...
seconds long, and the entire revolution thus lasts about
one hundred seconds. In the course of the film, the
rotation time is constantly reduced and at the middle
of the film, a full revolution is no more than six seconds.
The length of each individual shot is thus limited to
around .25 seconds. After this climax, the rotations again
decelerate until they have again reached the duration of
one hundred seconds at the end of the film. The film's
last image remains on screen for an unusually long time.
Unlike all the other shots, it doesn't end with a cut to
black, but rather a slow fade to black.

Idiosyncratic Panoramas

The particular form of the panorama in the chance films
is worthy of somewhat more precise inspection: next to
camera movement, the pan is a second fundamental filmic
strategy for representing landscape because, like the
former, it highlights the dynamic point of view and makes
topographic relationships visible.

Neumann chose a special, unfilmic form of panorama
for his films. He does not use a continuous sweeping pan,
but instead he subversively undermines the totalizing idea
of apprehending the visible world from a single predetermined point by intermittent still images. This kind of
panorama is clearly a construction.

The spatial consistency that a pan can claim for itself
is destroyed by the cuts between the individual shots.
The viewer is inevitably confronted with questions about
representation.

Instead of the dynamic of the panned image, Neumann
emphasizes temporal duration, in which each section is
shown, and in the process, moves closer to photography.

And finally, a complex relationship between subject
and the object of the view shown is another characteristic
of the Neumannian panorama. As a montage of stills,
its structure references the "transfixed moment" of the

classical landscape image. What is uncommon to it is the *fundamental separation* between viewing subject and viewed object (the landscape) or, in other words, the distancing of the viewer from the object of his aesthetic perception. It is only by means of this dissolution from his immediate space that a differentiation between the (lived) environment in which he *moves* and the aesthetic landscape, which he *views* from afar, becomes possible for the human being. The panorama is genealogically the exact opposite. It creates the illusion of the integration of the subject into the panoramic image. This singling out of the viewing subject makes the view corporeal: there is *someone* at the center of the scenery depicted. For the filmic panorama, the same is true: the viewer is implicitly represented in the image as well. At the geometric center of a perfect circle, he owns the privileged viewpoint of the representation.

In the intermittent form, in which the stills are strung together with jump cuts, the panorama nevertheless gains a paradoxical double form: as the "all-seeing perspective" of the 360° view, it draws the viewer's standpoint *as a corporeal subject* into the representation; and as a series of unmoving images—which, because of the rapid frequency of the cuts are no longer perceived as parts of a panorama—it simultaneously distances the viewer from the world depicted.

Here, the contradictory character of the whole undertaking represented by the chance films seems to be reflected: the goal is a view that eliminates the human, and thereby potentially conventional element from the production of the image. At the same time, the film is shot from a point of view, which structurally emphasizes this very human standpoint.

The Otherness of Neumann's Images

Within Rüdiger Neumann's work, the two chance films represent the most radical structuring of landscape and

are above all noteworthy with regards to the systematization with which they attempt a filmic representation of a
specific country. As described in the quotation at the start
of the chapter, the interest behind them is touristic: it is
an attempt to transpose the form of the postcard into the
filmic medium. Traditionally, the view used on a postcard
is meant to capture something worth remembering, or
something considered worthy of depiction. The postcard
in the recipient's mailbox is primarily a report about a
successful visit to a place worth seeing. In the ideal case, it
represents what the recipient should know in brief, or what
he already knows. Rüdiger Neumann's experiments work
against this principle of selecting significant scenes, which
essentially defines the postcard, just as it works against a
representative depiction of Germany. His films do not show
what is special or preselected.

But what do films show when they depict their locations
according to standard camera angles chosen by chance?
The places selected by chance operations are morphologically and topologically extremely varied: rural and urban
scenes, flat landscapes with broad horizons, and hilly
settings in which the camera is located on a steep slope,
revealing only the view of a grassy hillside. Neumann's
concept seems to have been successful: the mundane
is made visible, a modest and ordinary image of West
Germany that corresponds to an unprejudiced gaze
without aesthetic pre-formation.

The depiction of the ordinary, of the "not visually or
conceptually selected," is, however, a significant challenge,
since our seeing is in many cases so conventionalized
that it is virtually impossible to escape the standard. The
landscape is a subject in which aesthetic conventions have
been almost exclusively determinative in the choice of
depiction since time immemorial. As in hardly any other
tradition, there is a norm guiding the way landscape is
to be seen and shown in order to be acknowledged as

such. Georg Simmel's definition, for example, described the conventionality of landscape in our culture as "individuality" and "observing its parts as a unity", which is derived from nature by a "mental act" of the human being (Simmel 2007). Neumann attempted to escape these visual conventions:

> Through the consistent use of chance operations, conceived like mathematical chance operations, I wanted to avoid the learned cultural and pictorial concepts, seeing, just seeing, not rendering what is thought visible, but rendering what is seen thinkable.
> (Rüdiger Neumann, email from May 15, 2005)

Upon closer inspection, however, the individual shots comprising both films owe a debt to the aesthetic tradition of landscape: the shots, filmed with a static camera, all have a clear visual axis. They show a sharply defined, "attractively" framed (according to aesthetic criteria) section, a "unity" that "expresses itself in the continuity of temporal and spatial existence"—[35] by means of the panoramas generated one image at a time. In many shots, the horizon line is also visible, allowing the sky to enter the image as an important element of the classical representation of landscape.

35 From the definition of landscape in the aforementioned "philosophy of landscape" by Georg Simmel.

In addition to the static camera, the filming location seems to have played a role in achieving this effect. The system of chance operations—which, based upon the 1:25,000 survey maps, led to the locations for *Zufalls-Horizonte*—only generates seemingly precise points on paper. Within the actual topography, there are certain tolerances within which the film team works to choose the camera location. If, for example, the defined point falls at the edge of a forest, then this tolerance already implies an aesthetic decision about whether the camera is positioned inside or outside of the woods. In the same way, the topographical givens of each location influence the camera's definitive position: a river or highway can prohibit the positioning of the camera.

This variability within a limited range becomes even more obvious in smaller towns. There, as Neumann said in conversation, "it was pretty quickly apparent where filming could occur. In many towns there are only a few possibilities, perhaps one street, at which one can *really capture* the place."—[36] In these cases, the choice of camera position was dependent upon individual decisions. Despite the precisely formulated system and its narrow rule set, it must be assumed that the camera's position was located somewhat arbitrarily within a certain margin of error. Hence, it is not out of the question that cultural prejudice influenced Neumann's landscape images.

And finally, the choice of the camera lens used exclusively in both of the chance films also recalls classical landscape images: the short focal distance—[37] creates a generously framed image, which has a landscape-like effect. The subdivision of the panorama into individual shots emphasizes the relative power of the cadrage in comparison to a continuous pan. The use of a longer focal distance, on the other hand, would have resulted in a more detail-oriented shot, especially in the vicinity of buildings and other large objects.

A truly "other" depiction of the landscape, which remains uninfluenced by "learned cultural and pictorial concepts," cannot be found in the two chance films at the level of focus. Instead, the practice of the "unintentional" view is the source of their ability to create landscape images within the *formal* conventions of classical representation, which nonetheless undermine the *content-based* conventions. The montage of eighty-nine everyday locations, simply by virtue of their mass and the far-reaching *absence of the extraordinary*, becomes notable by virtue of its sheer quantity; the classical image form of the landscape remains present as a non-quotation. The extraordinary in Neumann's series of images becomes obvious only against the background of a lack of its counterimage.

36 Rüdiger Neumann in conversation, December 2, 2005. Author's italics.

37 Heim and Herzogenrath (1977) describe it as 10mm.

The learning curve in exercising the unintentional view can be observed through the years in Neumann's work. His films slowly free themselves from the system of chance operations, which forced the creation of images into a predetermined form.

The Construction of Paradigms through the Systematic Production of Images

The meaning of Neumann's early works, however, can also be legitimately discussed by focusing on systematization and the chance operations of image production as quasi-scientific means to reduce the images' contingency. What possibilities are afforded by this reductive instrument with regard to the perception of landscape?

By means of the exact repetition of formally identical shots at eighty-nine (or one hundred) locations in Germany and the restriction to only one focal distance, Neumann achieves above all the *formal comparability* of shots. He creates a *paradigm* through which, as in a visual grammar, different forms can be conjugated, all of which encompass the concept "landscape."

The intermittent panorama, the basic systematization, can be understood as a visual "part of speech," to extend the comparison to linguistics. Neumann himself writes: "I had the idea of creating something like a visual concept, with the help of fundamental filmic methods of depiction."—[38] This is a limitation of the filmic means as a way of achieving precision, which resembles a conceptual definition: a definitive, unambiguous visualization of landscape, in which the contingency of the real work and its visual representation are reduced. By means of temporal thickening of the images—analogous to overlaying data of different origin in the positive sciences—certain structures also become apparent. In this sense, Neumann's chance films function like a scientific atlas: they present "working objects" of a

38 Rüdiger Neumann in the aforementioned email, May 15, 2005.

quasi-scientific confrontation with landscape aesthetics, a typology of the German landscape offered as a standardizing gaze that eliminates idiosyncrasies and defines the scope of "normal" that can be applied to landscape. The power of standardization: the view that remains formally identical and that can rest upon natural and (more) urban topographies makes them all aesthetically the same. Why then would one wish to give the obviously similar views different names? "Landscape" seems an appropriate name for this kind of view.

Without wishing to overstate the degree or extent of influence these films have, it is important to note at this point of a well-known mechanism: the societal evaluation of a phenomenon follows the aesthetically normative power of a name given to it. Neumann's films are thus one tile in the mosaic, which the societal redefinition of the concept "landscape" has occupied since the nineteen-seventies in moving away from a near-natural towards an urban, artificial form. The formal proximity of Neumann's pictorial forms to traditional landscape representation acts in favor of this integration.

In the meantime, the conceptual identity of such topographically diverse areas has become a fundamental characteristic of our landscape concept. The perspective within which landscape is judged has shifted away from differentiating between different shades of the "natural"—[39] towards the question of scale: if in the past the scale was strictly defined by natural landscapes at one end and built environment at the other, this differentiation has become obsolete in relation to the dynamic landscape. Neumann's two chance films are early "symptoms" of the extension of the concept to include large-scale, unnatural built environments.

39 A rough scale within the spectrum between natural and artificial might be defined as landscape—cultural landscape—industrial landscape.

"Seeing, Just Seeing"

What is Charm? (GFR 1980)

Neumann's next film *What is Charm?* is based on an eponymous poem by Marcia Bronstein. The trail of images reflects two different planes: on the one hand, a poet who is seen in different situations reading her poem. On the other, views of urban to rural scenes filmed in the Hamburg neighborhood Barmbek, "in whose exact center" Neumann's desk was located in 1980.—[40]

With *What is Charm?* Neumann moved closer again to the strictly structuralist film tradition. The montage of images follows the sound montage, which derives from the poem's text. Contrary to the chance films, in which the relationship to language appears only implicitly in the paradigm of the production of images, *What is Charm?* is a linguistic game per se: Neumann analyzed the poem's text in advance according to word frequency, and attributed to each word one of the scenes filmed in Barmbek.

Temporal measure is given by the reading of the poem. At first, the film shows nine scenes from Barmbek which, with their original soundtrack, are shown for each of the nine sections of text. In the following sequences, single fragments of the poem can be heard. The soundtrack then includes only the most frequent words, such as "I," "and," and "ah" in a cut-up montage, while all other words are suppressed. The viewer thus gets the impression that the poem is minimal, made only of sounds. The image montage follows the sound and shows Marcia Bronstein in very short shots, in which she reads the parts of the poem that can be heard. In between, when no excerpts of the poem are being read, one sees an exterior shot with its original soundtrack. This shot is attributed to the unspoken word that in the poem follows the one just spoken by Bronstein.

The ratio between the two pictorial planes, Barmbek/ Marcia Bronstein, shifts increasingly because of this

40 Rüdgier Neumann in a letter to Alf Bold from January 20, 1980, in the Arsenal archive, Berlin. Here, too, one finds an indication of Neumann's predilection for geographic determinants.

structure, to the detriment of the landscape shots. The montage becomes faster towards the middle of the film, then decelerates towards the end again, when increasing numbers of exterior shots are replaced by images of the reading poet. The text is repeated fifteen times in fragments, the last time as an uninterrupted image of Marcia Bronstein reading. Slotted in between the individual cycles is a montage sequence of three shots, which remains the same: a street scene, the plaza behind the circus and an office building on a river.

As in the chance films, a kind of conceptuality of images is attempted here. If in the former, a fundamental method of depiction was attempted to create concepts (or word types), then *What is Charm?* relates images to words.

For the viewer, there remains the difficulty of not hearing the words to which images are associated and that the poem is only gradually accessible to him in its full length. Neumann does not think didactically: unlike Hollis Frampton in his pioneering structural film *Zorn's Lemma* (USA 1970), he does not prepare the viewer for the substitution of images for linguistic elements by gradually replacing letters (or words) with images. Instead, he replaces the images with words, which belong to a text the viewer does not yet know. The sequences of images thus change in each showing and offer no recognizable pattern.

Substituting individual words with landscape images, like the systematic order in both previous films, points to a paradigmatic function of images: images represent the entire world, like words, by means of the variation of basic forms. And like language, the meaning of landscape images also rests traditionally upon an arbitrary attribution. By choosing mundane images, Neumann points to this arbitrary relationship: the meaning attributed to landscape images of different eras is by no means inert.

Meridian—Oder das Theater vor dem Regen
(GFR 1983)

Neumann's next film is also underpinned by a precise prescription, which still concerns the choice of location, but no longer the shot. For *Meridian—Oder das Theater vor dem Regen*, Neumann traveled from Carrara on the Mediterranean along the tenth longitude east to Denmark. The journey traveled measures approximately 1,400 kilometers, and the film shows some 140 locations—which, according to Neumann's own information—were shot in ten-kilometer intervals, not more than ten kilometers east or west of the exact trajectory defined by the meridian. The imprecise camera location was subject to the filmmaker's measurements or was in part attributable to the (in)accessibility of points exactly on the meridian.

Neumann put the following text at the beginning of the film:

> When I was a young boy. I discovered a line in the pavement of the Alster Bridge in Hamburg, which marked the trajectory of the tenth meridian.

> I asked myself where the line would lead and what it would look like there.

> My longing for far away places was nourished by my grandmother, who moved from Hildesheim to Hamburg in 1965 and therefore counted for me and for herself as well traveled.

> I looked at the trajectory of the tenth meridian in central Europe: from Carrara on the Italian Riviera to Hirtshals in Northern Jütland.

> At the time of filming on *Meridian*, the American president Ronald Reagan said that, assuming the use of "Theater Nuclear Forces," a nuclear war occurring only within Europe against the Soviet Union was not unimaginable.

> Let us look again at where the nuclear theater might occur.

> Work on the staging continues.

41 The introductory text for the film has often been incorrectly quoted in one point. Instead of the sentence "Let us look again at where the nuclear theater might occur," it was often quoted as "Let us look at where the nuclear theater might occur. Neumann explicitly pointed out this shift in meaning to me in a conversation on December 2, 2005.

The second to last sentence of these introductory comments directly address the point of the film: "let us look again at [...]"—[41] *Meridian* is, like the two chance films, a phenomenological project. In fact, even more clearly than in both previous films, Neumann is driven by a political motivation. Given the threat, which was felt to be real in the early nineteen-eighties, Neumann wants to hold on to the place and time he *experienced* in his car before the possible catastrophe. *Meridian* is thus a kind of preemptive history writing, which is meant to serve as the memory of a landscape before its destruction. It is thus not only a cross section of Europe, in which the different topographies and vegetation from the south to the north are made apparent, but above all, the momentary capturing of a civilizing culture in the central region of Europe in the years around 1982–83.

What is new to Neumann's work is the free camera movement: the choice of location is no longer strict; the camera is not always static but often in motion; intermittent panoramas, which in part include flashbacks or "swish pans" instead of cuts, alternate with continuously filmed or singular shots of unspecific landscapes. The kinds of images and places, which have been chosen more or less consciously here, hardly distinguish themselves from the places found through chance operations in both of the stricter films. Once again, these are mundane situations and views: homogeneous landscapes without tourist or aesthetic emphasis, stretching across all possible middle European topographies. The practiced, unintentional gaze trained on the landscape seems to succeed even without strict chance operations in *Meridian* and in the following film *Archiv der Blicke* (Archive of Gazes, GFR 1983/84), which Neumann co-authored with Stefan Konken for the *Kleines Fernsehspiel* for the German TV network ZDF.

Images of Nature and Culture

With *Meridian* and *Archiv der Blicke*, Rüdiger Neumann's interest in cross-sectional films was apparently exhausted.

113

Even the titles of Neumann's two last films indicate that natural phenomena had become the focus of his interest. He exchanged Central Europe as his location for Scandinavia, where civilization grows increasingly thin as one moves further north.

Nordlicht (GFR 1988)

Nordlicht (Northern Lights), which Neumann filmed in collaboration with Stefan Konken, begins with a shot at dusk at the end of a street. This first shot is shown for almost a minute. The following shots are shorter, and they typify the film's programmatic development: out of civilization, into the natural landscape.

The second shot depicts a lake at dusk, on whose twilit shore a house is visible in the background. The next shot is shifted somewhat to the right relative to the first. The house has disappeared from view; in the prior image, the horizon was at the middle of the picture, but now it is on the lower edge. The third shot, taken with a longer focal length lens, shows only a cloud formation in the dusky gray sky, only barely bounded below by the woods on the edge of the lake.

Nordlicht develops its theme slowly thereafter, in calm, almost soundless shots. In sequences structured by location, the film initiates a journey characterized not geographically but rather by the landscape's colors.

Individual sequences show the green of a bright forest, saturated with sunlight and striated with the brown of wood and the gray of rock; the luminous yellow of an autumnal deciduous forest; the white of a mountain lake in snow; and the limey gray of a stony landscape. The colors are bewitching.

After some time, buildings appear again in the distance, only to give way again to luminous natural landscapes in longer passages. Smaller settlements appear in the distance, then intersecting roads and flat supermarkets with large parking lots in front of them. The snow recedes, the light is more muted. After twenty minutes, for the first time, there is a short sequence of the northern lights, which lend the film its title. Immediately thereafter, the film slips into winter, dominated by images of urban and agglomerative landscapes, filmed in an oppressive "unhappy, pale light" (Tode 2001).

This is a longer sequence, which collects joyless images of harbors or supermarkets, as well as street scenes. Only towards the end of the film do these images give way to a snowy landscape and the sun finally shines again.

The alternation between seemingly untouched natural
landscapes and cityscapes, which can only be partially
described here, demonstrates what Thomas Tode had
ascertained: Neumann did not undertake an "idolatry of
nature" (ibid., 123). Despite their often seemingly romantic
beauty, his images of nature are always broken. The
presence of human beings is not only visible in the obvious
images of civilization, but even in the most naturally and
simultaneously least hospitable (to humans) contexts,
Neumann shows traces of human presence. Snowdrifts
indicate the trajectory of a street in a seemingly endless
snow-covered plane; paths lace through woods; houses
and settlements can be discerned on the horizon, and
a telephone line runs through an austere landscape.

Unlike his early landscape films, in *Nordlicht*,
Neumann sporadically uses the ambient noise of human
sounds. Shots of natural landscapes thus immediately
suggest the presence of human beings. The noise of a
snowmobile seems overly loud and irritating after the
muted sounds of thinly settled regions; a man's shout
echoes across a seemingly uncultivated moor before a
house enters the picture frame. Still, it is not only this
form of deculturation of the natural landscape that
Nordlicht cultivates through the soundtrack montage, but
also a countertendency: in several shots at the beginning
and more markedly so in the final images showing
the northern lights, images of nature are accompanied
by music or restrained musical noises. The landscape is
transformed into a mystical and suggestive moment by
means of the soundtrack introduced: these moments are
snippets of a romantic attitude towards nature, which
are particularly alien given the sober perspective charac-
terizing the rest of *Nordlicht*.

Stein/Licht (GER 1992)

In his next work, *Stein/Licht* (Stone/Light), Neumann
does not use any obvious diegetic sound. The film, only

thirty-six minutes long, confronts nature in an even more radical way than *Nordlicht* had done. Once again, the first shots seem to have a programmatic character for the entire film: one sees a dirt road, which is soft from moisture amidst the sparse vegetation of Ifjordfjellet in northern Finland; it comprises essentially stone, moss and thin, stunted birches. The camera follows the road in the direction of the view, using a montage of motionless shots, each lasting a few seconds. The distance between camera positions is relatively large, so that the actual movement is not easy for the viewer to understand. As in the chance films' panoramas, motion has to be interpolated from the movement of individual elements within the image frame. Nonetheless, it is a movement into the deep space of the filmic image, which ends as the camera leaves the road and is engulfed in an extremely severe, hilly landscape of moss and other low-growing vegetation.

Fields of heather, edges of bush-like birch forests, and a landscape punctuated by football-sized stones do not indicate a single visible trace of culture. The trip leaves civilization behind, represented here only by a bad road.

Even more single-mindedly than *Nordlicht*, it leads into a region where the human being has no business. There is no one around; only the wind introduces a bit of motion into this inhospitable but breathtakingly beautiful landscape.

Stein/Licht celebrates the beauty and calm of nature. The placid montage lends the images a presence, which reflects the slowness and sublime quality of this landscape. A suggestion of romantic nature reveals itself in *Stein/ Licht* not, as in *Nordlicht*, in the soundtrack, but rather in the obsessive detail with which the wonder of the variation in natural form and color is represented. Using extreme close-ups of the smallest vegetative elements, Neumann shows how, even at its most austere, nature is still generous on a small scale and opulent in form and color.

Still, even if *Stein/Licht* remains devoid of human presence over long stretches and no larger settlements are shown—a loose settlement of perhaps fifty buildings with a harbor at the end of the film is the only hint of

permanent human presence—the will to domesticate the landscape through civilization is nonetheless visible in many shots: a stake such as those used to mark the road's trajectory in winter protrudes in the foreground; a log cabin stands in the midst of a woods; roads cross the most abandoned areas, demarcated periodically by telephone and electrical cables; felled birches wait for transportation.

This makes the greatest impression at the end of the film: unlike *Nordlicht*, *Stein/Licht* ends not with a series of natural images, but with the aforementioned settlement at dusk, the clearest indication of human presence in this inhospitable region. The search (in vain) for pristine nature ends with this image and accordingly, the circle from culture to nature and back is closed. Neumann himself described the film's development as the movement from culture (in the image of the dirt road at the beginning) to an "experience of light" and then back to the human being (in the image of the settlement),—[42] but the human traces even in the most pristine landscapes allow for another reading: *culture* marks the end of the film and relativizes the sense of pristine nature that the film seems to emphasize. In this way, as Neumann's most straightforward *nature* film, *Stein/Licht* is simultaneously a manifesto for the cultural penetration of even the most remote regions and the disappearance of "wilderness" in areas that at first glance seem, in their inhospitableness, unscathed and unformed by human hands.

42 Rüdiger Neumann in the aforementioned conversation, December 2, 2005.

Stein/Licht seems to echo an impression Neumann had while looking at a painting by Caspar David Friedrich:

> In Caspar David Friedrich's *Riesengebirgslandschaft*, he painted a tiny house, so small that it hardly has any meaning for the painting's composition. And in spite of that, it is so decidedly at a central point in the painting that one can never again think it away once one has seen it. (Rüdiger Neumann, email from May 12, 2005)

Even in the high north, in areas where "at least based upon appearances there must still be something originary, where nature is still itself" (Tode 2001, 124), the gaze is confronted by enculturation.

At the Transition to the Image of the Dynamic Landscape

In his time, Rüdiger Neumann was not alone with his view of the landscape, as evidenced by the early films of his Hamburg colleagues Heinz Emigholz and Klaus Wyborny, who were later to become influential.

Neumann's restriction on the gaze using a mechanistic filming method determined by chance operations is, on the other hand, unique. Unlike any other filmic oeuvre, his development over slightly less than twenty years to his final film *Stein/Licht* reveals an epistemological process. Starting off with the belief that conventions of seeing landscape could be set aside, a position that seems almost naïve from today's perspective, this process leads to an entirely different conclusion: at the end of his long, probing dedication to the landscape, the gaze, trained to see the topography in its mundane permutation, finds even in the most remote regions of the world the traces of human reconfiguration and thus the signs indicating the loss of pristine naturalness.

Seen as a whole, Rüdiger Neumann's work is located on a threshold: it stands at the transition from the classical aesthetic landscape to the dynamic understanding of the landscape. His works are not only interesting for the study of landscape representation, since they also took this step at the same time as, and apparently completely unnoticed by, the landscape theory that, motivated by John Brinckerhoff Jackson's texts, began to dominate the vernacular. Nor is it only because they document the actual condition of the landscape in this period. It is much more the case that Neumann's personal development also clearly describes the genesis of a paradigm through which land-scape is depicted today: initially, the filmmaker mistrusted his own gaze and his ability to "avoid the learned cultural and pictorial concepts." He therefore delegated the choice of location and the type of shot to a chance system, through which he hoped to train an unintentional, non-instrumental gaze by means of repetition and habituation. Only slowly did he let go of his self-made seeing machine and learn to trust his own gaze, now trained to see the everyday landscape. The subjectivity of perception and communication slowly assumes its rightful place as equal (and unavoidable) participant in its representation.

The result of the initial restriction is twofold: on the one hand, Neumann succeeds in standardizing his images, in analogy to a normative scientific experiment, so that they really do allow for universal applicability as is expected from a strictly reductive experiment. The landscape image in both films is still strongly marked by the classical landscape aesthetic: the filmic apparatus dictates the central perspective, which had marked landscape painting from time immemorial.

At the same time, however, Neumann appropriated for himself a new way of looking at the landscape, which was more independent from cultural clichés. By means of his training, he succeeded in partially freeing himself from the ballast of the cultural norms attached to the landscape image and in his later films, even without his self-imposed renunciation of formal liberties, showed the unspecific, everyday landscape free from compositional dictates. He freed himself from "rendering what is thought visible."

Ten years later, Simon Schama framed in words this independence from the experiences and conventions related to seeing, which Neumann struggled to set aside:

> For although we are accustomed to separat[ing] nature and human perception into two realms, they are, in fact, indivisible. Before it can ever be a repose for the senses, landscape is the work of the mind. Its scenery is built up as much from strata of memory as from layers of rock. (Schama 1995, 6)

The Pedestrian's Gaze

After these last few miles, I am aware that I'm not in my right
mind; such knowledge comes from my soles. (Herzog 1980)

Walking Perception

In the fourth century of our historical accounting, the
Greek philosopher Aristotle founded a school in Athens
in a grove dedicated to the God Apollo Lykeios. Lessons
were conducted while walking. For this reason, the school
soon received a new name: under Aristotle's successor
Theophrast of Eresos, it was called Peripatos, the school
of the walkers.

From Peripatos, a field of meanings and applications
for the concept "peripatetic" has emerged which, on
the one hand, encompasses the act of being in motion
without a goal and, on the other, includes the thinking
associated with it. Someone who is often in motion can be
described as peripatetic, as can the reader of a text that
is not linearly structured, but instead works with cross-
references. To follow a textual network of references and
perhaps to lose oneself in the process is understood as a
form of wandering (Bolz 1993).

Aristotle not only found a philosophical school in the
Lykeoin, but he also created a spatial practice, which until

today has been repeatedly deployed in various contexts. Walking is a form of forward motion that permits a spontaneous stop at any time, a change of direction, and the potential to consider not only what is worthy of being *seen*, but also the context and—not to be forgotten—the people one encounters. For this spatially framed wandering, which permits us the most complete bodily immersion in our environment, the artist and theoretician Guy Debord wrote the manifesto "Théorie de la dérive" (1976). Debord's text intended to return the city to the perceiving human for use. His "wandering" consists essentially in the description of urban atmospheric entities to which the human being exposes himself in the urban environment. The study of the effect created by these entities is what Debord named "psychogeography." Its purpose is to examine the influence the geographic environment has on an individual's perception, experience, and behavior. The primary instrument used in his experimental excursions is the body. The body reacts to emotions exactly in the way it leaves its mark on the dérive when it gets tired and begins to shun exertion, or will no longer accept exposure to the weather and ecological conditions.

Although it was established as a play-based form, the dérive had a concrete aim for the urban researcher: the creation of a kind of cartography to record atmospheric entities, (individual) primary axes of movement, and the fundamental structure of the city as a functional space. The subjective data from many samples is taken as the basis for a general image, which summarizes the city as a dynamic construction of daily use. The intention is to make "psychogeographical turntables," which surreptitiously makes the lives of city dwellers visible; contextual units are identified, although their specificity is not necessarily linked to the built environment, but instead resides in their atmospheres. The psychogeography thus comes to terms with the deficiencies inherent to the geographical cartography perfected in the nineteenth century: these show a city's topography and massing down to the detail, but nonetheless completely ignore its *spatial qualities*. The psychogeography does not relinquish the depiction provided by classical geography, but rather expands it by means of qualitative information on everyday human space, which deposits like sediment in one's experience.

Methods based upon subjective perceptual experience generally assume that all human beings are equipped with an, if not identical, then fundamentally similarly functioning perceptual apparatus and therefore collect comparable and cumulative sensual impressions. The individual maps that the dérive method generates also rely on intersubjective comparability and adjustment. The decisive image arises from the accumulation of as many similar maps as possible, if common (behavioral) patterns emerge that can be understood as expressions of societal praxis:

> With the aid of old maps, aerial photographs and experimental dérives, one can draw up hitherto lacking maps of influences, maps whose inevitable imprecision at this early stage is no worse than that of the earliest navigational charts. (Debord 1981/1958; 54)

Reference to the vague beginnings of classical cartography and its development from the unreliable observations made by sailors makes it clear that Debord took the dérive enterprise seriously, despite its playful approach. The goal of achieving a "constructive method of play" is tantamount to creating a new kind of insight about the city. A psychogeographical structure in which the "the distances that actually separate two regions of a city" are determined in a way that "may have little relation with the physical distance between them" (ibid.). Wandering may be aimless in its movement, but it has a method nonetheless. It has only been in the past decades—as architecture, planning, and landscape architecture arrived at the ground zero of an urban development based upon control—that Debord's seed seems to have germinated and the method of wandering has been more concretely reconsidered: as an expression of the confrontation with the complex sociology inherent to the urban development, which has become unavoidable with peripheralization. Walking is a practice cultivated in different ways in the work of the geographer Gerhard Hard (1970, 1989, 1995), the urbanist and sociologist Lucius Burckhardt (2006), and the architect Francesco Careri (2002).

Fragmentary Proximity

Walking is not only forward motion, but also a form of cognition. The pace is a human's natural velocity. Here, a body's identity and identification prevails with its tempo: "I know my speed just as I know the body that produces it," writes Paul Virilio (1978, 20).—[43] Its inextricability from the body, with its conditions and restrictions, produces a specific perception that differentiates itself from other perceptual modi inasmuch as it belongs entirely to us. While walking, the human being experiences his environment as a phenomenological adventure to which he exposes his entire body existentially. He is rewarded with moments in which he dissolves entirely into his environment and has experiences that are only possible through physical concentration.

[43] Translated from German by the author.

It is a gatherer's perception, not a hunter's, whose interest is focused on the distance in which his prey will suddenly emerge. The gatherer decides how long he will cast his gaze and he follows his nose. He is entirely at one with himself and his activity. His body is embedded in the environment, it becomes a part of it, and consequently his gaze is attracted to phenomena within reach. While walking, the body is all body, unprotected and exposed to the environment, which threatens again and again to attack him in his inadequacy. That which is close at hand is more acute than what is distant because it is more "threatening." With increasing distance, atmospheric stimuli pale and far-away sounds, even if physically audible, are cognitively blocked out.

Perception is detailed, but it is also selective. Especially in places as oversaturated with stimuli as a city street, the pedestrian's eye—like the collector's who schools his gaze—focuses on recognizing hidden objects using subtle clues and does so using as much time as it needs to interpret them correctly.

Selection and fragmentation are the primary characteristics of ambulatory perception. The French historian Michel de Certeau nonetheless emphasizes in his book *The Practice of Everyday Life* (1984) that walking not only imposes perceptual losses, but also opens a specific epistemological spatial potential. In the chapter "Walking in the City," he describes the view from the 110th story of the World Trade Center in New York:

> Beneath the haze stirred up by the winds, the urban island, a sea in the middle of the sea, lifts up the skyscrapers over Wall Street, sinks down at Greenwich, then rises again to the crests of Midtown, quietly passes over Central Park and finally undulates off into the distance beyond Harlem. A wave of verticals. Its agitation is momentarily arrested by vision. [...]
> To be lifted to the summit of the World Trade Center is to be lifted out of the city's grasp. One's body is no longer clasped by the streets that turn and return it according to an anonymous law; nor is it possessed, whether as player or played, by the rumble of so many differences and by the nervousness of New York traffic.
> (de Certeau 1984, 91–92)

It is *the* twentieth-century city par excellence that de Certeau chooses to be the object of his description: New York, planned in an enormous grid whose lines hardly bear any street names, but rather numbers and letters; a city of surfaces as if made for the panoptical viewing of those up on the 110th floor, who only see while impartially registering what happens below at an unreachable distance. The city of surfaces seems entirely ordered and organized, unchangeable, and stable. It is a fiction comprising comprehensibility and clarity.

At street level, a different city presents itself. De Certeau emphasizes the "certain strangeness" of the everyday (ibid., 93), based not on panoptical constructions and beyond the distanced view of an inanimate city, but instead nurtured by the practice of everyday life that peoples an inhabited city. Such cities resist legibility because they are too chaotic and multivalent for their entirety to be registered. They draw much more on knowledge of the place and the experience of pedestrians whose "knowledge of them is as blind as that of lovers in each other's arms" (ibid.).

It is walking that *generates* this city. Urban space is produced by the subject, by the body that relates itself to other bodies and perceives this relationship. Only a physical presence identical to the perceiving subject generates "here" and "there"—the most fundamental spatial distinction. In the state of unceasing decisions between spatial options, which we call "walking," the two shift constantly.

Corporeally engaged, the pedestrian is involved in situations that constantly force him to interpret what he perceives and to deal with the demands of the moment. This process of ascribing meaning transforms the associated space with every cognitive, will-based decision, just as the shifting of bodies constantly reconfigures space. In the act of walking, "a *migrational* or metaphorical city thus slips into the clear text of the planned and readable city" (ibid.). Maurice Merleau-Ponty described the difference between the two spaces as "anthropological" and "geometric" (2002, 1945).

Unlike the city of surfaces, the city of the pedestrian cannot be described in traditional ground plans and maps. Wandering cannot be represented in the temporal section topographic maps depict. Of course, the paths and places through which one has traveled may be drawn on a map, just as Debord's dérive demands, but the multiply drawn lines on the map "only refer, like words, to the absence of what has passed by" (de Certeau 1984, 97). Maps lack the "being in the world" and thereby the decisive element that lends the "act of passing by" its meaning.

In an analogy that is not only beautiful but also productive, de Certeau compares walking to a "speech act" (ibid., 97), a linguistic term describing the way any speech system is actualized by a specific act: from millions of possibilities, each speech act represents a specific way to use a language. It is different from others in its grammar, semantic and content-based phrasing, articulation and phatic meanings, which are carried as much by the manner of speaking as they are by the immediate content of the spoken words. By walking, we appropriate the city for ourselves, just as we appropriate language by speaking. The pedestrian makes a specific articulation, which can be attributed to his subject, but also follows an overarching grammar and the rules of the linguistic system (in other words, the laws of the city). It is the concrete application of systems, which de Certeau makes plain by comparing language and walking. The city is constantly updated by the action of walking and, in some cases, reconfigured by the needs resulting from it. As a consequence, walking becomes an encompassing societal force in a larger context: it influences the environment to the same extent as large-scale planning conceived at a structural scale.

Describing Paths

Thus, walking is an action, which transforms geometrically or geographically precisely definable trajectories into subjectively experienced paths. How can such paths be represented? One vague clue can be found in another passage from *The Practice of Everyday Life* (ibid., 119). De Certeau analyzes a study by C. Linde and W. Labov—[44] in which descriptions of spaces by their inhabitants were collected. The study showed that the majority of New Yorkers interviewed described their apartments in the form of paths. Directions were given as if the apartments were being navigated mentally. In opposition to that, there were only few narrations in map form, which operated with geometric locational descriptions such as "the dining

44 Linde, Charlotte; Labov, William, "Spatial Networks as a Site for the Study of Language and Thought." In: *Language 51*, 1975. pp. 924–939.

room is next to the kitchen"; this kind of description occurred in only 3% of the cases. Mentally, apartments are generally understood as routes—a direct translation of the daily appropriation of space.

For de Certeau, the depiction of space functions like an elusive description of small portions of a path (tour) and particularly noticeable items seen at each respective location (map). In one example, this combination sounds like this: "In front of you is a short hallway. Go through this hallway and turn left. You will see a door." To represent a path in language is thus nothing more than the attempt to create small units within an extended space and to lend each of them an individual order. De Certeau speaks not only about path and map, but also about walking ("spatializing actions") and seeing ("the knowledge of an order of places") (ibid.).

How can the perception of a pedestrian be translated into film? Before I look more closely at two films, I would like to offer some fundamental considerations on the translation of peripatetic perception.

The first order of consideration is the slow movement of the pedestrian and his eye for details. The relatively long and selective attention span in which details can be studied and, at the same time, the fact that the overwhelming portion of phenomena and perceptual stimuli are repressed is typical of this type of forward motion.

In addition to the necessary selectiveness with which stimuli are processed, another characteristic of human perception—which is particularly obvious while walking because of its bodily dependency—is the impossibility of *perceiving* without simultaneously *interpreting*: whatever our senses pick up is immediately evaluated in terms of its relevance for the subject. The pedestrian's gaze is never disinterested; ambulant perception constantly absorbs meaning.

Seeing at close range and the unhurried, concentrated gaze of peripatetic seeing can be more or less directly translated into a film's camera work. This can be accomplished, for example, by using close-ups and a low cutting rate, allowing the viewer to perceive the environment in detail.

Selection and interpretation—in other words, the fragmentariness inherent to perception—is translated in film using montage, which in itself is actually the organization of fragments. The way attention is guided by montage corresponds to the guiding interest of a gaze not tied to a place. The filmic cut also offers a parallel to the interpretive perception of real space, in which everyone focuses his attention on different things depending on his (visual) preferences and fixations, and puts other "landmarks" in the foreground: whereas for one person, a notable building is the central experience in "her" landscape, for another it will be a chance encounter on a simple park bench. The film has already made the choice between these options, and it compels the viewer to an entirely specific, pseudo-individual perception. Unlike walking in reality, there is in the cinema (in most cases) no "outside" that the viewer could alternately consider.

The filmic montage is thus an instrument for relating the "fluctuating" experience of routes taken. It creates small units as necessary for orientation: whereas the "spatializing action" (walking) can be represented both as shot in motion and as the ellipse-like cut between two reference points, the "knowledge of an order" relative to a singular point of orientation ("seeing") can be represented in an image. The question remains as to which orientation filmic fragmentation finally permits in its smallest unit: is it really a spatial orientation, or more of an orientation within the narrative, which is supported by the montage (within which space, too, might be accounted for)? This question can best be answered with reference to the analysis of specific examples.

Walking in the Cinema

The motif of walking appeared in the cinema as soon
as the camera became small enough to be carried by a
person. It is most common in *auteur* and experimental
film—although since the invention of the Steadicam, it
has become more common in mainstream film—where the
work process, which is usually determined by teamwork,
can ideally be reduced to one single person. The basically
lonely act of walking seems to have an affinity with this
kind of filmmaking.

Thus, for example, as early as 1927, Oskar Fischinger
walked with his camera from Munich to Berlin. He did
this not only out of sheer compulsion to move, but rather
because his business transactions in Munich demanded
a new start after his colleague had absconded with the
money from their partnership. Fischinger knew that he
was unable to repay the remaining debt. So he slunk away.
With his camera in his luggage, he decided to walk to
Berlin since his financial situation left him no other means
of travel. He documented his trip in a three-minute-long
film *München-Berlin Wanderung* (Munich-Berlin Walk,
GER 1927), in which several of the walking film's most
important motifs can already be seen.

However, because the majority of shots last less than half
a second (longer shots are reserved only for the passing
clouds), the true journey occurs *between* images. There
are only scattered sequences, which Fischinger filmed in
a way that roughly animates short portions of the trip in
a kind of stop-motion. For example, he shows his passage
through a small city with a splendid city gate in a kind of
cluster of brief shots, which create the impression of actual
movement. The majority of the images, however, bear little,
if no, relation to those that follow or precede them and only
show things, views and places that seemed to him worth
showing along his journey. Thus, the film's trip is represented almost exclusively as a sequence of reference points

that—viewed together—permit an (extremely coarse) orientation on the route between Munich and Berlin.

It is apparent even in this early example of a "pedestrian film" that Fischinger often does not show a landscape image at all, but rather portraits of people. Using close-ups of acquaintances made along his journey, he deploys their frequency and the close camera focus to document the fact that the pedestrian cultivates contact and proximity to his direct surroundings. His journey is thus not only a passage through the landscape, but an act of social movement.

The bond with the route expresses itself in other shots. An extreme top shot, for example, shows the muddy ground and, in the process, gives a small indication of the physical conditions to which Fischinger was subject. The route stretching before the traveler, which seems to extend far beyond the horizon, is also given its share of frames. Symbolic images such as these describe the dimensions as they were felt, relative to the distances to be traveled on foot.

The landscape shots can be grouped together. They do not show the world from a neutral perspective. The frequent appearance of roadside chapels and churches describe Germany's hinterland in the nineteen-twenties as a Christian region where the church literally stood in the village.

When it comes to actual landscape *images*, atmospheric details seem to have given the impetus to the shots: they show sunsets, light, and almost mysterious woods, or, for example, wind in fields of grain—places and moments that not only have an aesthetic effect on people, but also have a bodily component through which they appeal to the filmgoer. They communicate *aisthetically* a romantic feeling of well-being, a physical shiver or the recollection on a breeze one once felt on one's skin.

In this regard, *München-Berlin Wanderung* serves as a predecessor in the lineage of films to be analyzed.

They all treat walking as a physical action, which can only be represented by attempting to represent physical sensations.

In 1927, Fischinger had already approximated a repertoire of "conventions" common to walking films: among these are close-ups, semi-close-ups, and the interest for chance acquaintances made on the road; for faces, small gestures, and fragments of work that can also be found in a brief sequence in Agnès Varda's *Les Glaneurs et la Glaneuse* (F 2000). In this sequence, she juxtaposes the bowed posture of people gathering the remaining vegetables in a field with that of a city hobo rifling through the garbage at a vegetable market. Another moment is the image of the road, which vanishes in a straight line to the horizon. In the documentary essay *Spaziergang nach Syrakus* (Promenade to Syracuse, GER/AUT/CH 1993)—in which Constantin Wulff and Lutz Leonhardt describe their walk from Switzerland to Sicily in the footsteps of Johann Gottfriend Seume—this motif is repeatedly used. The film is subdivided into chapters, the first of which is entitled "On Foot." It opens with three sequential shots of the same motif: paths that vanish as straight lines into the horizon.

In *Spaziergang nach Syrakus*, there are more common motifs that cannot be found in Fischinger's film: the view from the edge of an asphalted, heavily trafficked road with which the marginality of the peripatetic undertaking is represented, and the evening or early morning view from the window of the room where the walker spent the night. And finally, the interest in the social conditions in the regions traversed, which had characterized the journey of their classical predecessor Johann Gottfriend Seume, who heatedly condemned the arrogance of the rich Sicilians for allowing their servants to suffer in the poorest conditions. Wulff and Leonhardt's gaze is also open to the society they come to know during their journey.

If walking and thinking are related (as Thomas Bernhard suggested in his seminal book *Gehen* (Walking 1999), and walking represents its own form of knowledge-gathering, then the German filmmaker Romuald Karmakar argues in a comparatively short journey on foot for the same relation between seeing and thinking. In a continuous shot at the beginning of his film *Land der Vernichtung* (Land of Annihilation GER 2004), the filmmaker walks with his camera along the long side of the fence around the former concentration camp Majdanek. As he does, he counts his steps. After seventeen minutes, when he has counted to more than 1,000, he has reached the end of the camp. Only then does the first cut occur. The rupture this sequence implies vis-à-vis the visual convention bears more than aesthetic meaning. By continuously walking for seventeen minutes, Karmakar not only stages an extremely disturbing beginning for his film, but also translates into film the dimension of the National Socialist's extermination of the Jews in a grueling visual experience. The relentless counting of steps echoes clearly the body count of the Jews murdered here. By marching along the fence, Karmakar finds an "image" that translates something not cognitively understandable into a physical experience—both for himself, who walked the stretch, and for the viewer who has to tolerate the torturously long shot in which nothing distracts from the horrors perpetrated by the Nazis on the far side of the barbed wire fence. The time the walker gains for his own thinking and the seemingly pointless and unchallenging activity turns against moviegoers, who had sought distraction. Karmakar compels anyone who *looks* to think.

In all filmic genres, there are certainly countless examples that make walking their theme; a more precise analysis of such films could be made fruitful for the work at hand. I have decided in favor of considering more thoroughly two essayistic films in the following section. This is because the reflective documentary film, with its tight weft of

135

image and text, objective and subjective perspectives, and often evocative (rather than explicit) forms of argumentation, is predestined to deal with both sides—the phenomenological *and* the cognitive perception of walking.

Peter Liechti: *Hans im Glück* (Lucky Jack CH 2003)

Since the mid-nineteen-eighties, the Swiss filmmaker Peter Liechti has moved between experimental short films and longer documentary or feature films. In a series of earlier short films (*Senkrecht/Waagrecht* 1985; *Ausflug ins Gebirg* 1986; *Tauwetter* 1987; *Théâtre de l'Espérance* 1987; *Kick That Habit* CH 1989), he developed his own craft as a cameraman in a way that visually characterizes his later films (and the films for which he was director of photography): Liechti uses his camera to search again and again for the personal in an image, to see metaphors, to find stories.

Especially in the internationally acclaimed artist's portrait *Signers Koffer* (Signer's Suitcase CH 1996), he demonstrates his artistic independence. *Signers Koffer* illustrates both the life and work of Roman Signer, and the approach Peter Liechti takes to an artist whose performances he has followed for decades with his Super-8 camera, and to whom he is bound by long-time acquaintance. His own "art" emerges in the way in which he depicts the artist's *personality*, his surroundings, and the circumstances of the filming, and allows them to become a speaking part of the portrait.

In *Hans im Glück: Drei Versuche, das Rauchen loszuwerden* (Lucky Jack: Three Attempts to Stop Smoking), walking plays a central role. The film depicts three hikes during which the filmmaker hopes to overcome his addiction. The simple program is reflected in an equally simple structure: the trip is repeated three times and at the end of each, the addiction is overcome—at first temporarily, then permanently. Each trip takes him from his apartment in Zurich to St. Gallen: "I grew up in St. Gallen. Where it all began, it's bound to find an end."—[45]

45 From the film's commentary.

The three marches traverse three different landscape types, because the journey is the reward. Eastern Switzerland, as the region between Zurich and St. Gallen is called, is well represented morphologically by these three walks: the northern route brings Liechti to St. Gallen via Lake Constance; the southern route leads through the foothills of the Alps and the Alpstein massif via Mount Säntis, the highest peak in the region; on the third hike, which leads in an almost direct line to its destination, he finally passes through the small cities of the Swiss plateau. Lake Constance, Switzerland's central plateau, the Alpine foothills and the Alpstein massif— this is the topography that adequately defines Eastern Switzerland. Above all, Lake Constance and the Säntis peak, visible from afar, are the two landmarks of the region on the basis of which it can be identified easily. A first layer of landscape representation is already achieved with these prominent views: this is Eastern Switzerland as a topographic and aesthetic spectacle.

But Liechti's interests are not primarily tourist attractions. As befits the radically personal motivation for this filmic undertaking, the film's gestures are radically personal. Rather than landscape attractions, Liechti documents the walks of a "homeless" person through regions that formed him culturally from childhood onward.—[46] Spoken commentary accompanies the flow of images and contributes diary-like notes and thoughts to the situations documented in the images. It instills order, identifies and interprets: the communications of a lonely hiker—plagued by nicotine withdrawal—who confronts his homeland and counters this imposition with incessant talk. The nature of this walk against addiction permits the camera to be used only at the pauses, whenever something appears that elicits the hiker's visual

46 Peter Liechti describes *Hans im Glück* in a fragmentary text on his website as a *Heimat* (Homeland) film for the homeless." See http://www.peterliechti.ch/page.php?en,0,13,0 (Accessed on November 18, 2005).

curiosity, or whenever the thought of a cigarette has to be overlaid by activity. The documentation has to remain fragmentary because the narration of the week-long sojourn follows the logic of a private relationship to the surroundings. At every moment, a detail can achieve particular significance or can evoke associations, which lead thought in a different direction. Reasoning—and with it, the filmic narration—slips occasionally from the visible world to the cognitively accumulated self, to recollections and growing internal images, which are visualized in the most diverse manner.

A visual and verbalized trace of interactions arises from this cinematographically experimental structure, an interaction between a constantly registering, lonely non-smoker and the exterior world. In *Hans im Glück*, the document of the author's emotional states and opinionated statements regarding the landscape exceeds greatly, in terms of realism, the topography that becomes visible. As a product of the walker's moods and vacillation, the landscape is subjectively connoted; it is presented in the train of thoughts described by the diary as much as in the images. It is also present in coincidental conversations, whenever an exchange occurs between dweller and landscape, and the viewer begins to associate both with each other.

Strategies of Subjectification

The experience of landscape communicated in *Hans im Glück* as a *filmic experience* must therefore first be considered by analyzing the strategies of subjectification. The types of framing and montage with which Liechti translates his perception are of particular interest in the following study. A second translation occurs between film and viewer. What does filmic subjectification offer so that the viewer is willing to acknowledge it as a plausible view of the world, even though this secondary perception of the landscape is not his own? And how is the reciprocity between "walking" and "seeing," between vectors of movement and reference point, translated into a filmic narrative?

A first general impression regarding the subjectification strategy in *Hans im Glück* can be derived from a brief sequence at the start of the film: a close-up of a full notebook, held by a left hand in which a cigarette smolders and the right hand, which guides a pen. In the background is a pack of cigarettes and an overflowing ashtray. One hears first only a high, synthetically produced sound, and children in the distance. As the pen touches the paper, a commentary begins: "In Mohammed's office at a frontier post to Angola, there was a poster on the wall with a skull and the inscription, 'Life is hard and then you die.'" The shot changes; one is looking down at a swing on which some adolescents are sitting and talking. The commentary resumes: "I've been smoking cigarettes for 30 years—all to my lungs, all to my heart." Once again, the shot changes. It is a close-up showing only the tip of a glowing cigarette. The sound of burning tobacco can be clearly heard. Finally, there is a fragment of the balcony from which the youths on the swing had been watched.

The ultimate form of subjectification is the use of "I." After a short tale from the border post in *Hans im Glück*, the film shifts to this "I" and stays with it for the rest of the film. The narrative's relative privacy is evident but is emphasized further by the image: one sees the hands of the person writing. The "I" of the commentary and the writing body are set in relation to each other directly by the simultaneity of writing and speech. This relationship does not remain abstract; instead, it is concrete in many of the film's shots (for example in the recurrent top shot of the walking feet). The camera's point of view plays along: the view of the notebook corresponds to the writer's subjective view. Finally, the story about the poster in the Angolan border post: the concise sentence "Life is hard and then you die" indicates on the one hand the essential theme of *Hans im Glück* and its author, one that can be read on every cigarette package: smoking kills. But at the same time, this beginning reveals the film's approach to (sound) montage. Angola, the poster, smoking, and Eastern Switzerland are associatively linked as they only can be in the consciousness of an individual.

Even before the film's title, four subjectivizing elements can be found:
— the "I" perspective of the commentary;
— the identity of the walker/filmmaker;
— the subjective view of the camera;
— the freedom of the dramaturgy to play with associations.

The Identification of the Narrating Voice and the Walker

The attribution of the commentary voice to the walker, which occurs through the use of "I," quickly becomes concrete during the film and allows the identification of Peter Liechti as a subjective narrator. The first reason for this can be found outside of the film. Only in the rarest cases do we see a film without prior knowledge, because the common facts are already known before the screening: general information about the production year and the author, the theme with which it deals. The pre-filmic knowledge about authorship contributes to a conscious decision that both the voice of the first person narrator and the writing and walking limbs belong to Peter Liechti.

At first, this is only a probable assumption, nourished by the suggestive simultaneity of writing and speaking in the shot, which shows the handwriting. The view of the hands and feet contributes a visible corporeality to the commentary's "I," which again indicates subjectivity. The shot of the feet becomes a leitmotiv that again and again recalls the embodiment of the view.

The hiker's identity becomes explicit when the automatic passport photo machine in the Winterthur train station

spits out Liechti's likeness on the first trek. With this quasi-official identification of the hiker (repeated somewhat later by a self-portrait in a mirror), the narrator's status is permanently changed: the film's statements have become grounded, calculable and, in a certain way, verifiable. From now on, the commentary voice can implicitly be attributed to the author and a real person.

This identification of voice, hiker, and author prove to be quite stable despite several disruptions. If one listens carefully, it becomes evident that the narrator's intonation and that of the hiker, heard in several chance meetings behind the camera, are not identical. In fact, during the credits, the narrator is identified as Hanspeter Müller. The dissonance between the commentary voice and the hiker's remains undiscovered in many cases, because the viewer has no reason to doubt their unity. Even if the intonations are not congruent, all other subjectivizing signals are so clear that they bridge this gap. Without hesitation, the viewer accepts the commentary as the author's statements, even if they are read by a professional voice.

Camera Style and Montage

Visually, the top shot of the hiker's feet, the shot of the writing hand, and the photo from the machine are the most important indications for the subjectivizing function of the camera work. This serves to identify the hiker and to anchor the action in Liechti's personal experience. The film thus creates for itself a reliable narrator: a person who really exists, with a body and sensations, just like we have.

But is it not only these shots, which suggest a personal point of view to us. It is a general characteristic of Liechti's camera style to insert individualizing components of image production into his shots. Especially the frames, which divert attention to chance meetings and details, are marked as "subjective." The gaze is, however, not only subjective; it is also bodily: the camera assumes only perspectives, which correspond to human sight. It never shows generalizing, overview-like perspectives taken from points that a corporeal human being could not simply assume. The shots always communicate the impression of the earth-bound nature of a real body: the slightly low perspective of a seated person on his surroundings, or the view from above onto the hands of someone sitting opposite are examples for these perspectives, which are easily identified relative to body-bound viewpoints.

Above and beyond that, the field of the shot transposes everyday proximity and distance, and emphasizes the affinity between these views and our own perception—in conformity with social practices, which determine what distances between bodies have been deemed appropriate. Behind the camera's position, a human body is palpable because the point of view corresponds to our body: we know the perspective from the back of a city bus, with empty rows of seats in front of us stretching up to the driver. Or the hasty sprint along a dark, damp pedestrian underpass—we know these views *as we know the body that produces them*, to repeat in modified form the Paul Virilio quotation cited before. The corporeality of these shots communicates with us more than visually, because we have experienced comparable situations *bodily* ourselves and empathize with them in the cinema.

Above and beyond the two forms of body-related shots, *Hans im Glück* also includes shots that do not offer direct indications of actual presence and nonetheless seem

143

attributable to a subject. The impression of seeing a specific perspective represented ensues only after viewing a series of shots: a camera style that does not change—a way of looking that stays similar—allows for the registration of visual interest and the impression of a coherent attention to the environment, which seems to indicate a single individual behind the camera. The camera style here is not corporeal, in the sense of a body-centered point of view, but the emergent "handwriting" points clearly to the gaze of a confident, experienced cameraman. The view can be attributed to a subject interested in the small gestures inherent to immediate proximity. Its significance rests not on what is depicted, but rather on the fact that it refers to the personality that thought such things worth recording. It simultaneously describes the world *and* the person who perceived it. Subjectivity reveals itself in *Hans im Glück*, however, not only in the images; it can even more easily be found in the film's narrative structures.

Landscape as Navigational Directions: "Seeing" and "Walking"

The landscape is *narrated* in a mode of radical solipsism much more than it is *shown*. This is particularly clear in a montage of paths that are traversed while walking.

As in the aforementioned depiction of the New York apartments, sequences alternate between "movement images"—[47] and views of significant places, which allow

47 The concept of "movement images" is used here in its literal meaning as an image which depicts movement and not in the definition made famous by Gilles Deleuze in his eponymous book (1986/1983).

for a rudimentary orientation in narration and geography. The landscape of Eastern Switzerland in *Hans im Glück* is fragmented. It is composed from singular views, which are only related within the narration of walking. It is thus not depicted in a literal sense, but instead is made palpable as a route in a kind of event and sensation protocol. This *narrative depiction of landscape* does almost entirely without the traditional panoramas and establishing shots, and instead conveys *atmospheres*: landscape *experiences* replace landscape *images*.

In the framework of this study, it is of course painfully obvious that *Hans im Glück* makes little use of traditional landscape images. The shots, for example, of the Säntis peak correspond roughly to the conventions of aesthetic depictions of the landscape: the peak rises at the image's center. Clouds hang in tatters along its flanks and the foreground is dominated by two smaller mountainsides and roofs, which frame the primary peak

almost symmetrically. It is a threatening, sublime image, similar to those familiar in classical landscape painting. In fact, with only very few views of this sort, the relationship to the tradition of landscape imagery is exhausted. Whenever the horizon can be seen in an image, the camera's interest is usually trained on elements in the foreground, whether people or buildings. Landscape recedes into the background.

The kind of seeing that Liechti cultivates in *Hans im Glück* arises clearly from the pedestrian's point of view and therefore creates a direct relationship to the landscape via the representation of landscape perception: on the one hand, closer and more "apprehensible" things enjoy the camera's particular attention. Aside from very few exceptional shots, the framing connects the view closely with the immediate environment. On the other hand, the sporadic alternation between close-ups and establishing shots, which represent the landscape or landmarks in a traditional way, evokes the fluctuating hybrid forms located between description and map described by de Certeau. "Seeing" and "walking" merge in a recounting of a space experienced in motion.

In the process, the establishing shots and the afore-mentioned subjectivizing, anecdotal views emphasize the act of *seeing*. They create relational points, which enable the viewer to orient himself. In the filmic representation, information on the routes is given by means of these markings, which are in reality already known to the hiker before his travels. Among these is, of course, the title at the beginning of the three treks and the periodic indica-tions given by the narration. The three chronologically related variations on the route from Zürich to St. Gallen are differentiated from one another by means of simply legible images, such as those depicting the impressive Säntis panorama or Lake Constance. Enough is thus done to orient the audience.

By the same token, brief portraits of places and situa-tions serve to ensure visual (if not geographic) orientation. The Säntis peak, for example, which becomes for Liechti a mental challenge as well as a physical one, is sketchily portrayed in eight shots; in the same way, the meadow at which Liechti's mood improves somewhat after the crossing, is made understandable with only a few cuts. In this way, the important stations along the route are strung together like memento photos: places where there was *something to see* on the trip.

Walking, on the other hand, is reflected in both the individual shots and the montage. Some shots show movements, which could be executed as easily by the filmmaker himself as by a proxy: next to the shots of walking feet are, for example, shaky shots of a breathless flight in a tunnel, or the view from a funicular gondola towards the approaching lower station. The departure from the peak, following a phase of stagnation and mental free fall, is staged in two symbolic images: the first, a gondola on a downhill trip disappearing into fog after only a few meters. The departure is thus depicted on an abstract level. In the shot immediately thereafter, the camera itself is on the descent. After a brief time, the soundtrack introduces a driving rhythm, which brings another invigorating element to the narrative and translates the resumed movement into musical terms.

Brief sequences such as these, alternating between relational points and space-creating forms of action, are the visual parallels to such verbal descriptions as: "There

you see a gondola. You get in and ride down into the valley." Such hinge points as these serve the film as a means to represent the journey's progress in extremely compressed form. Other shots, which can be understood as the filmic translation of dynamic moments, include the green figure on the traffic light, which indicates that the street can now be crossed; the yellow signs along the hiking trail; the view from the soon-to-be-crossed highway overpass down to the moving cars; passing trains; time-lapse accelerated snails, airplanes, and pedestrians. Even up to the metaphor of "passing" when a person dies, forward motion is a leitmotiv throughout the entire film.

From the Truth of the Individual to Socially Robust Knowledge

A subjective depiction like *Hans im Glück* cannot lay claim to any form of generalization in order to reclaim its status as epistemological instrument for *experiencing the landscape*. The example of *Hans im Glück* does show, however, that film can apparently succeed in conveying a personal perspective intersubjectively. The translation relies here, of course, not upon the reuse of conventionalized views, but rather on the individual balance between viewer and filmic proxy subject, upon a kind of empathetic participation by the viewer in the narration.

The basis upon which landscape representation rests in *Hans im Glück* is a subjective one, and walking is the vehicle for the production of experience. The precondition to intersubjective communication of experiences is the anchoring of the documentary narrative within a reliable narrator. This reliable narrator, whose perceptual apparatus is accepted as corresponding to our own, offers the viewer a bodily, aisthetic access to the subjectivizing elements of the representation, rather than the quasi-objective, conventional images of the traditional landscape representation.

The identification of the hiker as filmmaker—the historical, securitized human existence of Peter Liechti—offers the viewer the potential to build a relationship to the "I" in the film. This is constantly reconsidered in the cinema, in a similar way as in real encounters: both the camera's views and the commentary about the individual situations must be able to be related to a perceiving subject, which takes upon itself and experiences the act of walking *as a body*, while serving as a proxy for the viewer.

In opposition to traditional (idealized) landscape images, *Hans im Glück* creates only *momentary* documents of places, capturing in film a specific subject's translated perceptions at a particular time. These perceptions of the camera, or the cameraman with his camera, are commented upon by the voice-over on the one hand, and the framing and montage of image and sound on the other. The sequence on the Säntis peak can serve as an example of this re-contextualization of perception. In all the experiences documented by *Hans im Glück*, the author's momentary state of mind shimmers through with a definite coloration: the rage of the self-inflicted catharsis, the aftereffects of the deathly fear inspired by being unprotected in the thunder storm, the skepticism about the boastful ease of the day-trippers who ascend the peak in hoards using the funicular, or the dislike towards the stiffly concrete, solidly enormous architecture of this "space ship" at the peak—everything that is offered to the viewer's eyes and ears has already been processed many times over.

Naturally these sequences do not lay claim to a generalized status, but at least they indicate the "this-has-been" (Barthes 1981, 77) of the photographic image—the fact of existence in this world, in the moment at which the photo was taken, in front of the camera. Everyone, by virtue of his shared perceptual apparatus, can perceive the world in a similar way; for this reason, it is also communicable to others. Just as the elasticity of a branch from which a bird has just flown away can show us the nature of the wood of which it consists, we are also able, *by means of experience*, to decode the filter of Liechti's moods and to apply it to the reality we are shown.

We compare the subjective viewpoint of the camera, into which a specific corporeality is inscribed, with our own bodily schema. The landscape images thus exist within a narrative we know from daily life: inasmuch as we *recognize* the situations, we substitute for the missing images by means of assumptions and logical conclusions. Even the elliptical narrative form of the longer stretches of the journey is a figure we know from daily life, since we often repress the uneventful moments of a trip with the same thoroughness as occurs in the montage used in *Hans im Glück*.

Encounters with People

We have the presence of the filmmaker and his camera to thank not only for intersubjectively communicated landscape images, but also for a series of other data that are equally important to our impression of the landscape: most important are the people who take action, and who are the film's central interest because, unlike the deer, meadows, flowers, and stones, they have mastered language and are able to talk back to the camera(man). The characterization of the inhabitants contributes to the understanding of the landscape and to the knowledge of its history, since the inhabitants are often identified with the region in which they live: the mountain dwellers' reticence embodies the impassable higher altitude regions (for example, Liechti's alpine herdsman from the Säntis peak); the tall woman with long, braided hair represents the coolness of the far north; the image of the drinker has accompanied the "devastated" landscapes of Eastern Europe since the fall of the Iron Curtain. The landscape can also be represented as the site of a particular social reality.

Most encounters in *Hans im Glück* are only passing, but even in their brevity, they offer clues about the locations traversed. The homeland tourist at 2,500 meters elevation with a cigarette in his mouth, who has clearly not reached the mountain's peak through his own exertion, points to the social meaning of a peak like the Säntis: the "conquest" of the mountains has become a commonplace, and this rocky landscape has been entirely mastered and accessed. Anyone who exposes himself to it without protection, as Liechti does during his ascent, is acting anachronistically. The sense of threat relative to the mountain's natural force belongs to the pre-nineteenth-century world, when the engineer's spirit began to make the Alps accessible and thus to domesticate them. Today, peaks such as the Säntis have disabled access, and an excursion to the highest peaks is a ritual of self-verification for the people of the Alpine republic: they have made their once terrifying, mountainous earth subservient. The herdsman, who appears just before, is still identifiable with the template for the traditional Alpine inhabitant so well loved in tourism advertising, and is made relative as an archaic bearer of meaning by the "outer space" contrast provided by the mountain peak scenery.

Hans im Glück considers more thoroughly the condition of farmers on its two-time visit to Senn Sepp. The topic of the Alps and their inhabitants has a long, critical tradition in Switzerland, beginning with Albrecht von Hallers' poem *The Alps* (1729). It was cultivated as a myth from the time of the country's founding in 1848 to the Second World War and beyond: the Alps represent a territory that unifies Switzerland's different linguistic groups through its power of identification.

Once again, Liechti approaches this broad political topic from a personal angle and breaks the discussion's national political dimensions down into conversations and situations, which emerge from his two encounters with herdsman Sepp during his leisure time. During the second hike, Sepp is introduced in his traditional persona: he takes care of the cows and the husbandry of the Alpine economy. But then he acquires his own voice and a life beyond this secure mountain world populated by livestock. Sepp does favor the traditional regional celebrations, but he is also interested in a jazz concert to which he accompanies his daughter who, for her part, has little interest in dances performed in traditional Appenzell costumes. In winter, on the occasion of the third walk, the second encounter takes place. This time, however, Sepp is working in the distribution warehouse of a Swiss food corporation, an occupation that leads

the traditional image of an Appenzell Senn ad absurdum. Sepp's presence at the jazz concert and in the distribution center breaks the established connection between the landscape and its inhabitants, which, in the case of the Alps, is usually structured by the phantasms of purity, untouched naturalness, and unity with nature. In just a few images and conversations, the film reveals the simultaneous ambiguity and normality of the life that Sepp leads in the Alps and on the flatlands. The film does not construct a true contradiction within the confrontation between his two occupations. In an insightful gesture, it subtly indicates instead the discrepancy within the herdsman's double existence, which is apparently understood to be completely normal, and the foundational rhetoric of the "Alpine narrative" (Zimmer 1998, 652), which still partially forms the social image of life in the Appenzell Alps.

Hans im Glück shows the landscape while largely
avoiding the traditional images—which are still over-
whelmingly powerful in society—and instead counters
with a sociological and economic discourse. Precisely by
means of the subjectification of his narrative, Liechti
succeeds in *Hans im Glück* in presenting such diverse
aspects of landscape perception as mastering a hike, the
bodily experience, and a social image of the Alps in a
way that can be understood generally. Nonetheless, the
contingency of the landscape discourse, often felt to be
excessive, seems to favor attempts at order which open
themselves in all directions to multiple influences on
our understanding of the landscape. Films such as *Hans
im Glück* seem to affirm that the extreme subjectivity
inherent to walking in the tradition of Robert Smithson's
Tour of the Monuments of Passaic, New Jersey is still a
real working instrument with which artistic, visual media
can contribute to an understanding of our relationship
to landscape.

Jem Cohen: *Lost Book Found* (USA 1996)

The films made by the American Jem Cohen arise from
the uninterrupted act of collecting everyday images. His
camera work reflects this approach to production, his
films always exude the concreteness of the pedestrian
who skewers his environment with the gaze of someone
involved in its happenings. This production method, and
Cohen's specific perspective, are clearly demonstrated in
the film *Lost Book Found* (USA 1996), a film about the
peripatetic appropriation of New York's streets.

The film narrates in the first person the story of a
denizen who observes the city's constant self-renewal. It
covers a longer period of time, during which the narrator
is initially present as a street vendor in New York and
then quickly becomes "invisible" for those who pass him
on a daily basis. He meets a certain "Sidewalk Fisher"

153

whose ingenious instruments salvage urban flotsam from subway and skylight shafts. The narrator purchases a notebook full of lists from him—lists which record the most varied observations in a random order, and evoke a kaleidoscopic image of the city.

Shortly thereafter, the narrator loses his job. He leaves the metropolis for several years. After his return, he notes the extent to which the city has changed in the interim—and yet has remained the same. One caption from the book of lists summarizes this observation suitably: "Glass is a liquid."

He attempts to reaccess this simultaneously new and old city using the lists in the notebook he had purchased years earlier. The lists become an obsession; they proliferate themselves in his head. Everything he sees multiplies itself through association with similar things; his environment seems to him to be a stratification of stories and memories which can be accessed through clues gleaned from consumer relics which, discarded without intention or notice, have solidified into a visible urban crust. The sum of small, unimportant actions forms the city of his perception.

The Dweller's Perspective: Anchoring the Gaze
in the Body

The image of the city in *Lost Book Found* is stylistically characterized by Cohen's specific way of seeing: centered, discontinuous, associative, and driven by personal visual interest, which expresses itself in, for example, repetitive serial motifs. Even more pronouncedly than Peter Liechti, Cohen cultivates a form of filmic representation that concentrates on the specific moment and proximate things and events. He emphasizes the fragmentariness and the contingency of the specific way in which the world is seen while *walking*. He depicts the "other spatiality," which evokes a "disquieting familiarity" in the observer (de Certeau 1988, 96): the city as each person must walk and experience it. One can, along with Simon Schama, speak of an "archive of the feet" (Schama 1995, 24), which Cohen unfolds for his viewer. Similar to the direct experience of the city, the film communicates an *atmospheric* sense of the places depicted and the impression of immediate subjective experience.

This subjectification occurs on several levels, of which the most important is the first-person narrator, from whose perspective the story develops. In addition, the style of camera work, the montage and the sound treatment are important elements.

The individual's perspective is most clearly evident in the different shots, which suggest the camera man's bodily position: following a brief prelude with atmospheric images, as well as the film's title sequence, three views of the New York skyline are shown. The first image is shot from the middle of a space. It frames a window, which fills approximately half of the film frame. The frame and center mullion are drawn sharply against the backdrop of the illuminated nighttime city. Behind the camera, a light goes on in an adjacent room and is reflected in the windowpane.

The next shot is already closer to the window. Window frame and mullion are no longer visible, but the haze of a curtain or another reflection from the adjacent room is. It is only in the third shot—which unlike the prior shots does not follow an abrupt cut, but rather a quick fade-out and fade-in—that an unobstructed view of the city is shown.

The brief series of three images at the beginning of this sequence shows clearly the approach to a window as we experience it ourselves on a daily basis: an embodied view approaches the window in order to look out over the city from above. The movement through the room suggests a physical seeing subject (much like the viewer himself) and lays claim right at the film's inception to a special "spatialized" perspective. In contrast, the ensuing city views assume a neutral perspective and show the city as image. Only the subtle swaying of these shots, apparently taken without a tripod, indicates again the bodily nature of the gaze.

Like an echo of Michel De Certeau, the commentary voice-over locates the shot in an office building, from which the first person narrator is looking down at the city:

> I'm looking down from an office building. A Skyscraper. And twenty-six floors below almost all of the executives and secretaries have long since caught their taxis and commuter trains home. I look west, wondering how far over you can see. If it's possible to find 9th avenue from any of these office windows. Far away I hear a sound like the ocean.——48

48 From the voice-over of *Lost Book Found*. See De Certeau: The *Practice of Everyday Life* (1984/1980). Chapter VII, "Walking in the City," begins with the words, "Seeing Manhattan from the 110th floor of the World Trade Center." De Certeau juxtaposes to this seeing at a distance his practice of walking, the "elementary form" of urban experience, which plays with "invisible spaces" in which the pedestrian's knowledge "is as blind as that of lovers' in each other's arms" (p. 91).

The film's first spoken words already presume a movement, which is immediately thereafter also narrated in the image. In the act of thinking about the people who have already disappeared into their taxis and commuter trains, there is already an indication of the street level, which will also be reached virtually after a longer series of urban panoramas and slow fade-ins and fade-outs.

The now executed transition from the impressions offered from the height of a skyscraper to the shots taken barely above ground level of the wheel of a mobile vendor's stand ejects the viewer from orderly "geometric space" (Merleau-Ponty) into the disorderly, rich, bodily experienced "anthropological space" of the city as "urban practice" (de Certeau 1984, 93) and thus into the perspective that makes it impossible to comprehend the city's massive, parallel multiplicity. Seen from the twenty-sixth story, it appears comprehensible, like a map, objectified in front of the viewer; at street level, it is ego-based, colored by personal interest and memories. The spaces are no longer interchangeable, but rather acquire atmosphere and identity through smells, materials, and memories. They become characteristic, recognizable *places*.

The catalyst for this transformation is the vending cart, to which the first image of the second way to see the city is dedicated. It creates a narrative coupling, since it is the instrument with which the camera's "self" is initially exposed to the city in the following frames.

In the sequence described, the appearance of a body behind the camera is suspended in the films' diegesis. There are, however, also indications of a physical presence behind the camera's perspective that can be only be inferred by extradiegetic clues. At the end of the film, for example, several of the city's inhabitants pose in front of the gleaming background of the entrance to Madison Square Garden. They look directly at the camera. This direct address indicates a situation outside the film in which the people depicted have obviously posed *for the camera.*

This moment of communication with the camera indicates within the diegesis the non-filmic world in which the person filmed must have recognized the camera's "subject" and therefore waited patiently. The shot signals that real subjects are present, visible *in front of* and invisible *behind* the camera; they relate to each other within the respective image.

As a third evidentiary moment for the suggestion that the film has a concrete, acting subject, a direct interaction between a filmed subject and the subject of the camera can be cited. The Sidewalk Fisher hauls an object out of

the sidewalk ventilation shaft in the last shot of the film
and holds it towards the camera. He apparently does
not only do this to *show* the found object. By means of
two transitions, it becomes clear that Cohen and the
homeless collector have in fact had an interaction: for
one, the image of the outstretched hand is superimposed
with a framed metallic disk the size of a dollar coin,
shot against a pristine black background. Thereafter,
the first image, before it fades to black, is overlaid for a
fraction of a second with a portrait of the homeless man.
It is the only moment in which his face is seen—hardly
noticeable, becoming the subject of the film only for one
extremely brief moment.

The coin-like medallion, inscribed with N.Y.TEL.CO,
has actually become the filmmaker's possession, although
the transfer has apparently occurred outside the events
narrated by the film—a fact that indirectly points to the
subject behind the camera. Above and beyond that fact,
the discrete reference to the collector sheds light on the
filmmaker's presence: the censoring of his face can be
understood as protecting the homeless man, whose semi-
legal urban existence cannot lightly be made public, but
who nonetheless should be acknowledged for his contribution to the film's genesis. This respectful treatment of a
socially underprivileged person gives the observant viewer
perhaps the clearest indication of the (apparently socially
conscious) subject Jem Cohen, who assumes a perceptual
mode that seems familiar and mundane to the viewer,
even amidst the codes of filmic representation.

The identification of the viewer with the camera's view, underpinned by the filmic means described, is facilitated by hints, which operate on the limits of the subconscious and signal corporeal perception. In lieu of identifying the view with a subject who is present in the film, a technique that in theory offers the perfect example of how to integrate the viewer into the filmic text, the film forces the identification of the filmic image with one's own bodily gaze. The characteristic of cinematographic communication, which allows the viewer to imagine himself as the film's subject, is accomplished here in a manner similar to Peter Liechti's *Hans im Glück*, as affinity between seen and heard, and our own bodily feelings: the "suture" between what is presented and our own reality can be bridged by the viewer, because he can effortlessly integrate the represented view into his own bodily schemata.

Cadrage and Camera Style

The constant willingness to take notice of what occurs around him makes Cohen into a documentarian of chance. Many shots in *Lost Book Found* evidence that he simply had the camera close at hand at several moments. These are "found stories," as Siegfried Kracauer called these chance moments, in which the camera makes observations that themselves merge into a small story (Kracauer 1960, 245). In most cases, Cohen closes the "story" of these observations abruptly with a cut. He is apparently more interested in the fact of having *seen* (and filmed) these scenes than in tracking down the stories that could be woven from them. Like a flaneur, Cohen perceives the city and its life in an "anamnestic intoxication" (Benjamin 1999, 417) without involving himself in any way except atmospherically.

The scenes are filmed without a tripod, using a volatile, often slightly swaying camera, which responds quickly to the image's motion and is constantly reframing. In the process, the view is often set at a low height, pointing down at the pavement. It shows only legs, without the bodies that belong to them, and corresponds to the view of a pedestrian or to the easy perspective of someone who keeps his eyes on the ground in front of his feet, in order to see any obstacles in time. This downward-oriented view is one of the most obvious characteristics of Cohen's camera work.

Often, the camera crops its subject along the edge of the film frame: bodies, buildings, signs and the vendor's cart are framed fragmentarily. The recurrent motif of this cadrage are small whirlwinds, which occur on the streets and spin paper and plastic bags in a circle; people on the streets; storefronts with all kinds of cheap consumer goods; and the (in part faded) inscriptions on facades, telephone booths, signs and stickers on street lamps, and other urban infrastructure.

Montage

The montage in *Lost Book Found* can best be described as associative. One image seems to arise from another: for example, when the characteristic top shot of goods spread out for sale on the pavement is followed by a "wanted" sign attached to a street lamp reading "Wanted Color T.V. 873 6661 Joe," or when, in three sequential shots, the view of a sagging door with the inscription "Whole Chicken 55¢/pound—Chicken Cutlet 2.50—Chicken Legs 1.55" is followed by a detail of a picture of a chick taped to the door and then, finally, a scene showing a squatting man of Asian extraction who sets off a small hopping toy chick.

This montage follows human perception, however, and imitates the economy of attention inherent to the city dweller, focused on quick cognition. When, for example, images are located parallel to the commentary's stream of consciousness, then the montage follows the everyday association of seeing and thinking—the former is conditioned and preformed by the latter. It is only in response to the intellectual focus on the many handwritten notes posted throughout the city, prompted by the commentary, that the eye becomes receptive to the multiplicity of these notes, which reference God, conspiracy theory, and financial hardship.

The localization of singular elements in the cityscape occurs according to the rules of everyday perception, from overview to detail: a three-part montage sequence, for example, comes closer to the façade of a building decorated with enormous, faded letters. The first shot shows an establishing shot from a worm's eye view, with a view corridor to the "New Yorker" hotel (crowned with an inscription that stretches over several stories). The second shot shows a portion of a closer building whose weathered façade painting had not been apparent in the prior shot. Finally, the third shot focuses on the magnified letter "S", whose somewhat darker color contrasts with the brick façade, clearly in need of renovation for some time.

In classic film montage, this sequence of shots corresponds to the usual partition of a scene in an initial *establishing shot* and subsequent detail shots. In *Lost Book*

Found, however, the way that the montage *guides attention* can be understood as a translation of the practice of everyday cognition. The eye perceives a situation holistically in a few moments, only to concentrate thereafter on a detail. It speaks for itself that Cohen's initial image, whose depth of field and graphic composition inevitably lead the eye towards the inscribed "New Yorker" building, has chosen for its detail studies the unassuming and unspectacular subjects that are only evident to the flaneur's eye.

The most obvious characteristics of the montage in *Lost Book Found* derive from the lists that the first-person narrator finds in his book. These lists are expressions of an attempt to organize the world according to subjective categories. The montage takes up their structure, which groups similar things together. It follows the voice-over commentary with illustrative images, or works associatively and panoptically with sequences of motifs in which similar perspectives are grouped: the sequence of handwritten notes in the city; the sequence of provisionally glued and repaired items; the sequence of stores with aggressive discount signs; the sequence of heads and figures in storefront displays; the sequence of perpetual motion; and the sequence of weathered, illegible inscriptions.

The lists in the found book seem to categorize the city indiscriminately. Their order does not follow official rules or relate to public open spaces or normative urban furniture, but instead it creates an everyday encyclopedia of a single person, in order to facilitate his orientation within the world specific to his consumerism and life. It is a "counter-order", which does not apprehend the generic version of an international metropolis, but instead, the individual cartography of an inhabitant who *appropriates* the city on foot. The filmic sequences break off abruptly and are replaced, often without apparent connection, by new images, just as one thought replaces another when an external stimulus evokes associations in an unanticipated direction. The slow fade to black and fade-in to a new shot, instead of the use of hard cuts, seems to illustrate the associative appearance and disappearance of images and ideas in our inner eye. The montage thus creates a visual parallel to the intellectual flaneurism, through which the human being concocts his reality from sensual impressions, chains of thoughts and scraps of memory.

Sound

As an atmospheric element *par excellence*, sound is a decisive participant in the production of filmic space. In *Lost Book Found*, it is nonetheless often significantly estranged. There are two families of sound in particular, which together subjectivize the filmic narration: the original soundtrack of the film's locations (or rather, what the viewer would believe that to be); and music, chance voices, and voice-overs, which together create the illusion of an interior monologue that is directed towards the audience.

More than half of the film includes sound fragments, which were recorded on the streets of New York. The film sets voice-overs, which tell the story of an "I," against this background noise. Nonetheless, it only projects infrequently into the foreground, since incessant urban background noise naturally projects itself less into consciousness than does language—even though it is at times quite noticeable beneath the commentary—and tends to be ignored. Even if it seems not to have been recorded as a direct soundtrack, the environmental sound often follows the content of the images.

Often, single samples of this soundtrack are looped: short sentences repeat themselves two or three times and are lost again in other noises. This background soundtrack compliments and expands panoramically and atmospherically upon the limited perspective of the tightly framed camera. Sounds of this quality are responsible for a particular form of integration into the filmic narrative, since they cannot be explained only by seeing and hearing, or by the cognitive comprehension of the narration. Instead, they are predicated on a perception that is activated bodily and spatially. The soundtrack expands, atmospherically, space that is cropped by the cadrage. The viewer *senses* it—in most cases, he does not perceive it consciously.

The second level of sound is more closely related by content to the commentary text: a kind of narrator who repeatedly reads aloud passages and titles from the found notebook, as well as a single voice that apparently was recorded on the streets of New York; short bursts of music that fade in only to disappear again, and double the fade-ins and fade-outs of the images already mentioned; longer passages of spheric music, bells resounding for a long period, and music box sounds, estranged using a minimal echo, accompany the quotations from the book of lists.

If the commentary voice represents the subject's monologue in its extraverted form, then the dreamy, surreal sounds relocate this monologue within a subjective resonance chamber, as if the "I" were still somewhat indulging his recollections and associations.

At this point, the image of the city and personal recollections begin to intertwine and to form a subjective "image" of the appropriated city through a complex reciprocal relationship.

The long montage sequences communicate a similar experience to the viewer: here, neither commentary nor environmental noises accompany the associative tapestry of images, but rather only isolated, clearly extra-diegetic sounds or even total silence. In the context of the cinema, the temporary lack of auditory stimuli opens up an intellectual faculty that is similar to the one, which nourishes the flaneur in the city: it is the mixture of processing external stimuli and recalling ones own memories, in other words, of thinking and emotion, which one calls *experience*.

The Identification of the Viewer with the Embodied Gaze

It is important, too, not to forget the deviations from everyday perception in the representation of how the city is perceived: a film can only reflect reality naturalistically within the medium's limitations, and so the representation in *Lost Book Found* is not completely identical to a realistic perspective, but is instead an artistically reconfigured translation. In this sense, it would be an excessive simplification to expect that the point of view in *Lost Book Found* corresponds completely to that of the human eye (to say nothing of the ear). The significant deceleration of many shots, for example, is obvious—a visual stylization that vigorously contradicts actual visual experience. The camera is often at too low a height for the human eye, and the visual fragmentation already mentioned often permits the off-camera presence to intrude into the viewer's consciousness to an unusually significant extent.

The camera's eye thus does not *imitate* human sight, but instead, *interprets* it. If partial identification between the camera's point of view with the subjective point of view of the urban dweller is nonetheless possible, then only in the estranged form of the artistic translation of private, assimilated perception. *Lost Book Found* presents one subjective perception as an integrated "thick description" of that which the cognitive system "human being" makes on an everyday basis out of his observations. It constructs a bipolar image of New York City, which shows both the external reality of the city's goings-on as well as the *stream of consciousness* of a constantly interpreting and ordering narrating ego.

I have devoted this chapter to exemplary case studies, demonstrating the fact that landscape in film not only communicates visually, but also *kinaesthetically* (Vivian Sobchack). The examples prove that the filmic landscape communicates visually, auditorily and also physically by stimulating the faculty for memory within the viewer as *body*. The bodily "knowledge" deriving from a situation shown from a subjective perspective is immediately activated, since the viewer has integrated analogous situations in his bodily image: the film translates "what the fingers [already] knew" (Sobchack 2004). In cases in which it is represented not only visually, but also bodily in its specific way, then filmic landscape can be experienced both as visual representation and *actually* as a kind of immersive space in which the (imagined) body can *move*. To consider the relationship between film and landscape a purely aesthetic relationship, as the majority of studies on the topic tend to do, seems much too limited an approach in this regard.

Narrating Landscape

He believed that if he looked at it hard enough, he could cause the surface of the city to reveal to him the molecular basis of historical events. And in this way he hoped to see into the future.
(From *London*, Patrick Keiller 1994)

There are said to be certain Buddhists whose ascetic practices enable them to see a whole landscape in a bean. (Barthes 1974)

The fact that landscape can no longer be treated in contemporary theory only as an aesthetic phenomenon or as a "unity" of a comprehensive "piece of nature", as Georg Simmel did at the beginning of the twentieth century, has been stated emphatically several times. W.J.T. Mitchell, for example, describes landscape as a medium, which reflects the social structure. He supports this thesis by pointing out an often invisible, but topographically and communicatively effective aspect of the landscape, which can only be understood by reading clues: the landscape contains signs of its function and meaning within society, and thus always also materializes society's practices vis-à-vis space. The marking and reinforcement of boundaries, or the various conditions of maintenance or use in two adjacent areas, indicate property relations; formalized or ritualized paths which permit or prohibit access can indicate, for example, a particular meaning in the case of religious sites. The monoculture of linearly oriented rows of trees in a forest communicates industrial use (and undermines the sense of the natural environment); and the appearance of the vivid red, very rare corn cockle in a barley grass meadow in the middle of Osnabrück can be traced to the agrarian and nostalgic impulse of a group of students who planted a mixture of flower seeds in that public space (Hard 1995).

Implicit clues, such as these, to the internal essence of a place can be described as *narrations*, since most of these landscape factors as intellectual background are based on structures, which are communicated as stories. These are of course not stories in the narratological sense, as closed narrative forms with beginning, end and a full-blown narrative arc, but rather "narremes," or small narrative elements that first unfold their effects within a specific context. Matthew Potteiger and Jamie Purinton, who had devoted an entire book to the narration of the landscape, describe the quality of these narrations as follows:

> Narratives can reside in very ordinary forms, routine activities, and institutional structures. Behind the uniform setbacks, heights, and materials specified in standard zoning and building codes are social narratives of progressivism and countless adjudications of what determines health, safety, and welfare. As they develop from often competing interests, these landscape narratives often lack clear individual authorship. Constantly in process of being made and unmade, they become open narratives without the closure and clear plot structure of conventional stories. Therefore, understanding narratives on this level requires more than reading a historic inventory or visual survey; it involves special attention, methods, and time to engage the storied texture of a place. (Potteiger and Purinton 1998, 19)

However, it is not only architecture and the built environment that operate as narratives. The methodologies of (landscape) architectural theory—inasmuch as they are not focused on construction—are not based upon normative models, but instead on the description of complex relationships between architecture and environment. By means of description, knowledge in our society becomes organic and can be transmitted across cultural boundaries. The historian Hayden White went so far as to describe narration as a metacode, which is universally found in all mankind (White 1980, 6). Its value for human communication is its potential to fill gaps and to make the fragmented, open complexity of real conditions into an integrated, coherent and above all closed form. The coherence of narration corresponds, according to White, to a fundamental longing of humankind (ibid., 27).

The narrative form seems additionally to play an important role in the learning of everyday knowledge: thus, children can more easily recall complex spatial sequences if they are related to a story (Potteiger and Purinton 1998, 3).——[49] This same connection between thoughts and spatial structure is also known as a mnemonic technique: Cicero's Loci-method, for example, makes use of the attribution of ideas to spatial details.

[49] Potteiger and Purinton quote an essay by Stephen Trimble, "The Scripture of Maps, the Names of Trees: A Child's Landscape." In: Gary P. Nabhan, Stephen Trimble: *The Geography of Childhood*. Boston 1994.

In the third chapter, I examined the function of the overarching narrative in bridging landscape discontinuities and connecting fragments. The perception of the urban periphery served as one example, which only constitutes a unified experience through the "action" of driving. Overarching *narratives* create closure for the fundamentally open form of the landscape. Landscape becomes communicable by means of the narrative (and naturally by means of images); in many cases, we come to know it in the first place by means of stories. These stories help to identify landscape spaces as specific places, and to identify *us with them*; once they have triggered a learning process in a person or society, they can in some cases influence the actual landscape by providing instructions for dealing with a given topography. A prominent hill, for example, becomes the Acropolis *by means of a story*; Dealy Plaza in Dallas, the site of John F. Kennedy's assassination, became a "National Historic Landmark" *by means of a narrative*. It is easy to find examples such as these in every location.

Narratives about the landscape, such as these, belong to our most complex forms of interaction with the environment. They do not sever our environment from the material plane, but rather trigger a process of mutual influence, which interweaves *material* and *meaning* into the highly resistant amalgam of the landscape myth:

> It is not just that "places" serve to remind us of the stories that are associated with them; in certain respects, the places only exist [...] because they have stories associated with them. But when once they have acquired this story-based existence, the landscape itself acquires the power of "telling the story."——[50]

50 Leach, Edmund: "Conclusion: Further Thoughts on the Realm of Folly." In: Edward M. Brunner (ed.): *Text, Play, and Story: The Conclusion and Reconstruction of Self and Society* (1984, 358). Cited in: Barbara Johnstone (ed.): *Stories, Community, and Place: Narratives from Middle America.* Bloomington (1990, 120).

Landscape narrations are usually connected to the past. They describe occurrences that happened at a place; interests, which influenced its form; or often simply freely imagined stories (many with a religious background), which have persisted within a society. The process by which a landscape is captured in a narrative is facilitated inasmuch as both develop as a process, in other words, on a temporal basis. And stories need locations. They develop their particular meaning often only from a specific background, in other words, when they are *situated*; as already mentioned, spaces, on the other hand, are identified by stories, which give them a closed, communicable form.

The fact that narration and landscape are nonetheless not necessarily congruent has been demonstrated by Simon Schama's work, among others. Stories can accede to definitive power over a topography, and determine the manner and way in which a society deals with it. There are then two possible ways to transform a landscape: on the one hand, the physical-material, as cultivated by the landscape architect when he constructs a landscape. On the other, however, there is a mental-idea-based way, which the poet or filmmaker chooses when he tells a story which occurred at a place—or *invents* a story which attributes to that place a new position within society. This second way leaves the topography untouched, but transforms the essence of how society perceives it.

Ground Zero in New York is only the most significant example in recent history: a place that has been inscribed anew with a new narrative by virtue of historical events. As with all good topographic narrations, it is nourished equally by real conditions and by mythical exaggerations and ideological honing. Narration and landscape seem in many regards to be a fortunate combination. The example shows that the telling of stories about places and landscapes is not the privilege of the narrative media. It demonstrates, however, like no other historical event, that new stories are dependent upon their medial transmission in order to be effective by penetrating society.—[51] In film, this connection can be almost perfectly represented: the image-based medium provides a photographic description of the landscape on the one hand, and on the other, it is perhaps the most effective narrative medium available today. The cinematographic correlation of narration and landscape can in the meantime be so strong that it achieves what Edmund Leach described in the quotation above: Monument Valley, on the border between Utah and Arizona, has, since John Ford's Western *Stagecoach* (USA 1939), communicated almost in a single image the story of the courageous settling of the American West by whites.

The following examples thematize the power of narration for a society's perception of the landscape. They all demonstrate particular perspectives and are not to be understood as neutral documentations of the places portrayed, but rather as readings of their histories and current topographies. These films make possible a reading of clues in a second instance. The work on the filmic form corresponds here to that of a landscape theoretician who combines disparate elements in order to convey a holistic image of hidden relationships within a landscape's development. In the process, narration becomes a proven means for organizing meanings.

The films do not reflect a socially accepted opinion, but instead they enter directly into the maelstrom of

51 In the aftermath of the events of September 11, 2001, a whole series of films were devoted to the attacks on the World Trade Center, and to the rewriting of this new history of Manhattan in several directions. Worthy of mention are, for example, the conspiracy theory *Loose Change* (Dillen Avery, USA 2005/2007), which circulated in various cuts on the Internet; the documentary film about the reasons for the US's entry in the Iraq War *Why We Fight* (Eugene Jarecki, USA 2005); the fictional films *World Trade Center* (Oliver Stone, USA 2006), *United 93* (Paul Greengrass, USA 2006) or *11'09'01—September 11* (Various, UK/FR/EG/JP, 2002); the documentary *9/11* (Jules and Gedeon Nandet, F 2002) and *Fahrenheit 9/11* (Michael Moore, USA 2004), as well as countless other small, experimental films such as *No Damage* (Caspar Stracke, USA 2002).

perspectives, didactic opinions, common sense and public opinion in which they—possibly—can work slowly towards societal penetration. In fact, they do what every idea before them has in fact done, until they become the "objective" opinion of a whole society.—52

52 This definition for the way an idea prevails is true not only in society but in all areas of the competition among human ideas. As ally, I would like to quote here the French sociologist Bruno Latour: "Who will win in an antagonistic encounter between two authors, and between them and between all the others they need to build up a statement S? Answer: the one able to *muster on the spot the largest number of well aligned and faithful allies*. This definition of victory is common to war, politics, law and [...] to science and technology" [Italics by the author.] (Latour 1990, 23).

Gerhard Benedikt Friedl: *Knittelfeld—Stadt ohne Geschichte* (A 1997)

Knittelfeld is a regional capital township with a population of 12,000 in the Austrian state Styria. About 10 percent of the inhabitants are foreign and its unemployment rate is somewhat above the national average. There are hardly any special characteristics to be found there—at most the largest collection of railway conductors' caps in the world at the local railway museum. More commonly, the city is associated with the nearby military airport Zeltweg, or with the former Formula 1 racing stretch on the A1 highway loop in the area. Only recently has Knittelfeld made headlines through an act of political disobedience, when in September 2002, a group of members of the Freedom Party Austria (FPÖ) distanced themselves from the prevailing party line, which at that time was determined by the xenophobic populist Jörg Haider who led the FPÖ as a coalition partner of the Austrian People's Party (ÖVP). This event, however, occurred long after the premiere of the film, dealt with in the following paragraphs. It is therefore not considered in the film.

In 1997, the filmmaker Gerhard Benedikt Friedl devoted a 35-minute film to the city: *Knittelfeld—Stadt ohne Geschichte* (Knittelfeld—A Town without a History). Basically, his approach to this place is not guided by an interest in the Styrian landscape into which Knittelfeld is nested. However, in addition to the title, which makes clear reference to the landscape as it actually exists, the film's pictorial level comprises exclusively images of the town and its surroundings. There is one exception that will have to be considered more closely.

The film numbers sixty-four shots, in addition to the introductory and end sequences. Beginning with a panorama of the city shot from a raised perspective, they show street scenes, landscape establishing shots, rows of houses, green areas, driveways, parking lots, supermarkets, shopping streets, industrial zones, courtyards. They comprise a panopticon of daily views, which in their totality represent the small town and its immediate environs quite representatively. The camera's eye is aloof and distanced; it does not seek contact to the passers-by. In the soundtrack, too, the film distances itself from its surroundings. It only incidentally records sounds and conversations, which occur close to the respective camera location.

In addition to the background noise, there is a running commentary, erratic in its terse and monosyllabic word use, which recapitulates in broad strokes the notable events that took place between 1977 and 1996 in and around a local family named Pritz (name changed for the film): a sequence of crimes and violent acts, including: the beating to death with a stone of a soldier, a schoolgirl laid low by rifle shots, two fathers who may have been murdered, a murder committed with a screw driver during a theft, and the abuse and death of a small child.

Without recognizable emotion, free from personal interpretation and constantly mentioning the places' names and the localities, the commentary recapitulates these six crimes one after another, which (at least it is suspected) members of the Pritz family committed. Intermittently, it describes the social and temporal history of the region, mentioning, for example, the crisis within the local heavy industry during the nineteen-seventies and the physical urban transformations, which fundamentally transformed the city's face around 1990 with the construction of industrial and shopping areas far from its center.

175

Cross-references between Image and Narrative

There are countless links between image and commentary. In the film's second shot, one first sees a billboard in front of a hedge that conceals an adjacent residential area. The camera leaves this scene and pans over the country road towards the checkpoint of a military compound and then, after a cut, across the building belonging to the Kärtner Inn and beyond. The next shot shows another inn, in front of which two cyclists cross paths on the road. The commentary, which began in the first shot, summarizes the events of early summer 1985: the brothers Hugo and Herbert Pritz become involved in an argument about gambling debts at the Korn Inn with a soldier named Armin Haas, who is stationed at the nearby military airport. Herbert Pritz strikes Haas dead with a stone. Before they can conceal the corpse, the two brothers hide from the approaching townspeople behind the billboard. They are found, however, and the judicial process takes its course. The fifth shot has changed locations and shows a cyclist in the country. The commentary is silent for a moment.

Within the first four shots, three knots within a weft of clues between image and commentary have already been looped, in a way that begins to set the pattern for the entire film: the image of the billboard in the second shot is followed by the mention of the two brothers' attempt to hide after the soldier's stoning in the first shot. The Korn Inn, in which the unhappy card game occurred and led to the argument between the soldier and the brothers, is echoed in shots three and four by the image of the two inns. The bicyclists in shot four (as well as in shots five and six) reverberate in shot twelve's commentary, which reports on the death of Susanne Deboth, a schoolgirl who was biking when she was shot.

The list of connections between image and soundtrack is long and is not only limited in the soundtrack to commentary, but also, extends to the coincidentally recorded

The brothers hide behind a billboard.

Hugo Pritz is sentenced to 25 years in prison.

snippets of conversations when, as for example in shot forty-six, a PA announcement advertises a nearby business center, while the image takes up the recurrent theme of the new industrial zone on Knittelfeld's periphery.

The Small City as Model of the Provinces

Bert Rebbhandl places the film *Knittelfeld* within the Austrian literary tradition in which the provinces are repeatedly portrayed as the site of horror.—[60] Gerhard Benedikt Friedl's Knittelfeld certainly qualifies for this category. Nonetheless, it is still worth noting that the Pritz family's story cannot be described as representative for the regional capital—it goes without saying that the story is not mentioned in the city's official communication. Why then is a mid-size city tied to the extraordinary story of one of the families that lives here?

Friedl's choice is not arbitrary. The sixty-four landscape panoramas are recontextualized by the violent, sometimes senseless story. Of course the film's implicit attitude can be rejected as too extreme and particular, but in fact, the opposite is also true: Friedl *universalizes* an idea by bringing the narration of the crime together with the image of Knittelfeld in a closed, autonomous and, most importantly, easily multiplied and communicated form, that of the film. The filmic form, which, unlike a mere thought, is generally accessible, *inscribes this idea into the image of the landscape*. In other words, the Pritz family's story can be anchored in the image of the landscape by *Knittelfeld—Stadt ohne Geschichte* even more easily because the city did not have any story (or history) of its own, as the title maintains.

Friedl's argumentation thus describes the trajectory of (almost) every objective insight: society's convictions most often begin as the idea of an individual before they are generally accepted.

The communicative work draws upon the montage's high degree of precision. Whereas documentary films often exhibit a direct relationship between image and commentary, Friedl uses precisely constructed relationships, which cross-reference one another suggestively to achieve a kind of narrative estrangement that negates the possibility of specificity between image and commentary. The image of a bridge does not show the bridge from which Karl and Hanna threw the child. The same is true of the subsequent discovery of the corpse: the film does not intend to make the viewer believe that he is in fact witness to the discovery of the child, but instead substitutes shots of an arbitrary fire department exercise on the river, clearly as a proxy for the actual situation. These shots communicate that the occurrences actually happened at a different place, but could just as easily have happened here or elsewhere.

The densely woven evidentiary structures between visual and linguistic components are the precondition for the way in which the semantic levels contained in the text can inscribe itself into the images of *Knittelfeld*. By means of the particular montage, which distends visual and linguistic relations over several shots and repeats motifs several times, these structures spread pandemically through the entire film until the non-specific images of the small town are suffused with narrative meaning and a kind of leapfrogging occurs: the image of an arbitrary inn, the view of an arbitrary supermarket or a provincial shopping street with its small shops—they all begin to be associated with the crime with which the commentary has pointedly inoculated the small-town perspectives. The specificity of the situation shown is sacrificed to an eerie ubiquity in the narrative, for which Knittelfeld serves as background and model.

The fact that the filmic argument—that *Knittelfeld* is a proxy for the (Austrian) provinces—is generalized, becomes manifest in two shots which are also formal exceptions. One of these is the only panorama not shot in Knittelfeld or immediate environs; it shows the heavily trafficked crossing of the Getreidemarkt and Friedrichstrasse in Vienna. A pan shifts over to one of the most memorable landmarks in the city, the Secession building by the architect Joseph Maria Olbrich, which is crowned by a gilded dome. The image is an answer to the commentary from the prior shot, which reports on the public ridicule "in the broader region" stemming from the events in Knittelfeld; it fractures the film's geographic boundaries.

The second exception is an intermezzo in the description of the crimes after two episodes: the deadly shooting of the schoolgirl is followed by a description of an early moment in the family's history, when the Pritzes moved to Knittelfeld in 1977. Whereas the transition only offers the sober facts surrounding the next crime (place, time, actors), the commentary describes tersely the hardships in the metal industry as they took hold of upper Styria in those years. It mentions the lay-offs, subsequent workers' strikes and an amusing episode in Austrian industrial history, when the politicians tried to build a national automobile industry out of nothing. This information on the economic conditions and on sports in Austria in the late nineteen-seventies bears no relevance to the recounting of the crimes. At most, the fact that the father, Wilhelm Pritz, apparently found work in Knittelfeld despite the difficult economic situation, can be related to the family's history, since he was thereafter purportedly poisoned by his wife, as is subsequently revealed. Still, the details, unusual as they are for the film, present the opportunity to consider the conditions in Austria and the desperation of one provincial region that had apparently pinned all its hope on the establishment of an automobile industry—which itself suggests pure political propaganda (or helplessness).

Like the shot of the Vienna Secession building, this brief episode also looks beyond Knittelfeld to the situation in the entire country. The distribution note by Bert Rebhandl quoted above formulates the same impression: "[…] and so it is with this film, which does not tell the history of the town of Knittelfeld, but rather the history of a town *like* Knittelfeld."—[53] Friedl therefore consistently avoids images of the city's actual "landmarks." The city's parish church, the conference and cultural center, the central square with its sculptural fountains or the plague monument are absent, although these are the primary elements used in the town's marketing. Instead, the film shows excerpts of a city that, in its unspecific, Central European form, could be anywhere in Austria. Friedl makes as little of the difference between urban, periphery and natural landscape types as he does of the place's individuality. *Knittelfeld*'s "landscape" is the sum total of all Styrian topographies.

The exchangeability of the images and their reference to the fundamental lack of specificity of the Austrian (or Central European) small town is emphasized by means of panoramic pans in most of the shots. Just as *Knittelfeld* is synonymous with the sum total of comparable towns, so, too, does the panorama show the totality of the disparate monotony that dominates these localities.

The narration of the criminal Pritz family may only be a radical footnote in Knittelfeld's history, but for the topos of the provinces as location of horror, it is exemplary in the way it points beyond this peripheral existence and impregnates the image of the wholesome landscape with doubts. It is hardly possible to make this argument with

53 Italics by the author.

a greater sense of impending events than in the film's final sequence: the commentary describes the whereabouts of Karl, Hanna's brother who first beat her son into unconsciousness and then drowned him. The sentence is life imprisonment. While incarcerated, he refused to have any contact at all to his family. He does, however, cultivate correspondence with an "older woman from Düsseldorf" who has converted him to the spiritual sect *Fiat Lux*, founded by the faith healer Uriella. The image shown at this point depicts dense woods, which apparently stand at the crest of a hill. The camera pans at a stately pace along the woods' edge and finally reaches a monument: a coarsely sculpted stone block serves as a high pedestal topped by an iron cross—the "Tatzenkreuz," which immediately recalls the synonymous military honors designed in 1813 by Karl Friedrich Schinkel for Kaiser Friedrich Wilhelm III. The subsequent moment is extremely unusual for the film: whereas all the other cuts connect two entirely dissimilar perspectives, the next shot shows the same

cross in close-up, and thus makes explicit what was hardly recognizable in the prior shot. The center of the cross is occupied by a swastika, beneath which is written the year 1939. The film's final, immediately subsequent shot is a static establishing shot of the Mur valley bathed in warm, autumnal light. A military jet is just landing.

The formal break, the cut between the third-to-last and second-to-last shots lends the monument at the end of the film great significance. The repeated, magnified shot ensures that the swastika cannot be overlooked and that its date is recognized, as well as what the cross' form already implies: the monument dates to Austria's annexation to the German Reich. The latent threat, which emerges from the reappropriation of a Christian symbol into a Nazi symbol, is doubled by Friedl with the comment, in which Karl is described as a member of the Order of Fiat Lux. In analogy to the recoding of the Christian symbol by the swastika, Fiat Lux is also a perverse splinter group of the Christian church. The bigotry of the child murderer, who is apparently unwilling to deal with his family history, indicates the lack of reflection, the intolerance, and the insincerity that has marked the family history's trajectory. The image of the still-present Nazi monument raises this bigotry to the larger political and social level of Austria's way of dealing with its past.

The landscape's militarization is, at the end of *Knittelfeld*, ubiquitous and again references the story of the Pritz family with which the film began. It, too, is martial, although no military honors or monuments are accorded to it. The chain of murder and manslaughter is revealed to be a symptom of the society's precarious condition, resulting from the way it avoids dealing with its past altogether, or deals with it selectively, just as Karl Pritz refuses to contend with his familial responsibility.

The seemingly extremely arbitrary and, relative to an understanding of the landscape, insignificant episode of the uncontrolled Pritz family is, at the end of *Knittelfeld*, unexpectedly embedded into the landscape in a drastic manner: it is related to the political history, which has *actually* inscribed itself into the form of the landscape by means of monuments, military airports, and airplane flights. The martial is ubiquitous. *Knittelfeld* keeps the consciousness of this fact alive *in the image of the landscape*.

Thus, the essential argument made by *Knittelfeld*—as
articulated in the images—can be interpolated from the
landscape and the "division of labor" between image and
soundtrack: in order to understand the landscape around
the town (as seen in the images), knowledge of the social
interrelations is decisive (as could be heard in the narration of the commentary). Together, the two levels create an
inventory of clues, which have inscribed themselves into
the landscape by means of social, political, or economic
actions.

Knittelfeld is devoted to complex interstitial phenomena,
because it is only by analyzing the relation between society
and landscape image that one can explain why the contemporary topography around Knittelfeld bears the signs
of manifest and latent violence, which has apparently
penetrated into its inhabitants' everyday reality without
notice or resistance. This is witnessed not only by the
Nazi-era monuments or the military presence at this place,
but also by the quickly built industrial and shopping
complexes, realized without much sensitivity towards the
landscape, and by most urban situations whose exchangeability accelerates the provincial town's loss of identity.

Still, the primary impression left by *Knittelfeld* is
societal and political. The interest of the author Gerhard
Benedikt Friedl was likely not the landscape above all else.
Nevertheless, the way he works in *Knittelfeld* is very closely
tied to spatial observations. In the process, he takes care
"to be attentive to relationships in what is visible."—[54]
With his research into the Pritz family history and his
insistent observation of the milieu in which he lived for
two months while preparing for his film, he derived for
himself a reading of the landscape; he then sought to make
the conclusions drawn apparent to the film audience by
means of the precise choice of shots and the rudimentary
narrative. The decisive phase in the production process is

[54] The quotations in this section are taken from a letter written by the filmmaker to the author in August 2007.

the intersection of image and narration. Friedl describes the result as "a network of crimes that have activated the places and that settles onto the topography in the form of memory and thought." The retelling does not assume the form of a refined narrative. Instead, it provides only the scaffold of structural information, which can carry enough weight to motivate the film-goer's thinking, but remains open enough not to close it down again. It is an "activation of images/topography by means of storytelling."

Filming and writing are equally important activities in Friedl's production. The way in which the narration is grafted onto the image of the landscape proves to be a contextualizing tour de force, which reveals relationships that could not be communicated by the image alone. In other words, *Knittelfeld* draws in its own particular way upon the potential of the filmic medium in order to meld the narration and the image of the landscape, and to guide the viewer's eye. In the process, it returns to the beginnings of that transformation which Edmund Leach described in the quotation already cited: first, a story attaches itself to a place, and thereby impresses it onto the public consciousness. By means of the gradual assimilation of its narrative-based existence, however, the place slowly acquires the power to retell this story itself. Although no one would wish it on the city of Knittelfeld, Friedl's film demonstrates the potential to unfold its social effect in this way.

Mattias Caduff: *Peiden* (CH 2002)

One film that seems at first glance apolitical is Mattias Caduff's *Peiden* from 2002. Once again, the title describes a real place. This place is in Lugnez, an extremely pictur-esque valley in the Canton of Grisons, Switzerland, but a place under enormous economic pressure and suffering from growing emigration. This emigration not only destroys the social fabric of a population, which had for centuries remained very homogenous, but also has concrete consequences for the landscape: the slopes and meadows, once "tended" by the farmers and their cows, are left to themselves and revert to a wild condition within a few years.

Peiden is located within this context and thus participates in a long tradition of Swiss films. However, Mattias Caduff's Peiden separates itself vehemently from this ethnographic tendency in Swiss films, which consider the heritage of farming.——[55] The film distinguishes itself from these works in form and content: Caduff does not depict the lovely landscape of the Lugnez valley and its agricultural tradition. This is not only attributable to the concentration on the town and its inhabitants, but occurs with the knowledge that it is difficult "to tell an interesting story […] without inventing a lot." In other words, it recognizes the conviction that recourse to the tradition of the beautiful Alpine landscape today is comparable to pure invention.

55 Worthy of mention here are above all the films of Erich Langjahr, but also *Urmusig* (CH 1993) by Cyril Schläpfer, *Das Alphorn* (CH 2003) by Stefan Schwietert, or *Hinterrhein—Umbruch im Bergdorf* (CH 2004) by Lisa Röösli.

The film's first image, accordingly, does not show a panorama, but instead the filmmaker himself sitting at a table in front of a window. There is a lamp above him. Faint light in the window behind him indicates dusk. He holds a piece of paper in his hand from which he reads aloud: "My grandfather came from a tiny village in Lugnez. He had to emigrate some hundred years ago. At first to Chur, then to St. Gallen. He died before my birth."

The gesture and form of speech recall the classic form of "Once upon a time." Caduff is apparently telling a fairy tale—and as one knows, these are stories intended to uplift, but also to teach a lesson. This is also true of *Peiden*: the film tells, one after the next, the story of the twelve inhabitants who still remain in the village. Beginning with Margreta, the oldest and the only one to have been born in the village, he indicates the problems associated with this Alpine community, which has slowly transformed from an agricultural settlement to a vacation spot; posterity can no longer be expected, and the town petrifies with its increasingly elderly population—slowly, inevitably.

The fairy-tale gesture lends the story initially the nimbus of happily-ever-after and intactness. Accordingly, just after his introduction, Caduff shows extensively the old loom that Margareta keeps in her house. The images of sunlit mountains and fertile meadows, as they are often

used in the exposition of documentary films about the Alps, are absent in Caduff's film, but nonetheless, the old crafts—for example the nostalgia of an old loom—function as mild evocations of the "traditional" life in the Alps. The shots of details, which appear with noticeable frequency, achieve the same nostalgic effect: Margreta's flowered cup or the three apples on the threshold, which a neighbor has left for the filmmaker who has apparently fallen ill. Even if these shots cannot be read as direct references to the cliché of the Alps and Alpine life, they still represent moments evoking the values, which can be identified with the lived culture of Alpine village structures.

Immediately thereafter, however, the film describes, as if coincidentally, how the changing times have made inroads into Peiden. Several villagers still correspond to the modest, rural life that was typical for the region's inhabitants for centuries: Maria, the lay assistant in the church who has boarded the priest for three years. From her, one learns that she once ran the Restaurant Bad Peiden, which was open 364 days a year and answered to every (culinary) wish of its guests. Even today, quite elderly, she runs the household for the priest and her son Ignaz while also taking care of the church. To underscore the sequence, the camera watches her preparing "Capuns," a labor-intensive regional specialty, for dinner.

Margreta, mentioned earlier, had a similar life story: as a young woman, she worked in various hotels in Grisons until the Second World War forced her to return to Peiden, where she ran the household for her mother and her three brothers—until they all died.

Here are the virtues of the mountain dwellers: the modesty, the satisfaction and the lives spent working industriously. The lives of the two oldest inhabitants correspond in fact to the common clichés. But aside from these two traditional biographies, *Peiden* depicts exclusively modern lifestyles. Martin works four to five days each week in Winterthur for the marketing division of a large company and comes to the Lugnez valley for weekends where he cultivates the basic seeds for the first commercially available high-altitude ecological grasses. Ignaz is a self-employed truck driver on call throughout the entire Grisons canton. Celi lives in Domat/Ems and spends his weekends in the village doing community work. Katharina works in the village via Internet as translator and editor for the Swiss Federal Office of Gender Equality. Isteria is a school psychologist in Ilanz and devotes her spare time to computer concentration training, which translates brain waves into a kind of computer game. The couple named Harry is spending their sunset years in Peiden, after an active life that even took them to Hong Kong.

Almost as an aside, without particular emphasis, the commentary notes other facts, which determine the villagers' lives significantly but cannot be represented

in images. Among these are the circumstances that Katharina is the only one in the village who, via Internet, actually makes her living there; that Celi and Ignaz have more than once repaired Peiden's sewage and water system because there is no money to pay for it properly; that the only member of the village's choir who lives in the village is Katharina, who only moved there recently from Gösgen. Or that on August 1, Switzerland's national holiday, none of the inhabitants participate in the communal festivities, but that only with summer vacationers do children come into the village. Caduff makes clear that work and life in the Peiden of today has little to do with tradition.

In the film's final sequences, the commentary finally broaches the topic of loneliness. The priest describes it as the Peideners' characteristic: "Everyone is a village unto himself." Even Margreta, who died shortly after filming began, had told him that her last winter had been horrible. She felt alone and was fearful of pain. "How lovely it would have been, had you been here!" she had said, according to the commentary, to her distant relative the filmmaker.

The style of speech borrowed from storytelling and cultivated so explicitly by Caduff has a dual function. On the one hand, as he himself indicates in the end, he wants to refer to the difficulty implicit in telling stories from "everyday life," "without inventing much of it"—a standard problem in documentary films. The accentuatedly fairytale-like, even exaggerated-seeming gesture towards the narrative quality of the portraits presented confronts Caduff with the problem of subjectivity in a documentary film, while he *nevertheless* registers his ambition to do justice to its subject matter.

At the same time, however, the fictional gesture of the fairy-tale-like storytelling is a subversive means with which to represent the reality of Alpine life: it is a kind of intervention into the idea that the Alpine world is still in order. Recited in a harmless voice, the fragments of the villagers' real lives first develop their full effect as an afterthought. The film's form and content must be carefully compared to each other if the viewer does not want to be led astray by the film's soundtrack into reconfirming his own clichéd preconceptions.

One of Caduff's dramaturgic ideas accentuates Peiden's function as a proxy for the transformation of the Alps: even before the story of each inhabitant is introduced by an image of his or her respective house (the vacation homes that are not occupied year-round and their inhabitants

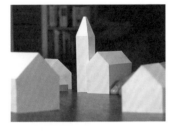

are absent), Caduff shows each house, even the church, in a model that he built himself out of simple paper, sited according to an interpretation of the actual topography.

The model *Peiden* tells a story about a little village in the Swiss Alps (it could also be a different village), but simultaneously, surreptitiously, between the lines, it also tells the story of the discrepancy between the reality and the traditional ideals, which hinder necessary structural changes. Because he *does not tell* the "official" narration of this central Swiss cultural landscape and shows everyday Alpine life, instead of picturesque mountain scenes, he is acting politically. To tell in the form of a fairytale what is *really* visible and what *in fact* determines everyday life in the Alps—"to see through the strata of memory" (Schama 1995)—is what makes *Peiden* subversive.

Stefan Kolbe and Chris Wright: *Technik des Glücks* (The Progress of Happiness, GER 2003)

The documentary film *Technik des Glücks*, by the two young filmmakers Stefan Kolbe and Chris Wright, is located in East German Zschornewitz, the site of what was once the largest coal-burning power plant in the world. After German reunification in the nineteen-nineties, the plant was shut down over time. The story is framed by an anecdote told at the start of the film by a voice-over: the grandfather served in the British Air Force during the Second World War and was commissioned to bomb the Zschornewitz power plant. The undertaking did not succeed because the pilot could not find the plant. The two filmmakers have the same experience today: they cannot find the plant because it has been completely dismantled in the interim.

The film's protagonists are former workers who share the hobby using video cameras to document their lives and even more so, the spectacular implosion of the obsolete industrial infrastructure. These men and women's video footage nonetheless enables the two filmmakers to show the enormous built structures that had vanished before they started to shoot the film.

The stories told by the plant's former employees, in addition to the video and super-8 footage they put at the authors' disposal, depict a lively, if provincial Zschornewitz. The scenes are populated with the local inhabitants; parties and celebrations are held; and in poems, stories and excerpts from instructional and fictional films associated with the plant, it is apparent that this was not just a place of dwelling, but also of work and life.

In contrast to these shots, often of poor quality, the film includes two categories of images that Kolbe and Wright shot themselves on location: sequences with former workers in their modest apartments and at their former places of work; and long, unpeopled shots, taken with a tripod, of views of the town as the two filmmakers found it at the turn of the century. Accompanying these images, fictive radio broadcasts are read, which for the most part report on daily, harmless police actions, or those which were of no consequence.

There are only few actual landscape shots in *Technik des Glücks*. It would be dubious to call the film a landscape film on that basis alone. And yet the viewer does get a specific idea of the area around the Zschornewitz plant because of the way the visual representation of the power plant's landscape is incorporated. By means of the found filmic material, it draws in many temporal levels and enables, even within a tight framework, a diachronic perspective, which covers the development of the area

from a small village to a significant industrial location in the Modernist era (with its own garden city) and its "decommissioning" by the reunited Federal Republic. The lone landscape *images* are not the only level on which *Technik des Glücks* describes the landscape: an internal "image" of the situation today (which can assert itself as exemplary for the conditions in the decommissioned

German east) is created by the weft of information on the social and economic space, as well as by the metaphor of empty fields, the location of what was once the largest anthracite coal power plant in the world.

The elements of this weft are presented to the viewer in a preinterpreted form: the two temporal levels—that of the "found" filmic material and that of the scenes filmed by the two authors—deploy the discrepancy between the activities shown in the two respectively, to insinuate the decline of Zschornewitz not as an industrial area, but as *Lebensraum*. The rigidity and stylistic restraint of the actual shots suggests the standstill to which the region

has come. Together with the amateur footage of the plant's detonation, the images of former plant workers in the ruins of their former place of work reveal the loss these people have suffered. Finally, the interviews about the economic situation make their precarious commercial situation explicit.

A chorus of elements thus communicates a complex image of the former industrial city: the political reorientation of 1989 is presented as an event that both ended brutally the prosperity of the area around the power plant and transformed the lives of its inhabitants into a kind of paralyzed hopelessness. *Technik des Glücks* shows the area around Wittenberg as a product of its volatile economic significance in the twentieth century and identifies the

195

reason for the emptiness of its landscape and people today in the region's vanished economic basis, and in an introspective insistence on what is past, which seems to be the only source for motivation left to the few inhabitants shown in the film. Coupled with the story and the life of those who today appear to be the losers of historical development, the landscape's configuration concretizes for the viewer the complex visual, historical, social, and economic threads in a way that simple depiction would not have accomplished. Or to use the terminology of Clifford Geertz, Gerhard Hard and André Corboz: *Technik des Glücks* is a *thick description* of Zschornewitz, which uses clues tracked by the two filmmakers to decode the landscape *palimpsest*. This makes visible not only the contemporary form of the landscape portrayed, but also the processes that have configured it topographically and socially. *Technik des Glücks* is simultaneously an analysis and an interpretation of the landscape according to the paradigm of clues, which, in recognition of the complexity of its subject, makes no claims to universal validity.

Political force arises from the film's approach: while it would have been easy simply to show the morbid beauty of the landscape, the film chooses the path that leads through contextualizing, multidimensional information, pointing to an obvious and acknowledged connection (if often ahistorically regarded and thus easily expunged from the picture): the political reorientation did not bring forth "flourishing landscapes"—[56] but instead, the decommissioning of infrastructure, production, and social identity.

56 In a television address on July 1, 1990, then-chancellor of the German Federal Republic Helmut Kohl used the metaphor of the "flourishing landscapes" to describe the future of the German Democratic Republic, which would be integrated into the GFR three months later.

Patrick Keiller: A Flaneur in England

A pronounced characteristic of Patrick Keiller's films is the careful framing of architecture and landscape. Keiller was an architect before he was a filmmaker. At the time of his architectural studies, the long tradition of the landscape image in England had been rejuvenated by a series of remarkable landscape films. In the nineteen-seventies and eighties, such filmmakers as Chris Welsby, William Raban, and Jenny Okun produced a large body of structural films, which exclusively considered the landscape and its objects. This loose artistic movement was the subject of an exhibition in 1975 at the Tate Gallery entitled Avant-garde Landscape Films; among its most important works are *River Yar* by Chris Welsby and William Raban (Dual projection, GB 1972), Chris Welsby's *Seven Days* (GB 1974), William Raban's *Surface Tension* (GB 1974–76), and Jenny Okun's *Clouds* (GB 1975).

Keiller does not see himself as a direct heir. He takes more of an ironic approach to the landscape, which has nothing in common with the planned chance operations of most of these structural films:

> I try to maintain an ironical attitude to the process of image making. I always think, "what is the most obvious way of making an image of this subject?" and then do it. (Pichler 1998, 52)

Only showing the obvious may be an accurate description of a few shots from Keiller's films. In general, however, Keiller's eye is primarily trained on those things that are so mundane as to have long become "invisible" in everyday life, in addition to his interest in official and officious spectacles (for example, the pompous parades in London, which have an established position in news reporting about the city). As the narrator at the beginning of *Robinson in Space* remarks, "The true mystery of the world is the visible, not the invisible [...]" (Keiller 1999, 5). Keiller's films *show* the visible by simultaneously *narrating* the invisible. In *London* (GB 1994)—as reported by the voice-over by Paul Scofield at the beginning of *Robinson in Space* (GB 1997)—Robinson had received the commission from a government agency to study the "Problem of London." He believed "that if he looked at it hard enough he could cause the surface of the city to reveal to him the molecular basis of historical events. And in this way he hoped to see into the future." The city as palimpsest which has to be read, the past as source for the development of he future—Keiller's Robinson seems to know his way around contemporary landscape theory.

Robinson carries out his studies in the tradition of the peripatetic by following three routes through London on foot and thereby ascertaining that the "Problem of London" is the English people's fear of the city and, above all, of the emptiness at its center: the financial district, which more or less corresponds to the area of the city's original Roman settlement. Only about 6,000 people live here and at the end of the workday it depopulates for the evening. London's actual identity, according to the narrator, is the *absence* of any identity: "London was the first metropolis to disappear." This pessimistic sentence ends *London*, which in image and commentary explicitly sets some of the cherished myths of the official London against the city that it *actually* finds in front of the camera. At the same time, it makes the involvement of British politics in London's cultural and social development responsible for the problems.

Robinson in Space (GB 1997)

The same first-person narrator appears in *Robinson in Space* as in *London*. He quickly bridges the years since the first study and reports that Robinson had contacted him again a short time earlier. A well-known, international advertising agency had approached him to complete a "peripatetic study" dealing with the "Problem of England." Robinson accepts the commission; the first-person narrator agrees to accompany him; above it all stands a motto, borrowed from Oscar Wilde's *The Picture of Dorian Gray* that recalls certain aspects of the prior film: "It is only shallow people who do not judge by appearances. The true mystery of the world is the visible, not the invisible" (Keiller 1999, 5).

Robinson in Space busies itself with showing the visible and reading the world's mysteries that are thereby revealed. The two researchers undertake seven trips through postindustrial England (and a detour along the Channel), which take them increasingly further into the north of England. With this movement, they take on an activity that was a partial contributor to the nation's genesis: it was only by means of the travelogues of the eighteenth century that the island was perceived as a whole. The idea of "England" but also the idea of "Great Britain" developed as a consequence of these descriptions (Burke 2006, 12).

The travels of Robinson and his companion quote this tradition. Like Daniel Defoe before them, whom the narrator cites at the outset, they cross the whole of England and thus communicate in temporally and geographically intensified form that which in reality is far apart and largely disparate. The journeys become a kind of compressor, a "binder" that permits the direct correlation of phenomena, which would be perceived independently of one another in everyday life. All of a sudden, typological sequences emerge that reveal not only the surface, but also the structure of England: England is slowly constituted as a postindustrial country at the end of a conservative political era,—[57] torn between the logic of a romanticized industrial production in the Victorian tradition and new forms of wealth creation based upon invisible, highly technical, globalized processes. And just as Daniel Defoe had been convinced earlier, the journey in fact created connections among distant social and economic phenomena, while at the same time integrating them into a familiar narrative. In the tradition of Defoe and his travelogue *A Tour through the whole Island of Great Britain* (1724–26), Keiller has his two fictive travelers unroll a huge amount of statistical data in accordance with the journey's subjective and interpretive

57 A few months after the premier of *Robinson in Space*, John Major's Tory government—which followed the eleven-year reign of Margaret Thatcher—was voted out of office after less than seven years.

mission. He thus creates an integrative, complex way of seeing that makes the data understandable and valuable for the viewer. The reading of clues in the visible universe of landscape topography creates a network of observations that at the end of the film coalesces into a usable form of argumentation and a plausible interpretation of England's contemporary development.

Traveling in Images

To this end, the picture plane in *Robinson in Space* is reduced: the journeys are almost exclusively documented in static shots. People hardly enter the images; instead, there are unmoving views mostly of landscape motifs.

As mentioned, the cadrage is structured with the greatest of care, so that even in the absence of motifs with classic beauty, the situations are depicted in aesthetic images. The shots do not, however, correspond to picture postcard views as travel guides favor them. Instead, they derive from the repertoire of J. B. Jackson's Landscape Three. They show everyday spaces of living (and working) in England. Even garbage dumps and buildings slated for demolition earn an appealing representation, usually emphasizing one-point perspective. They can be intensively studied and enjoyed thanks to the lack of motion and relative length of the shots.

For the depiction of the landscape, moreover, the static camera has another consequence: Robinson's trip is not shown in images. Keiller's shots do not show any movement, but instead, the places which, for reasons that initially remain obscure, were visited on the journey. All that remains is the commentary, which provides incessant temporal and geographic information to allow the viewer to follow the route on a map quite precisely. The ample mention made of place names subdues any doubts about the film's geography and grounds the situations depicted in the actual England of the nineteen-nineties. The pictorial level of *Robinson in Space* presents views and noteworthy details—but the act of moving through the landscape is only narrated.—⁵⁸

Property Relations. A Typology of the English Landscape.

The commentary has a story about each view, lending it additional historical and social content. In the accumulation of these stories, there are increasing clues about the film's actual story, one about an economic typology of the English landscape.

At least a dozen harbors belong to these typologies. For each, the viewer receives information about the rate at which it is frequented, the ratio of import and export, the primary goods traded, its ranking among English, European or even global harbors or owner consortiums. Note is taken of the production of ships or submarines at a location.

A further topic is the local offices of internationally operating companies and their production locations. They are contextualized with their production, the number of employees, the conditions of employment and often—again—the ownership conditions of the operating company.

These ownership conditions play a role in the shots, which show both the old walls of feudal aristocratic

58 Patrick Keiller himself has commented on this: "Sound is a much more appropriate medium for representing space, as it isn't constrained by the frame" (From the interview mentioned above, 52).

properties and new business complexes. The respective information is fundamentally the same: in the case of castles, manors, and extensive gardens, the anecdotes are about feudal structures, marriages, and rights of way; and in the case of modern business complexes, they are about familial interrelations among individual companies, the international mergers in the business world, and the global competition for market share.

For example, while images of construction site signage (first for a large science park, then for the new Beefeater branch office), a large factory complex, a frontal shot of the Oxford Spiritualist Church, and an older but well cared-for car in front of a brick house are shown, the commentary floats in a broad arc across disparate events, peppered with ironic observations on the private relationships that can significantly determine any venture's economic success:

> On the evening of June 12th, we arrived in Oxford, the King's headquarters in the Civil War, and Hitler's preferred capital had he occupied England. Most of what was once the Morris Motor Works at Cowley was demolished in 1993, and the site is now a business park owned by British Aerospace, who sold the Rover group to BMW in 1994. There's been little made of the fact that Bernd Pischetsrieder, the chairman of BMW, is the great-nephew of the late Alec Issigonis, whose innovative designs for Morris and its successors could probably have given the company a ten-year lead over Volkswagen in the European mass market." (Keiller 1999, 54)

The views of the entry to a classical English landscape park bounded with statuary are similarly accompanied by the rise of the Drax family to become the Earls of Charborough:

> Towards Dorchester, we passed Charborough Park. Col Henry Drax left Yorkshire after the Civil War and settled in Barbados, where, in a few years, from £300 in sugar plantations he acquired an estate of £8,000 to £9,000 a year. His successor married the heiress of the Earls of Charborough. (ibid., 93)

As the commentary insinuates, in the past, as in the present, England's landscape appears to be a territory in which property and power relations, and, in more recent times, economic interests, decide how things will be developed and what they will finally look like. Or, to use Pierre Bourdieu's words: beneath the surface of visible physical space as the camera shows it, the commentary reveals a social space, which can apparently never belong to its inhabitants, but rather is always determined by societal factors of power. Once it was the aristocracy and politics; today it is the global economy.

The disempowerment of the individual to assert himself physically in space is already clear in the frontispiece with which the commentator first begins his narration:

> Sitting comfortably, I opened my copy of *The Revolution of Everyday Life*. "Reality, as it evolves, sweeps me with it. I'm struck by everything and, though not everything strikes me in the same way, I am always struck by the same basic contradiction: although I can always see how beautiful anything could be if only I could change it, in practically every case there is nothing I can really do. Everything is changed into something else in my imagination, then the dead weight of things changes it back into what it was in the first place. A bridge between imagination and reality must be built [...]" (ibid., 1)

Disappointed in England's development and armed with much-appreciated British irony, the film draws a picture of power and ownership relations, which determine the topography in its essence. At no time did the lower classes truly participate in configuring their environments, but there is one decisive difference between contemporary times and the classic period of English landscape building: if it was previously an *apparent* power that configured the landscape, then today it is mostly *invisible*, structurally influential economic potentates that determine the face of the landscape:

The *Victory*, Nelson's flagship, is preserved at Portsmouth and is the principal monument of the eighteenth-century British navy, the largest industrial unit of its day in the western world, on whose supremacy was built the capitalism of land, finance and commercial services centered on the city of London, which dominates the economy of the south of England. Those of us aesthetes who view the passing of the *visible* industrial economy with regret and who long for an authenticity of *appearance* based on manufacturing and innovative modern design, are inclined to view this English culture as a bizarre and damaging anachronism, but if so, it is not an unsuccessful one. (ibid., 90)

Robinson in Space illustrates the differences and similarities of the two systems of domination in many shots. Visible from far and wide, and manifest materially in ways that cannot be dismissed, there are witnesses to the old power structures in the form of manors, castles, and expansive gardens and parks. Today, they are all easily accessible because they have been secularized and are looked after by the National Trust as museums.

Other than the old lords in their time, the new ones limit the representation of their power—if one overlooks the ubiquitous warehouses and factories that look the same everywhere—largely to billboards and directions signs they have positioned at the driveways to their gated, expansive corporate headquarters. To enter them means to see the true representative architecture of the twentieth century from close up. That is as impossible today for the average citizen as a visit to the manor was for the peasants of earlier centuries. Of course, those in power still manifest their claims to ownership by occupying space. But today, much less value is placed on representing architecturally the spatial aspects of this occupation, as was the case in the older regime.

The Periphery of the Visible

The narrator's assertions are not without humor, for example, when he dismisses the role of politics that was formerly quite influential, but today is nothing more than lackeydom in the way that international firms are courted with discounts, subsidies, and tax abatements:

> With the departure of Douglas Hurd for the *NatWest*, there remained three Old Etonians in a Cabinet of 23, about an eighth. Between 1868 and 1955, of the 294 Cabinet ministers who held office, over a quarter attended Eton, so that either Eton is no longer what it was, or, more likely, government is no longer an occupation that is so necessary for Etonians to be concerned with. (ibid., 25)

Mention of Douglas Hurd in this passage contains a hidden (but intentional) reference to the motto already mentioned that Keiller put at the start of his film. Hurd left his position as Foreign Secretary in July 1995 and went to National Westminster Bank Plc. (NatWest). As it relates to Robinson's obsession with the invisible, one event that occurred after the film's premier is worth noting: In December, 1997, Hurd was elected head of the *International Financial Servies*, London, a private organization that promotes the British financial sector, then called the *British Invisibles* (!). It derived from the *Committee on Invisible Exports*, founded in 1968.

The naming of this coalition of financial institutions makes clear that Robinson's fixation on visible and invisible, and his attempt to make the invisible apparent, do not only stem from fiction. To a greater extent, it translates into the discussion of the landscape the actual linguistic rules operable in Great Britain for the production of wealth by British firms abroad: bank transfers, insurance payments and profit sharing are described as "*invisible* exports." They are, as Keiller argues in *Robinson in Space*, (without ever being visible themselves) significantly implicated in the configuration of the British landscape.

Keiller's use of the concept of the invisible differs from the official one only in that, in addition to the actual invisible "goods" in which the modern economy trades, he also includes those flows and productions that want to remain invisible on the periphery of daily trajectories.

That which Keiller began with the film *London* in England's economic center is what he continues with *Robinson in Space* on the periphery. His work recognizes that it is precisely these peripheral regions that play an eminently important role in the new economy. In the first film it is the city, which develops an affinity for the invisible as a pure financial services center and thus hollows out the very idea of the city. In *Robinson in Space*, it is places "at the ends of roads" (ibid., 233) on which he trains his attention. It is here that one finds the production lines of companies that do not want to appear in the conscious minds of the end users with their goods.

The longevity with which these invisible economies impact the landscape's image is made clear by their sequencing and temporal densification in filmic form: the ports, power plants, garbage dumps, wire tap apparatuses, military restricted zones, business parks and distribution centers that function as part of this new "industry" appropriate increasing amounts of space—but they do not make visible an actual production, such as that which the traveler confronted with Nelson's flagship desires, in which people as workers were also involved.

The superiority of this industry as impetus to and basis for landscape development leaves traditional English landmarks as little more than a theatrical backdrop in *Robinson in Space*. Official England is happy to promote the richness of its tradition with the voice of the National Trust, among others, and thus nourish its national self-confidence. But Stowe House, designated by the National Trust as "Great Britain's greatest artwork," has been secularized since 1923 as a public school, and during the filming of *Robinson in Space*, one of six television adaptations of Jane Austin was being produced in Montacute House.

Between these two poles, that which Robinson identifies as the "Problem of England" becomes *visible* in the truest

sense of the word. England is divided between an old, traditional, industrial identity and one that is only now forming itself as a fundamentally new, post-industrial, national identity, in which politics can do nothing more than set parameters; at the same time, it finds itself in a global competition, which it often only experiences reactively. Ultimately, a company such as Ford decides itself whether the commission to build a new compact car goes to Dagenham near London or to Valencia, Spain—and thus impacts the short- and middle-term development potential of entire regions (ibid., 37).

Robinson in Space's approach recalls the work of another British author, who devoted himself intensively to the topic of the landscape: in his 1995 introduction to *Landscape and Memory*, Simon Schama established that the landscape can only really be recognized by working through the layers of cultural memory, which have determined the way landscape is dealt with and perceived over the course of centuries (Schama 1995). For Robinson, it is the ubiquitous romanticizing of the English heritage, which prevents England from *actually* being perceived after almost two decades of Tory government and the rigorous privatization of state operations: "It's only shallow people who do not judge by appearances." Or they do not look closely enough. So it is that the northwest English city Blackpool, with its extensive entertainment offerings, provides the key to his utopia: "Blackpool stands between us and Revolution" (Keiller 1999, 194). In the brightly lit cityscape, the human being's true nature is evident inasmuch as it allows the products of consumer industry to draw it in and overwhelm it.

The polemic motto from the beginning of the film, according to which the real mystery lies in the visible and not the invisible, has proven true in its own way: by identifying and organizing in a *visible* line-up the traces of "invisible" economies, which have taken on the form of landscape as he found them on his travels, Robinson has arrived at the correct questions. It is not fundamentally impossible for the human (or camera) eye to identify the invisible essence of the driving economies. It is much more human ignorance, or in other words the lack of cultural heritage, and the entropy of the landscape, that make it impossible to recognize such things in everyday life. The way to overcome this is the point of narrative *densification*. It imposes an order onto images and thoughts by means of temporal and spatial collection. It brings together disparate landscape elements and makes legible the structures which are apparent, but which disappear in the white noise of everyday life.

With his studies of London and England, Keiller proves that the "molecular basis of historical events" can in fact be read in a certain way on the surface of things—if one has a 35 mm camera, knows how to tell a story about the landscape, imposes some order on entropy, and wants to close the gaps that come into being in everyday perception, because reality is too complex for integrated perception.

Volko Kamensky: Landscape Myths or the Happy Island in the Roundabout

We are standing in front of an empty, disused place, in the middle of space dedicated to traffic; its function and form are normed by regulations with the goal of insuring traffic safety. The island in the middle of the traffic circle—an entirely functional element of landscape design. With its circular form and its central island, it provokes contemplation, and promises to return something to the streetscape that traffic had driven away: the beauty of the natural and the traditional, miniaturized in a circle, whose radius is normally two lanes' width—a vacuum that absorbs ideals of nature. It is a ubiquitous happy new midpoint of a traffic condition, which in its earlier permutation as ordinary crossing had only an invisible center to offer.

Volko Kamensky dedicated a film entitled *Divina Obsesión* (GER 1999) to this element of our everyday landscape, which owes its existence to mobility. In 1996, he was filming in France, where the large-scale experimental construction of thirty-five traffic circles in the city of Quimper in 1982 could count as an unsurpassed success: in one fell swoop, the city in Brittany was freed from its traffic problems. No more chaos on the streets, no more traffic snarls. "From one hundred to zero," according to the "pope of German traffic circles" Prof. Werner Brilon in a telephone interview. The "roundabout" began its rapid victory through all of Europe, where the problem of automobile intersections is now completely subdued.

Kamensky's interest in this locus of wonder is evidenced in the various discourses that he—with some irony—uses to give weight to the twenty-seven-minute discursive journey, which moves from traffic planning to metaphysics.

The film begins with an artificial night sky and a humming sound. One of the white points in the black background gets larger and is finally recognizable as the earth: the iconic blue planet, the largest scale view of the landscape "earth." A cut and we find ourselves in a suburb in France in 1996. Having just landed, we are already in motion—apparently in a car—with our view perpendicular to the direction in which we are driving. In slow motion, newly built, identical row houses flit by surreally from right to left, and once the last one disappears from the frame, the film's actual movement starts: a circular trip from orbit to orbit, with the traffic island always at the center of the image. A metaphysical journey begins.

Spatial Estrangement

Traffic circles are built for automobile traffic, and thus the driver's perspective is the standard perceptual mode for this landscape situation. The driver's gaze is distracted

211

by the traffic island: before entering the traffic circle, he looks left to see whether another car could prevent his entering; later, he shifts right in the direction of the desired turn-off. It all happens quickly. The slightly tense concentration on the traffic prohibits the driver from looking more closely at his surroundings. The formal qualities of the traffic island do justice to this fact. It is intended to ease unconcentrated perception by virtue of its large forms, and to keep to a minimum the amount of perceptual effort needed to understand the overall situation. The operative formal golden rule is thus that the role of the traffic island is to keep the driver's eyes away from what is happening on the opposite side of the traffic circle so that he is not distracted from what is happening in his immediate frame of action. A raised elevation is preferable. The circle's configuration is consciously perceived, but then immediately suppressed, in order to deal with the traffic situation at hand.

The driver's perspective is therefore not self-determined or contemplative, but rather one which is consciously directed by the planned environment and limited in its normal attention span, directly dependent upon the viewer's speed. *Divina Obsesión* thwarts this normal perspective with three estrangements, which prepare the film viewer for the insight that this apparently clear and morphologically seemingly simple traffic layout is, on the contrary, an extremely complex cultural achievement far beyond traffic and landscape planning-based issues.

The most obvious is the *deceleration* of driving speed. The film does not represent the view of someone in a car, but rather, that of what would seem to be appropriate to a pedestrian. One has time to study the traffic island's form in detail. Using this simple intervention, Kamensky destroys the fragile balance among built elements and transient everyday perception while motorized. At once, the elements of the traffic island seem out-scaled, too massive, the forms too clear, the icons too crude. This collapses the place's visual coherence, which otherwise appears to us—the motorized populace—in our daily lives too obvious really to notice. In exchange, its landscape qualities, which would remain unregistered in normal traffic circle "use," earn our attention.

At the same time, a second impression arises, which is typical of slow motion sequences: as disproportionately large and grotesque as the elements in the traffic circle may be, as intensely as the lush plantings exude bourgeois self-satisfaction, it is nonetheless true that the slow, floating, disembodied movement of the gaze communicates the feeling of the sublime, which lends this disturbed, disturbing landscape dignity.

The second estrangement comes into play as reinforcement for this focusing of attention onto elements that would normally not even be perceived: the fact that the camera is pointing perpendicular to the direction in which the car is driving.

In the driver's standard perception, the area around the circle is separated optically from the center island by the roadway. In view of the Divine Obsession however, it is in the background. The adjacent area and the design of the island thus engage in a direct relationship, relative size is accentuated and the elements of the traffic island tend to shift into the out-scaled.

Even the film's panoramas are estranged. While the area around the traffic circles is presented as a more or less normal landscape panorama, the central island revolves in the foreground in the opposite direction, and thereby thwarts visual convention by breaking with the classical form of landscape representation. The viewer no longer stands in the imagined center of the representation, but instead rotates around a point outside of it. The corporeality of the view is thus shifted. It moves simultaneously into the center of a rotational movement where, according to the conventions of the panorama, it would have to find itself again, and out of it, into the panorama around it. *Divina Obsesión* shows *eccentric panoramas*—a genuine filmic form of this classical motif.

In order finally to close the space that *Divina Obsesión* creates, one must carefully distinguish between real and filmic space. Kamensky presents multiple geographically distanced real spaces, which he splices into a single, consistent movement using hard cuts. He does so by carefully equalizing the rate of travel before and after a cut. The viewer should not be conscious of the transition from one space to another, and the impression of a continuous car trip should not be disturbed by the montage.

Since every traffic circle is exited onto the road from which it was entered, the filmic motion culminates in an absurd and *impossible space* when measured against our real-world scales, a space that can only arise in the moving image. The physical reality would keep us captive in an eternal, seedy pendulum-like movement between two traffic circles.

Not so in the wonderful universe of *Divina Obsesión*. Here, the filmic space constructs a *single, apparent continuum* from several geographically distant spatial elements and creates a paradox, consisting of twenty-three consecutive spaces. Driving on the traffic circle becomes an endless loop. Circle upon circle accrues, undisturbed by the Euclidean impossibility of this fact. At the end of this fantastic journey, the viewpoint frees itself from its earth-boundedness and rises to the sky: under the glistening Southern sun and beneath the eyes of a house-high female figure, the voice of Peruvian singer Yma Sumac reaches the highest notes of her enormous range and lends the impossible scenery additional exoticism. The final image draws parallels between the traffic island about which the mystery of Quimper revolves, and the sun as center of our planetary orbit; thus, the frame of *Divina Obsesión*, which ranges from patented traffic solutions to metaphysics, closes ironically.

Kamensky illustrates the associated cultural historical implications of the traffic circle, which can also be drawn from those responsible for traffic circles, with visual non sequiturs that interrupt the flow of the traffic circle's movement: the image shifts immediately to a neutral white background, against which a hand pushes picture postcards into the middle of the frame. Four of these postcards are integrated into the flow of the never-ending traffic circle's movement (See image on page 222). They all show circle motifs from various cultural contexts: a dance scene; a garden design in the form of a shallowly sloping amphitheater; an urban parking lot; and a religious procession that leads around a Madonna statue in a circular enclosure. The circle is implicated as a symbolic, empty form, which is filled culturally with content. Even the decision to design the shots so that the motifs remain recognizable as postcards indicates the inscription to which the traffic circle is subject from many sides: convenient, mailable, ahistorical, and without context, postcards with their verso open for any message, to be filled with interpretations in any number of ways. The traffic circle is the postcard of street traffic.

A Space Takes a Bow

As the preceding description of the final shot already suggests, the film's soundtrack is at least as important as the image. In addition to music, the soundtrack uses three telephone interviews, which the filmmaker conducted with German proponents of traffic circles. The conversations touch on themes within which the traffic circle is functionalized and filled with meaning. Naturally, the conversation at the film's beginning circles the primary meaning of the traffic circle as an element of traffic safety. This is, however, only the basis for further interpretations of the phenomenon.

Prof. Werner Brilon of Bochum University, referred to admiringly by colleagues as the "pope of the modern German traffic circle," states:

> From the point of view of the design, the center of an intersection is asphalt; it's ugly, inaccessible and invisible. From far off, you see nothing. Whereas with a roundabout you can see the middle from all sides, it is nice.

But what exactly is the middle? Helmut Nikolaus from the Traffic Department of Euskirchen has a clear idea:

> I keep saying this is the only place on the road where a motorist has to bow, right? He kneels down, in the true sense of the word [...] normally, traffic signs dominate, you know [...] whatever is in the middle dominates, and here for the first time a certain space, a creative space, moves into the center and the traffic is pushed aside, right?

Traffic that has been pushed aside is traffic that cannot do damage. A tranquil, feel-good space is generated in the middle. The traffic circle apparently not only solves traffic problems, but also those calamities that the car brings with it for life on the street. Werner Brilon explains how that happens:

> Think of an ugly street in a big city. It stretches over ten intersections, the whole stretch is ugly and it's endless in a way. People who live there have no feeling of security. Now imagine such islands every 500 meters, each with a bit of green, each with its own design [...]. Then people are likely to think they are in a homey room—I'm exaggerating with my choice of words—but, and this can be proved by sociological or psychological institutions, such spaces make the people who live there feel at home. You have a claim in which you feel at home.

The impression that the traffic circle has to carry with it no less than the yearning for nature felt by traffic planners is complete when Helmut Nikolaus evokes the unity between mankind and nature by describing the traffic circle as "natural," following a "a natural flow [...] that has actually been rediscovered", with which traffic planners try "to create a self-regulating circulation in the true sense of the word."

The claim that the traffic circle is somehow a rediscovered natural regulating principle is a bold redefinition. From artificial intervention in nature as a built traffic artery, the traffic circle is recoded as natural *circu*lation: from antinature to *false nature* (Barthes 1991, 134). *Divina Obsesión* comments on this outrageous ideological occupation of the traffic circle by means of the estrangement of images already mentioned and the remarkable use of music. As is usual in other works by Kamensky, this commentary remains subtle in relation to the attribution of such unquestioned absolutism as is undertaken in the interviews.

The Space Straightens Up

Initially, the slow motion effect, as has already been mentioned, makes the rhetoric around the traffic circle transparent by undermining the coherence of larger-scale spatial relations and representing the center island as a cultural landscape of the late twentieth century: a landscape element decorated with disjointed scenography and distorted in its proportions that can assume every desired form in any arbitrary location. But by inscribing it visually with a kind of sublime quality, the slow motion effect also does justice to the multiplication of this wonderful space's meaning. The traffic circle becomes apparent as the product of projections; if these projections are analyzed structurally, the contingency of our era and the culture of the superlative are legible in an exemplary way. To quote Roland Barthes freely: the whole world in a bean!

The music underscores the representation's ambiguities and irony. Kamensky devotes the same attention and precision in his films to the sound montage as he does to the composition of the images. Excerpts from seven different musical pieces are montaged to the interviews, all of which can be understood as a commentary on the image and as an extension of the interviewee's commentary. The predominant motifs are those that evoke a romantic idea of the genesis and on occasion offer a counterpoint to the film's content—for example, using futuristic and somewhat artificial synthesizer sounds. A brief introductory track of traditionalizing bagpipe notes is set to an image of a huge terracotta amphora on a large center traffic island; Nikolaus' psychological and natural-mythical interpretation of the traffic circle is, in the end, accompanied by romantic guitar and violin music, which slowly climaxes in a dramatic twist and prematurely ends the interview with a kind of whistle. Without warning, the music moves thereafter into a very loud symphonic passage, in which pompous violins accompany the appearance of enormous steel flamingos, and thus translate the wonder and insanity of modern traffic circle interpretation into sound. Finally, it culminates in the image already mentioned of the Sun King with a song by Yma Sumac, which moves into astonishingly high notes and ends abruptly with the sound of bells.

Akin to the way slow motion is used in the images, the musical interventions comment upon and contrast with the rhetoric in the interviews, but maintain the gesture of poetic sovereignty. In the soundtrack, too, Kamensky avoids overly obvious means to make his authorial voice clear. The ease with which he develops simple means to establish and maintain the balance between myth and material, fascination and critique of the traffic circle, evidences a unique capacity to transpose documentary arguments into precise and yet always subtle filmic ideas. He elegantly translates the complexity of the social narratives, which actually influence landscape-forming decisions by consolidating a wealth of factors that inscribe themselves into the traffic circle, and thus contribute to an understanding of this hugely successful topographic element. The film makes clear that this landscape form can only really be understood through the thick description of the multiple discourses behind the *idea* of the traffic circle. The film achieves the documentary densification of this idea almost without notice, since the elements of the associated rhetoric are integrated into a short, cumulative narration, which can only gradually be reached by the viewer's active effort to interpret it. This narration is the decisive distribution channel for the social knowledge about the landscape offered by *Divina Obsesión*.

James Benning: Panoramas of the American West

> The value [of Benning's films] for students in academic fields such as American Studies, Environmental Studies, and Cultural Studies could be considerable, if only those who teach in these fields were aware of Benning's work. (MacDonald 2005, p. 4)

Prior to his most recent film *Ruhr* (GER/USA 2009), produced by Westdeutscher Rundfunk (WDR), the American filmmaker James Benning worked only with 16 mm film. The decision against 35 mm was essential for his working method, since it permitted him to realize his films by himself. A single person can both transport the equipment needed over greater distances and also operate it without additional help. Thus, Benning can travel around in his car, without organizational machinations or high costs, and film in the most remote places.

At the end of 1999, Benning completed his 35th film *El Valley Centro*. Like his earlier works, it premiered at the Internationales Forum des Jungen Films in Berlin. It inspired an unexpectedly positive reception. When the Forum presented the *California Trilogy* in February 2002, in a special program, the trilogy was preceded by its reputation as a set of extraordinary landscape films. In addition to *El Valley Centro*, it included both of the films that followed, *Los* (2000) and *Sogobi* (2002). Benning's films were astonishing in their stringency, conciseness, and entrancing images of his proximate environment: in thirty-five unmoving shots in each film respectively, he portrays southern California, where he has lived since taking a professorship at the renowned CalArts School of Film and Video.

The fact that this work rekindled an interest over the long-term in the filmic representation of the landscape was not really expected. Of course, there were at that time already films that thematized the landscape with similar focus, but none of them accomplished what Benning was able to do with his trilogy: within a very short period, his films became a reference point for the depiction of the landscape and influenced a string of filmmakers and artists.—[59]

59 Benning's influence is more than clear, for example, in Bernhard Sallmann's *Die Lausitz 20×90* (GER 2004). A patient observing of the landscape over a long period of time is also characteristic of Sharon Lockhart's *Pine Flat* (USA/GER 2005). The film was shot in Benning's second area of residence, a remote location north of Los Angeles.

The California Trilogy

The three parts of the *California Trilogy* share an identical structure. They consist of thirty-five unmoving shots, each 2.5 minutes long, a duration derived from the length of the smallest commercially available 16-mm reel of film, about 2 minutes and 47 seconds. Each scene corresponds to one reel, which was shot completely without interruption and usually including the sound. The beginning and end are cut, in order to eliminate the inevitable bleaching out caused by the light that enters during the changing of reels. A 2.5-minute credits sequence with information on the filming locations and their ownership follows the shots. The completed film lasts 36×2.5 minutes, a total of 90 minutes. The reference to the classical standard film length is unmistakable and underscores Benning's desire to be part of the evaluative context for the cinema and film.—[60]

60 It must be noted that after finishing the trilogy, Benning began to treat the three films as a unit and to show them in direct sequence, interrupted by two fifteen-minute intermissions. Thus, a standard showing of the *California Trilogy* lasts five hours.

In the construction of the images as well, the shots in the trilogy have commonalities: in almost all cadrages, the fine line of the horizon is visible. It is located primarily at the middle of the image, and only varies its position minimally. The lens is the same in all the shots: Benning uses, according to his own information, only a Bolex with 10 mm focal length, with the focus set on infinity (∞) and the aperture set on f11. The short focal length creates images that correspond fundamentally to the perspective typical of classical landscape painting, accentuating depth of field, and making movement appear to be sharply accelerated if it moves along the viewing axis, either towards or away from the camera. The focal depth is quite pronounced because of the relatively high aperture value, and includes the entire space except for the immediate area.

Benning pursues a representational strategy, which we have already come to know in Rüdiger Neumann's films.—[61] The formal rapprochement with the typical landscape representation creates a connection to established traditions of images and seeing, but at the same time, many landscape *types* are juxtaposed with their opposites: next to natural landscapes, Benning shows industrial parks, monocultures, or visibly contaminated areas. As in Neumann's films, it is the very form of representation and the seriality of equally important frames that suggest the landscape-ness of the views offered, not the individual topographies. The series of formally unified images has a homogeneous effect and, because of its cultural weight, the category of "landscape image" is assigned to shots, which, if considered in isolation, would not necessarily be seen as landscape. The stringency of the camera work is thus the key to understanding the trilogy as landscape films.

[61] See above.

The trilogy's three films describe the three territories constitutive of Californian water management. *El Valley Centro* was filmed in the enormous agrarian-industrial areas in California's central valley, which stretches from Los Angeles to San Francisco and beyond. The second part, *Los*, describes the typological variety of Los Angeles County and as a consequence, the corresponding urban conditiono of the completely controlled Central Valley landscape. *Sogobi* concludes the trilogy

El Valley Centro
(1999)

with a—putative—counterpoint to the industrially
and urbanistically configured landscapes of the two
preceding films: with desert, fallow, and left-over spaces,
it focuses on the remaining naturalness in California's
territory and on those areas that provide water for the
rest of the state.

El Valley Centro (USA 1999)

El Valley Centro begins with a shot filmed at the shore of
a lake with a glass-like surface; in the background, it is
bounded by rocks and a white line at the water's surface.
In the lower third of the framed shot is a circular hole
in the lake, through which white, foaming water pours
down to a point far below. One can hear the sound of
rushing water. The explanation for the hole is given to the
viewer only at the end of the film, when the film location
is described by name: *Spillway. Department of Water
Resources. Lake Berryessa.* The artificial lake, some one
hundred kilometers north of San Francisco, serves as
a water reservoir and is controlled by this spillway.

Immediately thereafter, without an intercut to a black
frame, this shot is followed by a view of blossoming fruit
trees, below which the ground is carpeted with white
petals. This is the first of a family of images that show
agrarian land in the most varied of forms: cropland,
watered by sprinklers, worked and harvested by tractors,
or sprayed by airplanes. The third shot shows a plowed,
watered field. It thus forms a kind of synthesis between
the two prior shots—and one later notices—the kernel of
the narration of the landscape, which leads to the sources
and to the users of California's water.

The fourth shot: a garbage dump. Mountains of dark
refuse are moved and worked by trucks. This shot also
belongs to a family of thematically similar views of non-
agrarian "production": a freight train, which rolls slowly
through the image; a burning oil well spewing black smoke;
an earthmover standing in deep water as it excavates a

river delta; a wind farm with hundreds of wind mills, which stand in several kilometers of gently rolling meadows; or the spectacular shot of a cargo ship moving at a stately pace through a slightly rising landscape of crops—the canal that serves as waterway is hidden by the low camera position.

A third pictorial theme includes humans pursuing recreational activities: fishing in a drainage canal; repairing a sports car; or training for a competition.

The brief accounting of shots makes clear the three types of images which comprise *El Valley Central* and through which the implicit politics of Benning's work is manifested:
— Cultural and agrarian landscapes (the picturesque gaze);
— Non-agrarian infrastructural landscapes (the industrial landscape);
— Activities of the inhabitants (the social landscape).

El Valley Central and *Los* are related to each other by a thematic bridge between the first and last shots: the end of *El Valley Centro* shows a pumping station and the concrete conduits of the California Aqueduct; the opening of *Los* is a shot of an old canal in the Los Angeles Aqueduct, which brings water to the city—two images of the water regime in California that are graphically and typologically equal in value.

Los (USA 2000)

With *Los*, Benning added an urban accompaniment to the first agrarian part of the trilogy. In it, he portrayed the larger urban region of Los Angeles: in addition to the well-known bird's eye view of the "grid" of urban blocks, the film shows views onto street corridors, intersections, enormous billboards, shopping centers with their parking lots, and a plane landing at LAX; but also of cattle herds, deserts, wetlands, and landscape scenes with dusty roads

Los
(2000)

that can also be found in expansive Los Angeles County. The third theme dealt with in the images ranges from Latin American gardeners in an upscale gardens, to homeless people in the streets, to an exterior view of the central prison in Los Angeles.

Much like *El Valley Centro*, these shots are also parts of three visual themes, which correspond to series of images from the prior film:
— The official, urban, and touristic image of Los Angeles (the picturesque gaze);
— Industrial, post-industrial, and landscape situations (the industrial landscape);
— Activities of the inhabitants (the social landscape).

As in *El Valley Centro*, Benning designs an additional narration that shadows the usual narration of Los Angeles and makes it relative. But unlike the case of Central Valley, this differentiating of Los Angeles' image not only means a more complex view of the place portrayed, but also includes an intramedial component, which is tantamount to the demolition of one of the most famous urban myths of our time. As Thom Anderson demonstrates in *Los Angeles Plays Itself* (USA 2003), a film consisting of hundreds of film quotations, it is a myth that was to a large extent generated in the cinema. Los Angeles is the most filmed city on the planet. No other is as well anchored in the filmic collective consciousness.

Sogobi (USA 2002)

While the first two parts of the trilogy considered the industrially developed landscape thematically, which runs counter to the aesthetic landscape gaze, Benning devotes the last portion to the "classical beauty of the wilderness" (MacDonald 2005, 12). The film's title is borrowed from the Shoshoni Nation's language and means "earth." Whereas, in the other two parts, the absence of human order appeared as an exception to the norm, the opposite is true here: human traces and human presence mark an almost violent-seeming intervention into the timelessness of the natural landscape.

On the other hand, the connection to the preceding film is found in the last, or first, image respectively: the thirty-fifth shot of *Los* shows the ocean at the Puerco beach in Malibu. The first shot of *Sogobi* also shows the Pacific Ocean, this time, however, a sea otter refuge near Point Sur some 150 kilometers south of San Francisco. As in the first two parts of the trilogy, Benning creates a connection using an *image of water*.

With the thematic connection between *Los* and *El Valley Centro*, and *Sogobi* and *Los*, Benning created a filmic super-sequence of 3 × 90 minutes, but he goes even further with another connection: *Sogobi* and *El Valley Centro* are set in relation to each other by the same means, so that the three films form a closed loop in formal terms. The first image of *El Valley Centro*, as already mentioned, shows the perfectly calm surface of Lake Berryessa, whose water drops into the circular abyss. The image echoes at the end of *Sogobi*, which shows the same location but at low water levels. While the shot in the first film is astonishing because of the unexpected crater in a *seemingly natural* landscape, the shot in *Sogobi* reveals the *artifice* of the entire situation: the low water level reveals that what had before seemed an inexplicable hole is actually a concrete conduit that is rounded on its interior face. In the background, which, apart from the white line at the water's surface, seemed to be a natural shoreline, one can now see the dam, which holds back the water. The slightly shifted framing supports this changed reading. Both images summarize a basic theme of the trilogy in a simple dialectic: what seemed to be *nature* proves to be *culture*. Anything to do with water is not left to chance in California.

Sogobi
(2002)

This play of opposites corresponds to the fact that the accent of both images is set against the primary narrative lines of the two films: whereas in *El Valley Centro*, the eye notices what is natural against the dominant industrial cultural landscape, the final image of *Sogobi* stages the intervention made by the artificial lake into the landscape. Small shifts such as these make it clear that Benning prefers cultural antagonism, which often reveals itself through unassuming traces, rather than views that are free of contradictions. The well-conceived positioning of the two slightly divergent views of the same situation emphasizes the subtlety of Benning's narration of the landscape.

While in each of the first two films there are three different discernable types of images, there are only two in *Sogobi*: humans are entirely excluded from the third part of the trilogy. They are replaced by motorized vehicles, whose occupants are scarcely recognizable. There are thus two types of images:
— Classical landscapes with a naturalistic atmosphere (the picturesque gaze);
— Traces of human presence (the industrialized landscape).

The two groups correspond in turn to two of the types, which had already been introduced in the two preceding parts. On the one hand, these are the picturesque images that can be described as typical of the topography portrayed, because they deliver the usual narration of the respective landscape representation: in the case of Central Valley, the extensively used agrarian and cultural landscapes, and in *Los*, a mild form of the images of the (dystopian) city, as it is determined by countless films and recalled on demand from cultural memory. These two series of images are joined in the third part by the classical picturesque image of the natural landscape in the tradition of the paintings of Thomas Cole or Thomas Moran, the photographs of Ansel Adams, and finally, the films of John Ford.

The anatomy of traces left by human presence in *Sogobi* bespeaks the non-agrarian infrastructural landscape from *El Valley Centro* and the industrial, post industrial, and landscape situations in *Los*: all three offer a counter-image to the canonical reading of the scenery subsumed under "cultural landscape," "city," and "natural landscape." They point towards the transformation of space: through the exploitation of its subterranean resources or other forms of land use, landscape is transformed into an economically deployed resource. But the degree to which the traces of landscape's econonmization are openly legible is a measure of the degree to which they can be easily overlooked, because they do not correspond to the usual "narration" of the landscape. The "strata of memory", as Simon Schama has named the cultural or individual preformation of landscape perception (Schama 1995, 7), have also inscribed themselves into the Californian topography; what is wild in the city, and what is "domesticated" in the wilderness hardly register on one's consciousness. One needs a gaze that penetrates through those layers in order to see what is really there. Filmic montage, as Benning deploys it, makes this possible. Traces that are normally hidden and reveal different formal interests in the landscape—the witnesses of the formal power inherent to "invisible" discourses in the landscape—are made clear by means of juxtaposition and a gaze that takes the time needed.

Human Beings and Landscapes

The third type of image in the first two parts deserves particular attention. Although the human being was located time and again at the center of interest, even in the classical landscape (and only vanished entirely from it fairly late, if sporadically), Benning's quotations of human presence point towards a fundamentally new interpreta-tion of the landscape. In terms of the history of motifs, humans first appear in landscape painting in the context of idealized scenes—longing gestures towards a golden age of human existence. Thereafter, Romanticism stylized people in paintings as proxies for the view represented. The staging of the "view over the landscape" became a repeated pictorial theme, an implicit indication that "landscape" is only created by the human gaze.

In the *California Trilogy*, Benning returns to an older tradition: the human being is located in the landscape without pretense. He does not look, but instead, he works. The kind of work has not changed fundamentally in comparison with the classical precedents: the ground is still—if more intensively used—at least in part worked by hand. But something is in fact different: those in the fields are no longer the hard-working poor, but native white, *largely self-sufficient* farmers, as in the Depression era of the nineteen-thirties, when Franklin D. Roosevelt launched the "New Deal" and the Farm Security Administration hired photographers and filmmakers, whose campaigns were so successful that they founded a new myth of the American farm culture. Today's workers of the land are Spanish-speaking immigrants, poorly paid wage earners working for huge conglomerates, which dominate contemporary agriculture. It is important to discuss the political significance of this observation.

The appearance of human beings elucidates the essence of Benning's working method: he registers scenes, which he finds after careful research and often multiple visits to a place. The decision to shoot usually occurs on the spur of the moment, when the conditions seem ideal. Without staging, the filmmaker challenges situations, which Siegfried Kracauer called "found stories" (Kracauer 1997, 245): those moments of coincidence between the film-maker's subjective desire for expression and the found material physicality, from which the camera extracts a "story." Or as Kracauer formulated it, "The demand for the story, then, re-emerges within the womb of the non-story film" (ibid., 213).

Among these images is also the monotonous training of a female rider, who in the fourteenth shot from *El Centro Valley* rides several times with great regularity towards a goat, in order to catch it with a lasso and take it down; the unexpected traversal of a freight train in the twenty-ninth shot of *Sogobi* or the regular lawn mowing of a Latin American immigrant in frame twenty of *Los*; but also moments independent of human activity such as the unmediated wind blowing across a field of poppy flowers. Shots such as these are jewels, rewarding hours of waiting; they narrate the landscape embryonically: "just articulate enough to convey a shade of human interest..." (ibid., 246).

Found stories can have a particular effect as singularities of landscape representation: by means of a micro-narration associated with the here and now, the visual (and auditory) scenes represented are raised to the status of a phenomenological situation. It presumes the presence of a subject, a subject who physically perceives the situation and makes it extraordinary as a *particular moment* by virtue of his attention. Above all, the found story is meaningful for the person who perceives it, because that person develops a *consciousness* for what is special about that moment; because the exceptional quality of that moment has forced itself upon him. The reasons for this are manifold in nature: a recollection, a bodily shudder, a feeling of happiness, the perception of astonishing beauty.

The film viewer in turn sees (and hears) not only a representation of the landscape (and its sounds), but also becomes a silent participant in the action, which has the character of an experience in that it affects him sensually, corporeally, or spiritually in a particular way. He *experiences* the scene mimetically in a secondary instant. That means: not only as an arbitrary stream of images and sounds, but actually as a specific situation laden with meaning, which evokes a pre-filmic constellation in his consciousness.

By means of the found story, the film viewer acquires
a privileged access to the landscape represented: the
secondarily experienced story and the image of the landscape intertwine to form a whole. The combination speaks
to the audience at a material level, which it shares with
the film author and the world represented, and which can
be empathetically understood. Rather than a distanced
observation, it offers identification with the scene.

Still, let us return to the representation of human beings
in the landscape. Naturally, the presence of humans or
of traces of human action offer the most obvious "stories"
because, as consciously undertaken *actions*, they interrupt the monotony and indifference of nature. Many of
them intertwine to form a larger-scale narration, which
stretches through the entire film. Not only can these
"super-narrations" influence the film's interpretation, but
they can also spread over the landscape represented. To
explain this, I would like to backtrack a bit.

The understanding of a landscape draws generally on
both the knowledge of its topographic qualities and the
tight integration of landscape factors with those of society,
history, or economics. The image of the landscape located
in the foreground of public discussion always refers to an
enriched "image" of the landscape. This is most obvious
wherever a perspective canonized by society inextricably
implicates a landscape and its inhabitants. Film is not the
only medium to establish the stereotype of post-Warsaw
Pact Eastern Europe as an ecologically devastated or,
on the contrary, an entirely wild and untouched natural
environment, which was bound to the social and societal
misery of its inhabitants. Alcoholism is widespread in this
stereotype, as is familial violence and deep ignorance of
world politics and culture. In countless films produced in
the nineteen-nineties, mostly in Germany, the connection
between landscape image and social downward mobility
served with painful obviousness to characterize the
regions that could be (re)discovered beyond the former

Iron Curtain: landscape and inhabitants are depicted in a rough parallel as hopelessly retrograde.—[62] The correlation of the rough Alpine landscape with its gruff, rather unwelcoming mountain people in many Swiss films is of the same generality,—[63] as is the depiction of Finland's barren stretches and the loneliness and silence of its inhabitants, as they appear in Aki Kaurismäki's cinematic successes. The parallelism of two "images" leads slowly in these cases to a kind of metonymic connection: the mention of the one involuntarily awakens associations with the other. The name of the respective region soon serves as a moniker for both: in "the East" are the echoes of the "flourishing landscapes" and environmental catastrophe, as well as of a region in which the inhabitants find solace from their desperation in collective alcoholism. After the transformation, the landscape of Eastern Europe is no longer only understood as despoiled or gone wild, but also as poor, remote, and retrograde.

The comingling of a landscape image with the characterization of its inhabitants leads us to the center of Benning's filmic landscapes. The difference is, however, that he does not offer clichés, but instead takes up topics, which are inscribed into the landscape through specific forms of use. He inverts the way of working just described and uses the power of filmic representation in order to create alternative associations, which have not (yet) achieved society's approbation. His understanding of landscape is founded explicitly upon the contextualization of topography and societal themes. His films cultivate a form of landscape representation that favors a spatial perspective in which the social and political reality is integrated as a factor.

The Politics of (Landscape) Images

In California's central valley, Benning became aware of widespread, well-planned irrigation systems, which makes the extensive use of land in this dry region at all

62 Better-known examples for films that operate with a reduced, clichéd representation of the "East" are, among others: *Asta E* by Thomas Ciulei (GER/ROM 2001); *Absolut Warhola* (GER 2001) and *Die Mitte* (GER 2004) both by Stanislaw Mucha. The film *Workingman's Death* by Michael Glawogger (AUT/GER 2005) evidences aspects of this stereotype in an episode about illegal coal mines in the Ukraine.

63 For example, Fredi Murer's *Wir Bergler in den Bergen* (CH 1974); the Farmers' Trilogy, and other films by Erich Langjahr (CH 1996–2002); or *Die Insel* (CH 1993) by Martin Schaub.

possible. Today, the valley produces a quarter of all the food consumed in the entire USA. Benning's shots show these irrigation systems. Six of the thirty-five shots in *El Valley Centro* deal with water management infrastructure in the valley. An additional seven shots implicate the topic of water indirectly: they show desert-like or at least very dry regions, in which little vegetation grows beyond pioneer plants. In contrast to these are three shots with more or less natural-seeming water availability. Benning counters these sixteen shots with thirteen of extensively used agricultural land, whose dependence upon irrigation is obvious.

The larger topic of *El Valley Centro* becomes clear in this accounting. The two other parts of the trilogy open up other facets: the meaning of water fluctuates, depending on the respective context in which it is seen. *Los* and *Sogobi* represent water management as a question of power: certain spaces consume the water that is drawn from others. The topographies, which we see in the trilogy's 105 shots, have acquired their contemporary forms by using technically induced methods of transporting water hundreds of kilometers; without these means, huge portions of Southern California would still be desert-like. These deep-rooted historical reconfigurations are the key to understanding Southern California's topography. Wherever the camera's registering eye sees gardens, fertile ground, and livable land, the montage points us to the historical dimension of the landscapes, which exist there today.

The appearance of human beings in the trilogy at this point has even greater depth. While Southern California is associated above all with a specific type of young, body-conscious men and women on surfboards, Benning portrays an entirely different social class in its natural environment: the population of manual workers, comprising almost exclusively people of African or Latin American origins.

He consciously does not feature glamorous people in the films—especially in *Los*—who enjoy the privileged side of the sun-kissed metropolis. He does not present the house owners in their gardens, but instead the gardeners with Latin American roots who push the lawnmowers in parallel swaths—like the harvesters on the immense croplands in *El Valley Centro*. He shows the field mainte-nance worker of Dodger Stadium, rather than a baseball game. He shows the field workers in Central Valley who hoe weeds with their backs bent. Finally, he directs atten-tion—from a distance enforced by fences and prohibiting signage—to the inmates of Wasco prison. Nowhere in the US is this cheap labor more plentiful than in California. They remain invisible behind the high prison walls—only audible through chants and scansions, which reach the camera from a distance.

Latin American immigrants instead of white Americans, workers instead of stars. With the conscious contrast to the official narration of Southern California as the freest place on earth, where everyone can realize himself, Benning shows a different, dark side of the American landscape: the land that was taken from the indigenous peoples of North America beginning in the eighteenth century in bloody conflicts has, since its settlement, been a place of colonization by whites.

The choice of locales and moments in which the majority of those seen are not those with higher social and society standing, but instead people of color, shifts the colonial past of the American landscape into the depiction of Southern California and shows its contemporary topography to be more or less a direct product of ethnic persecution and the exploitation of cheap labor. This is apparent in the third part of the trilogy, in which colonization, which had been present in the background of the two prior films as a social theme, is projected onto the landscape. Whereas the first nine

245

shots in *Sogobi* could give the impression of completely untouched nature, the loud intrusion of a firefighting helicopter hauling water from the Truckee River in the tenth shot is a significant break. It becomes clear that the natural beauty of "Sogobi" is not beyond the sphere of human influence. Further shots reveal the extent of economically induced interventions: twelve locations show an explicit relation to the human presence in this landscape. The oversized billboard in the Mojave Desert is no more than a somewhat harmless starting point. The following shots show clearly the exploitation of the state's uninhabited regions: timber extraction by Sierra Pacific Industries; cement extraction at Big Bear Mountain by the Mitsubishi Corporation; a military convoy on a sand trail at Twenty-Nine Palms; and a rectangular reservoir for salt extraction (in possession of National Chloride), to name only the most spectacular images. The witnesses to human influence in remote areas drive home the fact that wilderness and free nature no longer exist in California, except in the romantic imagination. Water management is here, too, the binding element through which both forms of colonization are compared: Sogobi is a landscape from which the human being draws water in order to use it in other places for agricultural production or for the needs of Los Angeles' urban populace. At the same time, the land to which the water is brought, is the location in which the socially weaker portion of the population is exploited. Land and inhabitants are two sides of the same larger logic. The mention of the film locations in the film's closing sequence thus sheds light upon not only the place, but also property ownership. In *El Valley Centro*, there is not a single shot for which the landowners are not listed.

There it is again, the "history" that enables understanding because it bridges discontinuities and creates coherence in places where, in reality, contingencies prevail. In the 3 × 35 stationary shots of the trilogy, an aspect of the space portrayed becomes clear, which could easily have been overlooked without the filmmaker's intervention to thicken time and geography—that unseen, complex background of the landscape that cannot be depicted in simple images. The radical concentration of the phenomenology of these places and the overview of 105 situations in only 270 minutes gathers the commonalities of the most diverse topographies and facilitates a richer understanding of the landscape.

Even if it is not a classical narration, there is a *narrative understanding* in the film (or through the course of the three films), created by the clustering of shots that share related content.—[64] *The California Trilogy* can thus be seen as a filmic form of "thick description," which conveys Southern California as a complex *product* of its historical development and phenomenological components.

The two poles of this narrative production of the landscape—the understanding of its historical context and its phenomenology—can be analyzed distinctly among films made before and after the Trilogy. Benning developed and formulated the combination of narrating historical events and representing landscape aesthetics even more radically than he did in the Trilogy in his earlier films. On the other hand, his interest shifts in the films made after 2001 more strongly towards the phenomenology of the landscape, and as a result, he experiments with a kind of "pure" filmic landscape aesthetic.

[64] I am aware that I have strained the classical concept of narration here in a way that will not meet with unanimous approval. Consideration of the landscape has, however, shown that the narrow definition of the narrative as is widespread in film (and literature) studies is in need of critique in order to deal appropriately with the variety of narrative forms in our culture. See Potteiger/Purinton 1998 and Bal 1997, p. 220.

(Hi)stories of the Landscape: *Deseret* and *Four Corners*

Before the *California Trilogy*, Benning worked for around ten years on another series of films, which can in retrospect be seen as a tetralogy. In it, he attributes history (or stories) to landscapes and thus generates a perspective within which he wants them to be seen. Unlike the trilogy, he uses a classical voice-over and titles in these films.

The four films' landscapes are distributed across the entire USA (*North on Evers*, USA 1992), contemporary Utah (*Deseret* USA 1995), the four corners region between Utah, Colorado, New Mexico, and Arizona (*Four Corners*, USA 1997), and a stretch of land in Southern California, ranging from Death Valley to the area just across the Mexican border (*Utopia* 1998). The shots are usually filmed from a tripod. The montage varies, however, in its strictness, depending on the soundtrack used respectively. Except in *North on Evers*, this includes an off-camera narration through which the landscape images are recon- textualized. I will limit my analysis in the following to the two films *Deseret* and *Four Corners*.

Deseret

Deseret bears as its title the first European name of the territory today claimed by Utah; the Mormon settlers there gave the territory the name before its assimilation into the USA. Benning procured all issues of *The New York Times* for the film, while searching for reports that had appeared in this "central organ" of the still-young USA about the area later known as Utah. The first story he found was dated March 19, 1852, about a half year after the newspaper's founding. From then until December 21, 1992, he found countless other articles, from which he finally chose ninety-three, which he edited to eight to ten sentences each while making sure that the original syntax and sentence length remained. A narrator reads the reworked articles, to which Benning matched the montage of shots he had filmed in contemporary Utah. Every episode has the same number of images and spoken sentences. In the first image of each respective sequence, the date of the publication is superimposed. The individual reports are separated from one another by a transitional image, in which the soundtrack originally recorded when filming the image can be heard.

This formal organization brings about an acceleration on several levels over the course of the film and elucidates the developments in both the way that reports were put together and the way they were communicated: both the average length of sentences and the lag between event and report decrease over time. If transmission took three months in 1853 (evident in the date of a massacre on government troops by settlers in Utah on October 26, 1853 and published in the *Times* on January 25, 1854), then event and report begin to converge, occurring on the same day towards the end. The montage reflects this acceleration inasmuch as the shots become shorter and the cuts more rapid as the sentences decrease in length. Parallel to this development, the transitional images between individual episodes are reduced with each occurrence by the same factor. The acceleration of speech and reporting are thus registered in the visual experience of the filmgoer.

Metaphorically, the montage points to the continual integration of the Mormon state Deseret into the United States, a development that the Mormon settlers in the east vehemently resisted for a long time. This is also reflected in the Times reports, which document the increasing incursions of both the central US governmental power into the peripheral regions of its sphere of influence, and the Mormon settlers on the land of the Native American indigenous peoples: reports from mutual offensives in threats, bloody confrontations, and massacres thread through the entire film.

In this first thematic major theme in *Deseret*, Scott MacDonald discusses the "development and decay of that series of ways of life that are encoded in this particular geographic area" (MacDonald 2001, 341). Benning uses *The New York Times* reports to narrate the collision of lifestyles among Native Americans, Mormons, and US governmental power as an utterly endless process of land acquisition. And since each of the three cultures brings its own form of land usage with it, and thus quickly inscribes

Deseret
(1995)

itself into the topographic form of the landscape, the ethnic conflicts leave direct landscape-based clues.

A second primary concern of the film, the appropriation and exploitation of land, makes itself known very carefully: if the first reports are about the difficulty of taking over land, about territorial conflicts, and the harshness to which people were exposed by the rigors of nature; then the tone shifts over the course of the reports made in the nineteenth century. At first, there are notices about the region's accessibility, for example, the building of the railroad. Later, it is the increasing numbers of reports on land exploitation and environmental problems that set the tone. The article from May 3, 1900—about an excavation accident with 250 casualties—is emblematic of this transition: it ends with an indifferent remark about the costs, which the contracted firm suffered by virtue of the catastrophe (while the environmental costs are not worth further mention). Two reports later, there is an article on the nationalization of 17,800 acres, which are to be transformed into a military shooting range and training fields. In the years after the Second World War, the topics shift towards large-scale considerations of the landscape, based upon the building of dams (1958); atom bomb tests (1963); nerve gas tests on cattle (1968); different industrial large-scale complexes, whose terrain is widely polluted (1984); the (stymied) construction of military test complexes for biological weapons (1988); the death of entire smaller cities because of the delayed consequences of radioactive pollution in uranium mines between 1947 and the 1960s (1990); and the disposal of polluted earth from Michigan at a special dumping site in Utah (1991).

A formal intervention iconically represents this twofold annexation of the land: with the fortieth report, from January 1896, about the official acceptance of Utah's statehood, the film switches from black and white to color. The break indicates a new era: land annexation moves into its second round, and the exploitation of (spatial) resources gathers momentum.

The use of color in the second half of the film, in which the destruction and misuse of land reaches catastrophic proportions, also makes clear that with this exploitation, the earth's riches suffer, but not the land's inherent beauty. The images in the second part are even more bewitching than before. Even where the full measure of industrial destruction is obvious, the landscape's visual representation can still be aesthetically appealing. It reveals a topography that seems to outlast all human interventions and does not reveal its lamentable state on its surface.

Which images of Utah can be seen in *Deseret*? Benning frames his images expertly and requites the desire for classical landscape views with breathtaking shots. Every episode relates, however, to the report in the *Times*: one shot each is filmed at the location at which the event in question occurred, and literally *shows* the landscape's decline and blemishes, which are described in the report. In Benning's work, the connections are in any case never unambiguous: only a few of the shots in question are identifiable with reference to the events described in the reports. In the other cases, the decision is left to the viewer to consider which shot could have been filmed at the historical location noted in the narration. To correctly locate the newspaper texts requires—like a real visit to an historic location—the search for clues.

Deseret's narrative space is determined by two contradictory factors: the association with each respective locale emphasizes the direct relationship between the historical narrations and the landscape. By choosing, however, not to identify the images and to show views from all parts of contemporary Utah, a kind of generalization simultaneously occurs. In the end, it is not the individual events that are of interest (although many of them are noteworthy), but instead the narrative space that the overview of all reports and images defines. Only in this generalized space does a differentiated concept of Utah's landscape and the history of its statehood as the forty-fifth state in the USA unfold. It is a conception that diverges quite clearly from the typical writing of history.

The synthesis of the two large topics of ethnic conflict and the changing forms of landscape usage implies a direct relationship between forms of societal control and topography, which is transposed into encoded clues. What becomes clear in *Deseret* is also true of the later trilogy: although he travels with a camera, Benning treats the landscape not only aesthetically, but rather uses the emphasis on its historical dimension to indicate its spatial aspects. He understands its *Gestalt* as a product of social processes. He represents it as the product of a gradual but—for many—painful transition from an indigenous hunter and gatherer culture, to one based in farming and agriculture, and finally, to a supra-regional, capitalist industrial culture. *Deseret* thus makes clear that the image of the landscape seen in isolation does not facilitate any real understanding; only the reading of the under-lying reasons that have resulted in human actions can help to decode the clues of the past landscape condition and thus, today's topography.

Four Corners

In the following film, Benning remains loyal to the geographic region he had come to know during the filming of *Deseret*. "Four Corners" is the name for the border region between the states of Utah, Colorado, New Mexico, and Arizona, which is characterized by orthogonal land boundaries.

Four Corners consists of four equally long chapters, each of which has three parts. The film is bracketed by the beginning and end: at the start of the film, the bracket consists of the title and a 2.5-minute shot of a bonfire, accompanied by a traditional song ("Song for the

Journey," played by the Native American musicians, Little Wolf Band). At the end of the film, there is a quotation ("Sometimes dreams are wiser than waking," Black Elk) and a two-minute shot of contemporary trailer homes in a Hopi Indian settlement, accompanied by the song "I Sang the Blues" by the Last Poets. The song's lyrics describe the brutal history of the Native Americans' banishment.

The four chapters are each introduced by a title, with white lettering on a black background that scrolls down across the screen. They tell the story of an artist in exactly 1,214 characters. The following shot shows a work by the artist, to which the voice-over narrates a historical event from the Four Corners region. The narrators of the four stories are filmmaker friends of Benning's and Benning himself, who reads his own story in the second chapter. Each of the narrations contains 1,186 words. Each of these circa 8-minute shots precedes sequences of thirteen images of the region described, which in turn last exactly forty seconds; their only soundtrack is what can be heard at the place depicted. In the precise and obsessively executed game of numbers, and in the strict formal organization, is the echo of Benning's past as a mathematician and author of structural films.

Unlike *Deseret*, in which the image/soundtrack relationship can be relatively simply deduced from the history of Utah and its inhabitants, *Four Corners*, like the title of the region described, makes references beyond its geographic borders. For instance, the four artists who introduce the chapters are Claude Monet, who spent his entire life in France; Moses Tolliver, a black artist from Alabama; Yukuwa, a fictional artist from the second century AD to whom Benning attributes Anasazi cave drawings in the Four Corners region; and Jasper Johns, who lived in New York and became famous for his American flags. Their stories, excepting that of the fictive painter Yukuwa, reveal no relationship to the Four Corners region.

Four Corners
(1997)

By the same token, the four narrations—which are read in relation to the artists' works—do not all originate in the region. The first is the story of Richard Wetherill, who was known as the discoverer and exploiter of the Native American cliff dwellings at Mesa Verde and was shot in June 1910 by a member of the Navaho nation, in revenge for mistreating a Native American. In the second story, Benning describes his own past and the (racial and immigration) story of his native city, Milwaukee. The third episode introduces, in a broad narrative arc, the settlement of North America by the Anasazi and other tribes, whose genealogy can be traced to contemporary Native American nations. Finally, the fourth story is the history of Farmington, a small town in New Mexico, and of Benjamin Benally, a well-educated but—within the American economic system—opportunity-less Navajo who died in 1974 as an alcoholic, murdered by white youths, for whom attacks on drunken Indians were apparently a rite of initiation.

In addition to information on the era of settlement and the conflict among cultures, each of the stories describes facts about the topography and the land's natural resources. It is a story of natural resources: gypsum, which works as a natural fertilizer; coal, gas, and oil, which were found and exploited in the twentieth century within the Four Corners region. The land use is mentioned, the appropriation of grasslands for raising cattle, and the successes in grain production. Mention is made of waterways such as the two rivers La Plata and Rio de los Animas, on account of which the Native Americans called the region near Farmington "Land between the Waters"; and finally, there is mention of pollution caused by oil extraction. Thus, transitions between historical givens and the landscape are established.

The thirteen shots that follow the narratives are filmed with the original sound at the locales of each story (with few exceptions, the soundtrack is not reworked). These are

Chaco Canyon in the first, Milwaukee in the second, Mesa Verde in the third, and Farmington in the fourth episode. As in *Deseret*, they are mostly depicted in static shots: the proclivity towards classical landscape cadrage, central perspective and symmetry in inhabited regions, and a camera usually placed at eye level, are also determinative of the images in *Four Corners*.

At first glance, the artist biographies, the narratives, and the choice of narrators seem disparate, because the geography of Four Corners promised in the title offers only a partially satisfactory background for them. Aside from this (obvious) relational framework, however, there are connections that do not correspond to the geographical location, but instead form a narrative cluster: for example, the narrator of the last story, Billy Woodbury, and the artist Moses Tulliver, are both African Americans. Both have backgrounds associated with Benning's narration about Milwaukee and the racial problems of this Midwestern city, where a poor, white, working class systematically excludes an even poorer, black, working class. The Korean Yeasup Song, narrator of the third story, references the Asian origins of Native Americans (and thus of the fictive artist Yukuwa), who crossed the Bering Straits twenty thousand years ago. The German filmmaker Hartmut Bitomsky, who reads the first story, shares Monet's European background; the old world, according to Benning, is part of the (official) historiography of the USA, in which the native peoples of North America are excluded. Furthermore, Benning understands his own voice in the second story, finally, as a reference to his country's immigration history. He is descended from German immigrants.

Four Corners plays on several levels with settings taken from American history, which are organized relative to the topics of migration, racial identity and power structures. Similar to *Deseret*, the film provides a complex and highly fragmented picture of the ethnic conflicts, which thread themselves through the history of the US and its territories. The landscape as locus of these conflicts emerges in front of the audience in a two-fold process. First, by means of the four narrations, the imagination is inspired by means of information about topography, history and inhabitants. Both in their content and their order immediately prior to the images of the locus of action, they contextualize the images that follow. *Four Corners* uses the four stories to create a specific prior knowledge in the audience. The thirteen views that follow seem to echo these stories and simultaneously to verify the narration because of their indexical relationship to the real world.

On the other hand, the melding of human fate, historical occurrence and landscape view create an overall impression that is more than the sum of its parts. The cave dwellings in Mesa Verde in the film's third segment can, for example, be understood through the information on early agrarian Anasazi culture as witnesses to an early high civilization. The ensuing decline of this culture—the division of the Anasazi people into Hopi and Navajo, followed by defeat at the hands of the brutally governing Spaniards and of the US troups—is still present in the narration of the second segment and is reflected in the traces left in the landscape by the bitter struggle for power in what is known today as the Four Corners region.

The image of the landscape does not only follow the narration chronologically in this case, but also in terms of content. In the process, the audience is instructed in a way of seeing that involves evaluating images aesthetically and also *reading clues*. The historical events introduce a new level of meaning into the depiction of the landscape by declaring it is the *scene of the crime*. The landscape space in these shots analogously becomes evidence of what Roland Barthes called the "this-has-been" of the photographic image (Barthes 1981, 77), reconfigured narratively to suggest a predetermined reading: "This is the landscape in which history has taken place."

The associations to artists and geographic locations make no claim to generalization. The references to different cultural circles in the choice of the four artists and narrators, or the (personal and biographical) connection between the Four Corners region and Benning's native city of Milwaukee, are commentaries that—for the audience—are at best decoded using clues gleaned from interviews. The connections seem too remote and the historical interrelations too extremely foreshortened.

Instead, these references are part of a radically centered argument, which, additionally, is not pursued in a way that allows the audience insight into it. It inevitably raises questions about the status of representations relative to historical reality.

The situation in the Milwaukee of Benning's childhood, for example, as his neighborhood went through a painful process of gentrification in the late twentieth century from a German to a purely African-American area, serves as a model for the much less well-known parallel occurrences in the southwest US. By insisting on a similarly positioned ethnic conflict, Benning raises consciousness of the fact that the war of repression is an oft-ignored component of the history of US American settlement in the West. The repression of alternate versions of history holds for him the key to dealing with history: the invention of "history" is not the exception, but rather the usual form of official history writing:

> If I'm gonna make up my history, let me make it up the way I want to make it up. And you can criticize it, but if you criticize that, criticize all history, don't just criticize mine.——[65]

[65] Benning in conversation with the author on May 28, 2006.

The process, by which historical identity is formed, is a question of power decided in the domination over the writing of history. *Four Corners* can be understood as an attempt to correct through repetition that which all writing of history does when it incorporates the depiction of the landscape. A symbolic form becomes laden with meaning that corresponds to the purpose and intention of the respective representation.

In the official written history of the American West, the heroic stories of the dangerous settling in Indian territories have determined the narrative that became largely inextricable from the image of the American landscape in the twentieth century, mainly through the agency of Hollywood film productions.—[66] Landscape images have proven a more powerful conveyor of the intended messages than language or writing, and the cinema has contributed decisively to the creation of societal identity in the West.

66 John Ford's Westerns should be mentioned first here: *Stagecoach* (1939), *My Darling Clementine* (1946), *Rio Grande* (1950), *The Searchers* (1956), and others.

In *Deseret* and *Four Corners*, Benning uses the same powerful set of tools in order to inscribe meaning onto the landscape: he re-encodes the symbolic content of images using alternative narrations, so that the newly generated way of seeing the Four Corners region (and with it, the entire USA) is capable of competing with the one sanctioned by society. Consequently, the success of this strategy lies no longer in the power of the filmmaker, but rather in that of the viewer.

Typologies: *13 Lakes*, *10 Skies*, and *Casting a Glance*

Following *Four Corners* and the film *Utopia* (USA 1998), not discussed here, *The California Trilogy* can in retrospect be seen as a kind of hinge in Benning's work, fluctuating between the narrative experiments described and films that focus radically on phenomenology. After the extreme minimalization of narrative means in the trilogy—which goes hand in hand with a stronger concentration on the image—Benning turned to his next project, filmed in 2004; this project does not center on the narrative construction of landscape identity, but rather on its visual representation and in particular on the function of time for the perception of the landscape.

This body of work includes the two films *13 Lakes* and *10 Skies* (USA 2004), which share an identical structure, as well as *Casting a Glance, RR* (USA 2007), and *Ruhr* (GER/USA 2009). In place of the barely three-minute rolls of 16 mm film used in the trilogy, Benning exposed eleven-minute rolls in each of the first two films, again for a single shot. In the final montage, the overexposed beginnings and ends of each roll are omitted, so that takes are ten minutes each in duration. As the titles imply, the films comprise thirteen or ten shots respectively and last accordingly 130 or 100 minutes.

13 Lakes and *10 Skies*

In *13 Lakes*, Benning filmed thirteen large North American lakes in the same way: the tripod stands with one leg in the water, the camera more or less at eye level, pointed at the water. The timing of the shot is so minutely planned in advance through extremely time-consuming observation of the light qualities that Benning can film atexactly the moment that, in his opinion, shows the "particular" of each respective lake:

> The idea of the film is quite simple. It's to first look at the lakes and look at the ways the light reflects on the water and the sky in thirteen different locations in the United States. So it's really an aesthetic study of light in the way light falls on water and the way it's going to move [...]. And yet since I picked thirteen lakes that are very different, I want to film them in such a way that you can compare the light on water, but I also want to present something in the image that tells you what's special about this lake. So that's the difficult part.——[67]

67 James Benning in Reinhard Wolf's documentary film James Benning: *Circling the Image* (D 2003).

The second film in this brief creative period, *10 Skies*, shows ten variations of sky and passing clouds. The view to the heavens is unobstructed: trees, buildings, poles or other high objects are excluded from the frame. The only intervention in the filmic representation of carefully chosen locations and moments is the collage of noises that were filmed, if from the camera's location, then not necessarily synchronically with the filming of the image.

13 Lakes
(2004)

10 Skies
(2004)

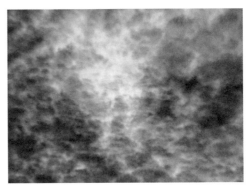

Films that show ten minute-long, static shots of the surface of bodies of water or of passing clouds make demands on the audience far beyond those placed by the trilogy films, with their 2.5-minute shots. They break radically with the usual audience economy in the cinema and facilitate an entirely different kind of seeing experience: a precise observation of the landscape (or the cloud formation) becomes possible, which—apart from the reduction of phenomenological data within the cropped frame—is only different from the real perception of the landscape in that the givens of cinema compel the immobilized audience to be patient and determine its view of the landscape through the framing.

The unusual length of the shots has as a consequence that the viewer's concentration is lost before the end of the shot. Instead of observation, another mode of seeing arises after a certain time is elapsed, which might be called mental flaneuring. The sheer duration makes the viewer's prior knowledge and all his stored associations part of the filmic experience. The image of the landscape merges immediately with the viewer's meandering thoughts to create an overall impression. The radically emphasized temporal parameter makes the mental *construction* of the landscape filmically palpable: it emerges as a product of phenomenological perception and of reckoning up with the "strata of memory."

In *13 Lakes* and *10 Skies*, Benning seems no longer to influence the audience's interpretation of the landscape in his role as author, but seems instead to want only to evoke that interpretation by means of reduction to filmic phenomenology. Viewing leads to the formation of constructions made up of topography and subjective elements; thereafter, one is always reminded of them time after time if one catches oneself daydreaming and returns to a brief moment of attention for whatever changes have occurred in the meantime.

The typical characteristic of this kind of seeing is the hiatus. It is the product of the discrepancy between the slowness of ongoing landscape developments and the boundaries of human attention. The organization of seeing parallels the perception of processes within primary landscape perception according to the length of the shots. The experience of duration is even heightened by the cinematic apparatus. In both films, the viewer experiences with uncommon clarity the process-based transformation of the landscape, and does so within his own, theater-seat-bound body.—[68] The experience of filmic landscape is a bodily experience in space and time, in which the physicality of primary landscape experience is captured in a transformed state. In other words: the experience in the cinema corresponds to a bodily, cinematic eye "located in the world" (Sobchack 1992)—to the impression of a visual and haptic representation of the world.

James Benning expressed himself similarly in an interview:

> However I do think that unconsciously all the work that goes into making an image somehow ends up in that image. That might be a bold statement, and I don't think an audience could tell you the exact facts—it's a subtle feeling. For instance, when you see the sand blowing in the Death Valley with such intensity, you don't know the story of how difficult it was to make that shot and how I was almost delirious from the 130-degree heat and the 45-mile-an-hour winds that were dehydrating me, but I think the shot itself has such intensity that you almost feel that that could be the story. I'm hoping that's true (MacDonald 2005, 12).

Whether his hope is realized must be decided anew each time a viewer experiences visual situation. As the statement above demonstrates, the thought that the viewer's corporeality negotiates between the reduced cinematic experience and the pre-filmic real experience seems to have found its way into the practice of filmmaking.

Within Benning's entire oeuvre, it is here that the aesthetic components of his landscape hermeneutics seem

68 The experience of duration in relationship to the image of landscape had already been probed before Benning—for example, by Michael Snow or Chris Welsby—as part of cinematic experience. Snow's *La region centrale* (CAN 1971) is famous: it is a more than three-hour panoramic camera sweep for which Snow built his own motorized apparatus in order to be able to move the camera like a sphere in every direction. Chris Welsby's *Drift* (GB 1994) shows a single, seventeen-minute shot of a gray lake, which almost unnoticed transitions to an equally gray sky.

clearest: in order to represent what is "particular" about a landscape, it is not enough for him to make its material substance visible. Instead, it is the combination of topography and perceptual situation that must be taken into account. The former is the product of social, political, or economic processes; and the latter includes the light that has been captured on the film, the actions in front of the camera, and the choice of an appropriate point of view from which to capture these qualities. Above all, it is the choice of the camera's location, which makes clear that the filmmaker's intervention and interpretation are ineluctable components of filmic representation. As objective as Benning's images might seem at times, the aesthetic insight, which his films facilitate, always contains a subjective component.

Casting a Glance

After completing the two typological films *13 Lakes* and *10 Skies*, Benning turned to a place that he had first visited while filming *North on Evers* and had since then passed through several times on his routes: Rozel Point on Utah's Great Salt Lake, where Robert Smithson's Land Art work *Spiral Jetty* is located.

Between 2005 and May 2007, Benning traveled monthly to Utah in order to film Smithson's artwork, which had been underwater and largely hidden for almost twenty years. As the lake's rising water level threatened to flood the railroad trestle, which crosses the lake from east to west, work began on pumping water out of the lake on a grand scale, in order to lower the water level. The undertaking not only protected the trestle from flooding, it also meant that Smithson's Spiral Jetty reemerged from the waters. The water level—which has fluctuated significantly since then—and the respective light situation mean that the artwork looks different upon every visit.

Casting a Glance uses a trick to communicate the history of visibility of *Spiral Jetty* and its environs: Benning annotates the water level, which he filmed over a twenty-four-month period, with dates in years from the past three decades. He thus creates a pseudo-portrait of *Spiral Jetty*'s history.

The ending credits are the first indication that the film was made between May 2005 and May 2007 and thus that the dates in the shots are misleading. The audience is covertly shown the ontological status of the images as an *analogy* to the times at which the dating shown *could* have occurred.

By attributing two moments in time to each shot, which was generated in a specific pre-filmic here-and-now, Benning emphasizes that it documents the landscape as it really existed at a given time. However, by means of the "counterfeit" dates, Benning lends each shot a narrative function that serves as a bearer of meaning within the filmic system's own laws. Each take, dating from between 2005–2007, stands *for* a landscape no longer in existence from *Spiral Jetty*'s thirty-six-year history; it does not *depict* but instead *narrates* the work's unexpected fate of decades-long submersion.

The fact that some of the fictive dates correspond to particular events in the nimbus of *Spiral Jetty* or in Benning's life—such as Robert Smithson's death in an airplane accident on July 20, 1973, or the birth of Benning's daughter Sadie on April 11, 1973—lend the fictionalization an associative documentary framework, which is similar to the effect known from earlier Benning films. The portrait of the artwork is recognizable as a broad, contextualizing concern, with its genesis and its own interpretive connection to the landscape to be described.

For the informed viewer, who is not exclusively interested in this central work of Land Art, the game with the falsified dates in the images is reminiscent of *Spiral*

Casting A Glance
(2007)

Jetty's historically documented fortunes; but it is also a homage to the transformability of a place and to the larger processes of nature that can be read in a place. The same landscape appears—depending on light, season, natural changes—to be constantly changing. In Benning's depiction, the twisted berm in the lake can be seen not only as one of the most important artworks in American history; even more so, it also becomes a catalyst, which makes the landscape's constant change palpable.

Casting a Glance makes a landscape experience accessible, whose media-based acceleration is "unnatural." For human perception, however, it achieves a comprehensible and above all visually communicable form by means of its temporal densification: only in this way are temporal processes, which take more time, *legible* in the landscape. The example of *Casting a Glance* shows that the way in which we (can) perceive the landscape has been changed lastingly for some time.

Activating the Viewer

Over the past fifteen years, James Benning has produced an oeuvre that with the exception of *Ruhr*—his most recent film to date—is dedicated to the American landscape. Since 1992, he locates the landscape in an interpretive framework, in which it is read not only aesthetically, but also as a meaningful player in a societal context. The image is for him a means with which to make "the innermost nature [...] able to be aesthetically experienced" (Vöckler 1998, 278). To achieve this, however, over the course of the development in his method described above, an increasingly active audience is required. Benning progressively only offers the contextual information with which the landscape images can be culturally ordered through implication, although in no small measure, by his own admission:

> It [the *California Trilogy*] reduces the variety of ways that I am giving
> you information, but the amount of info is maybe more. It's more
> hidden but it needs a more pro-active audience, an active eye, an active
> ear to listen and an active mind to draw conclusions from that one shot
> and then from the accumulation of shots. (Pichler and Slanar 2007, 172)

The initial concentration on the narrative, in which the
landscape was tied to its own history and cultural and
intellectual background, indicates the extent to which
Benning is conscious of his responsibility as author, not
merely transposing facts about the landscape into a visual
form, but in fact interjecting his own convictions into the
portrait. Using commentary and text titles, he explicitly
directs the interpretation of images towards everyday
stories (*North on Evers*), about the treatment of the other
in the US (*Deseret, Four Corners*), and about the economic
power structure (*Utopia*). The American landscape—especially that of Utah, the Four Corners region, and Southern
California—are not only depicted in these films, but also
read as historically laden topographies in conjunction with
historical events.

The role of interpreter shifts in the trilogy more
strongly towards the viewer. Confronted with the structured collage of images, he is not required to *gaze* upon
it without much commitment, but instead *to interpret*
what he sees. The clusters of related motifs, such as water,
migration, and work, guide his attention in the process.

In the two typological films *13 Lakes* and *10 Skies*,
Benning almost entirely dispenses with narrative elements
and simultaneously limits his authorial contribution to the
choice of camera location and framing. He leaves the field
of interpretation almost entirely up to the viewer, who in
contending with the sheer duration of a ten-minute shot
cannot help but reflect upon himself and his situation as
a consumer of landscape representation. Thus, Benning
points more explicitly than before towards the presence
of the viewing subject in the cinema, who consciously or
not interprets and orders. Simultaneously, he implies the

subjectivity of the landscape *experience* as a factor in the evaluation of a landscape. As duration increases, the viewer's associations and uncontrolled lines of thinking assume a function that becomes an integral component of seeing and understanding the film. At the same time, the landscape's duration and presence gain the *haptic quality* of a real bodily experience that corresponds to a great extent to time spent in the real landscape, if not in strict physical terms, then structurally and formally.

Finally, Benning instrumentalizes the efforts towards interpretation by the author and viewer playfully, in a very different way, with the "counterfeit" dates in *Casting a Glance*. Benning shows the historic thirty-six-year development of *Spiral Jetty* in proxy images, as a compressed narration after the fact. In eighty minutes, he makes a landscape process visible, whose slowness would defy the living eye. The occurrences of Robert Smithson's *Spiral Jetty*, which *cannot be depicted*, can be *experienced* medially, inasmuch as they are *narrated* filmically.

Understanding the Landscape Filmically

You doubt what I say? I'll show you. And, without moving more than a few inches, I unfold in front of your eyes figures, diagrams, plates, texts, silhouettes, and then and there present things that are far away and with which some sort of two-way connection has now been established. I do not think the importance of this simple mechanism can be overestimated. (Latour 1990, 36)

Studies on "Attention Restoration Theory" (ART) have shown in recent years that nature has a positive influence on the regeneration of the human capacity for concentration. The psychologist Rita Berto examined the connection in 2005. In empirical field tests, she showed that observing images of nature in contrast to those of urban landscapes can improve human cognitive performance.

Three years later, Marc Berman, John Jonides and Stephen Kaplan repeated the experiments in a slightly different form: they tested the attention of control groups before and after they had taken a walk in an urban or natural setting and/or had looked at images of one of the two topographies.

The comparison of the four groups showed that the results of the group, which had either walked through the city or looked at urban images as a form of regeneration did not show significantly changed results in the tests that followed. On the other hand, the group that had been exposed to nature or to images of nature did significantly better after their regeneration phase.

In both studies, there is surprisingly little attention given to the fact that the positive effect was also the same, whether the subjects were physically exposed to a primary experience of nature or whether "nature" was communicated to them only *secondarily* by means of images.

The studies mean essentially nothing other than the fact that the value of primary sources for the communication of experiences is questionable in cognitive and psychological terms. Nature appears to have eminent meaning for the cognitive functioning of the human being—the ontological form in which it is made accessible seems, on the other hand, only secondary. Its recuperative power cannot only be transmitted materially.

Whether the possibility of secondary communication is open for spaces and topographies other than the natural is a question not answered explicitly by the studies. Their findings, however, offer a strong indication for the fact that medial representations in general transmit at least a portion of the experiences that are unique to the sensation of the primary (natural) situation.

For research into images, this means access to an interesting new research area, to which I could contribute only a beginning in this book. What are the consequences that must be drawn from the fact that primary and secondary accesses to spatial experience apparently have much in common and that visual media do not only transmit visually, but literally make experiences possible? Does the ubiquitous medial communication of knowledge of the world assume a function as the producer of knowledge, especially of subjective qualities, thus integrating *physical* and *haptic* comprehension in addition to the cognitive?

There are theoretical starting points deriving from a film studies perspective, which try to explain the way in which films function relative to lived experience. A few of them have central meaning for this book, above all the work on spatial experience and the corresponding production of emotion. The books and essays quoted share, by and large, the fact that they either postulate an affinity between the materiality of film and of human corporeality, and study the image of the human body as the trigger for an audience's empathy, or attribute to the filmic image (or video image) haptic depictional qualities that transpose themselves onto the viewer's body. It is my hope that the examples in the second part of my study compliment and expand these theories, above all in relation to an aspect of research into emotions often forced into the background: the communication of emotions and experiences that, predicated on associative visual (and auditory) connections in the cinema, are based on bodily experiences the cinematic audience has had in similar situations. This kinesthesia—a kind of auto-empathy, evoking knowledge of the world and situations stored in the body—is something I have tried to represent as the source of relevant reactions to the depiction of space and landscape.

Images of things can release emotions within us if they resonate with our experience and provoke sensual communication (Merleau-Ponty). But it is not only the things that act emotionally upon the viewer, but also ways of viewing that correspond to our everyday visual practice. It is possible to attribute a specific corporeality to a view captured by a movie camera; a view that communicates directly with the viewer's body by addressing a "tacit knowledge", (Polanyi 1966, Schön 1983) stored within it. I have tried to cull this aspect of camera work and framing, which can evoke emotion in the films of Peter Liechti and Jem Cohen, and to demonstrate that the films do not only communicate well-known places and situations using "quotations", but can facilitate haptic experience using the association of their camera work with the body.

For the effect of (filmic) images on our cognitive and emotional system to be visible at higher resolution, there is a need for intensified attention to be trained on the effects of visual representation on our bodily-emotional experience. Given the contemporary significance granted to the topic of emotion, research in the coming years will certainly generate further points of reference and attempts at explanation.

Next to the haptic and emotional communication of landscape via film, there is another aspect I believe is central when discussing the relationship between film and landscape. The possibility of medially transmitting an experience through images, as evidenced by the studies in psychology already mentioned, implies—when it works—that increasingly, narrative aspects must be taken into account in analyzing the relationship of nature and landscape, and their medial communication. This is true because the capacity to tell stories is fundamentally the societal function, which determines visual media, above all naturally film. Nonetheless, there is naturally a terminological problem here. The visual narration of designed environments, as seen in various examples, has no specific form, but instead builds upon associations with existing societal conventions, myths, and ways of thinking. They have a narrative effect because they bring stories anchored deeply in the viewer to the surface. It is actually not possible in these cases to speak of narration, in the sense of the classical terminology, which has motivated such ancillary constructs as "narreme" or "narrative"—neither of which are entirely satisfying. A valid term for these "externalized" forms of narrativity, which also assume an important role in dealing with other human artifacts, such as design objects or fashion, has not yet been found. I have therefore limited myself to the concept of narration.

It is not only because of the inadequate terminology and the lack of clarity it produces that the examination of these kinds of narrative connections is a delicate enterprise. An additional difficulty is the fact that the relation between landscape and story is characterized by arbitrary interpretations, which are often not codified intersubjectively, but instead derive from a background of private experience. Moreover, every interpretation of the landscape is inevitably subject to cultural differences. One should nevertheless not underestimate the effect that implicit narrations have on the judgment we pass every day on the landscape.

In this regard, too, I have only been able to offer certain analyses of the power of storytelling in the second part of the book. These stories are not only effectual in their narrative universe; they also extend very concretely into the reality of our value systems and our ways of dealing with landscape, inasmuch as they shift internalized images and associations, which always and inevitably underpin our judgment—and with it, our actions.

It is not only in relation to the landscape that there is a great need to examine those forms of narration, which follow a non-classical dramaturgic structure, and to come to understand the way they achieve their effects in everyday life. Other areas of design in which objects are created, which play with our knowledge of the world and our associations, could also be similarly scrutinized, in order to argue for their dissemination and to influence consumer decision-making.

Above all, in respect to their active integration in the design process, narrations seem to me still neglected— although in the past, many of the most successful designs certainly drew their persuasive power from the history (or stories) that they implicitly told to their users. This is the point at which the promise of nature in a landscape park, the promise of technology in a smartphone, and the promise of social acceptance in a popular shoe brand move nearer to one another. They all draw deeply on the culture of our everyday communication, which, at times, is particularly well represented and open to analysis in film.

I hope that this book about films as hermeneutic means in landscape architecture succeeds primarily in one area: the contention that the films presented here are interesting as "thick descriptions," to reference Clifford Geertz, not only in artistic terms as the basic material for (form-giving) considerations. Because they articulate both verbally and visually the promise of their subject, landscape, they are in my opinion much more aptly described as part of an expanded theoretical toolbox that has been examined far too little—a way of creating visual theory.

Appendix

James Benning: Prints of his films are available through these sources, among others: Arsenal Berlin, Filmmuseum Wien, Filmmakers Coop New York etc. A DVD-Edition of James Benning's films is being released by the Österreichischen Filmmuseum in cooperation with *Edition Filmmuseum*. The first DVD was published in 2011. The series is ongoing.

Mattias Caduff: *Peiden* (CH 2002). The film can be acquired for viewing from the author (http://www.caduff.info).

Jem Cohen: *Lost Book Found* (USA 1996) and his other films can be ordered for viewings from Video Data Bank in Chicago.

Gerhard Benedikt Friedl: *Knittelfeld—Stadt ohne Geschichte* (AUT 1997) and *Hat Wolf von Amerongen Konkursdelikte begangen?* (AUT 2004) are available as a double DVD in the *Edition Standard: Der Österreichische Film* as number 98 (http://www.derstandard.at/oefilm).

Volko Kamensky: *Divina Obsesión* (D 1999): The film can be acquired for viewing directly from Volko Kamensky (volko.kamensky@web.de).

Patrick Keiller: *London* (GB 1995) and *Robinson in Space* (GB 1997) are available as a double DVD from the British Film Institute (http://filmstore.bfi.org.uk/).

Stefan Kolbe, Chris Wright: *Technik des Glücks* (D 2003): The film can be acquired for viewing directly from the authors (http://wright-kolbe-film.de/).

Peter Liechti: *Hans im Glück* (CH 2003): The film can be acquired for viewing directly from the author (http://www.peterliechti.ch).

Rüdiger Neumanns: *Zufalls-Horizonte* (GFR 1980), *Archiv der Blicke* (GFR 1983/84), *Meridian—Oder Theater vor dem Regen* (GFR 1983), *Nordlicht* (GFR 1988), and *Stein/Licht* (GER 1993) are available as a special edition in book form, along with numerous texts, from Materialverlag (http://www.hfbk-hamburg.de/). A DVD-only edition of these films is available as an Arsenal Edition from the Filmgalerie 451 publishers (http://www.filmgalerie451.de/).

Anderson, Joseph D.: *The Reality of Illusion. An Ecological Approach to Cognitive Film Theory.* Carbondale 1996.

Andrew, J. Dudley: "The Neglected Tradition of Phenomenology in Film Theory." In: Bill Nichols (ed.): *Movies and Methods. Vol II.* Berkeley 1985.

Appleyard, Donald; Lynch, Kevin; Myer, John R.: *The View from the Road.* Cambridge, MA 1964.

Arnheim, Rudolf: *Art and Visual Perception. A Psychology of the Creative Eye.* Berkeley 1974.

Asendorf, Christoph: *Super Constellation. Flugzeug und Raumrevolution.* Wien 1997.

Augé, Marc: "From Places to Non-Places." In: Marc Augé: *Non-Places: Introduction to an Anthropology of Supermodernity.* London 1995. pp. 75–115.

Bachelard, Gaston: *The Poetics of Space.* Boston 1969 [1957].

Baier, Franz Xaver: *Der Raum. Prolegomena zu einer Architektur des gelebten Raums.* Köln 1996.

Baier, Franz Xaver: "Erected Space. Zur Ästhetik des Lebensraumes." In: *Kunstforum International.* Vol. 143, 1999. pp. 130–140.

Bal, Mieke: *Narratology. Introduction to the Theory of Narrative.* Second edition. Toronto 1997.

Balázs, Béla: *Early Film Theory: Visible Man and the Spirit of Film.* New York, Oxford 2010 [1924]

Barthes, Roland: *Camera Lucida.* New York 1981 [1980].

Barthes, Roland: *Mythologies.* New York 1991 [1957].

Barthes, Roland: *S/Z.* New York 1974 [1970].

Baudry, Jean-Louis: "The Apparatus." In: *camera obscura 1. A Journal of Feminism and Film Theory.* Berkeley 1976. pp. 104–126.

Baudry, Jean-Louis: "Ideological Effects of the Basic Cinematographic Apparatus." In: Bill Nichols (ed.): *Movies and Methods, Vol. II.* New York 1985. pp. 531–542.

Bazin, André: "The Ontology of the Photographic Image." In: *Film Quarterly*, Vol. 13, No. 4 (Summer 1960). pp. 4–9.

Bazin, André: "The Evolution of the Language of Cinema." In: Leo Braudy; Marshall Cohen (eds.), *Film Theory and Criticism. Introductory Readings.* New York 2004 [1958]. pp. 41–54.

Bellamy, Robert V. and Walker, James R.: *Television and the Remote Control. Grazing on a Vast Wasteland.* New York, London 1996.

Beller, Hans (ed.): *Handbuch der Filmmontage.* München 1993.

Benjamin, Walter: "The Work of Art in the Age of its Technological Reproducibility (Second Version)." In: Id.: *The Work of Art in the Age of its Technological Reproducibility and Other Writings on Media.* Cambridge, London 2008 [1936]. pp. 19–55.

Benjamin, Walter: *The Arcades Project.* Boston 1999 [1983].

Benjamin, Walter: "On the Mimetic Faculty." In: *Reflections.* New York 1986 [1933]. pp. 333–336.

Berg, Jan; Hoffmann, Kay (eds.): *Natur und ihre filmische Auflösung.* Marburg 1994.

Berman, Marc G.; Jonides, John; Kaplan, Stephen: "The Cognitive Benefits of Interacting With Nature." In: *Psychological Science.* Vol. 19/No. 12, 2008. pp. 1207–1212.

Bernhard, Thomas: "Walking." In: *Conjunctions*, 32, Spring 1999 [1971]. pp. 7–66.

Berto, Rita: "Exposure to restorative environments helps restore attentional capacity." In: *Journal of Environmental Psychology.* No. 25, 2005. pp. 249–259.

Beuka, Robert: *SuburbiaNation. Reading Suburban Landscape in Twentieth-Century American Fiction and Film.* New York 2004.

Böhme, Gernot: *Für eine ökologische Naturästhetik.* Frankfurt/Main 1989.

Böhme, Gernot: "Die Natur im Zeitalter ihrer technischen Reproduzierbarkeit." In: *Kunstforum International.* Vol. 114. 1991. pp. 166.

Böhme, Gernot: *Atmosphäre.* Frankfurt/Main 1995.

Bollnow, Otto Friedrich: *Mensch und Raum.* Stuttgart 1963.

Bolz, Norbert: *Am Ende der Gutenberg-Galaxis. Die neuen Kommunikationsverhältnisse.* München 1993.

Bordwell, David: "Modelle der Rauminszenierung im zeitgenössischen europäischen Kino." In: Andreas Rost (ed.): *Zeit, Schnitt, Raum.* Frankfurt/Main 1997. pp. 17–42.

Bourdieu, Pierre: *Distinction. A Social Critique of the Judgement of Taste.* Boston 1984 [1979].

Bourdieu, Pierre: "Physischer, sozialer und angeeigneter physischer Raum." In: Martin Wentz (ed.): *StadtRäume.* Frankfurt/Main 1991. pp. 25–34. (From the Manuscript of the conference on Poverty, Immigration and Urban Marginality in Advanced Societies, Maison Suger, Paris, Mai 1991).

Branigan, Edward: *Narrative Comprehension and Film.* London, New York 1992.

Breidbach, Olaf (ed.): *Natur der Ästhetik—Ästhetik der Natur.* Wien, New York 1997.

Brinckmann, Christine N.: "Abstraktion und Einfühlung im deutschen Avantgardefilm der 20er Jahre." In: Id.: *Die anthropomorphe Kamera und andere Schriften zur filmischen Narration.* Zürich 1997a. pp. 247–276.

Brinckmann, Christine N.: "Empathie mit dem Tier." In: Alexandra Schneider et al. (eds.): *CineZoo.* Basel 1997b. pp. 60–69.

Brinckmann, Christine N.: "Somatische Empathie bei Hitchcock: Eine Skizze." In: Heinz B. Heller; Karl Prümm; Birgit Peulings (eds.): *Der Körper im Bild. Schauspielen—Darstellen—Erscheinen.* Marburg 1999. pp. 111–121.

Brinckmann, Christine N.: "Die Rolle der Empathie oder Furcht und Schrecken im Dokumentarfilm." In: Matthias Brütsch et al. (eds.): *Kinogefühle. Emotionalität und Film.* Marburg 2005.

Bruno, Giuliana: "Site-seeing: Architecture and the Moving Image." In: *Wide Angle* Vol. 19 Nr. 4 (October 1997), "Cityscapes I."

Bruno, Giuliana: *Atlas of Emotion. Journeys in Art, Architecture, and Film.* New York 2002.

Burch, Noël: *Life to Those Shadows.* Berkeley 1990.

Burckhardt, Lucius: *Warum ist Landschaft schön? Die Spaziergangswissenschaft.* Berlin 2006.

Burgin, Victor: *In/different Spaces. Place and Memory in Visual Culture.* Berkeley 1996.

Burke, Andrew: "Nation, Landscape and Nostalgia in Patrick Keiller's Robinson in Space." In: *Historical Materialism*, Vol. 14, Nr. 1. 2006. pp. 3–29.

Careri, Francesco: *Walkscapes. Walking as an aesthetic practice.* Barcelona 2002.

Carr, Stephen; Schissler, Dale: *The City as a Trip. Perceptual Selection and Memory in the View from the Road.* In: *Environment and Behaviour.* June 1969. pp. 7–35.

Carroll, Noël: "On being moved by nature: between religion and the natural history." In: Salim Kemal; Ivan Gaskell (eds.): *Landscape, Natural Beauty and the Arts.* Cambridge 1993. pp. 244–266.

Carroll, Noël: *Engaging the Moving Image.* New Haven 2003.

Clarke, David B. (ed.): *The Cinematic City.* London 1997.

Collot, Michel: "Points de vue sur la perception des paysages." In: *L'Espace Géographique*, 3, 1986, pp. 211–217.

Comolli, Jean-Louis: "Machines of the Visible." In: Stephen Heath; Teresa de Lauretis (eds.): *The Cinematic Apparatus.* London 1980.

Comolli, Jean-Louis: "Technique and Ideology: Camera, Perspective, Depth of Field." In: Bill Nichols (ed.): *Movies and Methods.* Vol II. Berkeley 1985. pp. 40–57.

Conan, Michel: *The Crazannes Quarries by Bernard Lassus: An Essay Analyzing the Creation of a Landscape.* Washington DC 2004.

Corboz, André: "The Land as Palimpsest." In: *Diogenes*, Vol. 31 (121), March 1983. pp. 12–34.

Corboz, André: "Entlang des Wegs. Das Territorium, seine Schichten und seine Mehrdeutigkeit." In: Id.: *Weg der Schweiz. Die Genfer Strecke. Von Morschach bis Brunnen.* Fribourg 1991.

Corner, James: "Eidetic Operations and New Landscape." In: James Corner (ed.): *Recovering Landscape.* New York 1999. pp. 153–169.

Corner, James: "Theory in Crisis." In: Simon Swaffield (ed.): *Theory in Landscape Architecture. A Reader.* Philadelphia 2002 [1991]. pp. 20–21.

Corner, James: "Representation and Landscape." In: Simon Swaffield (ed.): *Theory in Landscape Architecture. A Reader.* Philadelphia 2002 [1992]. pp. 144–165.

Corner, James; MacLean Alex S.: *Taking Measures Across the American Landscape.* New Haven 1996.

Cosgrove, Denis: *Social Formation and Symbolic Landscape.* Beckenham 1984.

Cosgrove, Denis; Daniels, Stephen: *The Iconography of Landscape. Essays on the Symbolic Representation, Design and Use of Past Environments.* Cambridge 1988.

Crary, Jonathan: *Techniques of the Observer.* Cambridge 1992.

Cullen, Gordon: *Townscape.* London 1961.

Currie, Gregory: *Image and Mind. Film, Philosophy, and Cognitive Science.* Cambridge 1995.

Currie, Gregory: "Narrative Desire." In: Carl Plantinga; Greg M. Smith (eds.): *Passionate Views. Film, Cognition, and Emotion.* Baltimore 1999.

Curtis, Robin: "Immersion und Einfühlung: Zwischen Representationalität und Materialität bewegter Bilder." In: *montage/av 17/2/2008: Immersion.* Marburg 2008. pp. 89–108.

Cytowic, Richard E.: *The Man Who Tasted Shapes.* Cambridge 1998 [1993].

Daniels, Stephen: *Fields of Vision. Landscape Imagery and National Identity in England and the United States.* Oxford 1993.

Darby, Wendy Joy: *Landscape and Identity. Geographies of Nation & Class in England.* Oxford, New York 2000.

Daston, Lorraine; Galison, Peter: "The Image of Objectivity." In: *Representations 40,* Fall 1992. UCLA 1992.

de Certeau, Michel: *The Practice of Everyday Life.* Berkeley 1984 [1980].

de Jong, Erik A.: "Der Garten als dritte Natur. Über die Verbindung von Natur und Kunst." In: Ingo Kowarik; Erika Schmidt; Brigitt Sigel (eds.): *Naturschutz und Denkmalpflege. Wege zu einem Dialog im Garten.* Zürich 1998. pp. 17–29.

de Lauretis, Teresa; Heath, Stephen (eds.): *The Cinematic Apparatus.* London 1980.

Debord, Guy: "Theory of the Dérive." In: *Situationist International Anthology.* Berkeley 1981 [1958]. pp. 50–54.

Debord, Guy: *Society of the Spectacle.* New York 1995.

Deleuze, Gilles: *Cinema 1. The Movement-Image.* London 1986 [1983].

Deleuze, Gilles: *Cinema 2. The Time-Image.* London 1989 [1985].

Diener, Roger; Herzog, Jacques; de Meuron, Pierre; Meili, Marcel; Schmid, Christian: *Die Schweiz—Ein städtebauliches Porträt.* Basel 2005.

Dyer, Richard: "Film, Musik und Gefühl—Ironische Anbindung." In: Matthias Brütsch et al. (eds.): *Kinogefühle. Emotionalität und Film.* Marburg 2005.

Eisenstein, Sergei: "Montage and Architecture." In: *assemblage* no. 10. 1989 [1937]. pp. 111–131.

Eisinger, Angelus et al. (eds.): *Stadtland Schweiz. Untersuchungen und Fallstudien zur räumlichen Struktur und Entwicklung der Schweiz.* Basel 2003.

Endell, August: *Die Schönheit der grossen Stadt.* Stuttgart 1908.

Entrikin, Nicholas J.: *The Betweenness of Place. Towards a Geography of Modernity.* London 1991.

Fechner, Renate: "Natur als Landschaft. Zur Entstehung der ästhetischen Landschaft." In: *Europäische Hochschulschriften.* Reihe XXVIII. Kunstgeschichte Bd. 64. Frankfurt/Main 1986.

Fecht, Tom; Kamper, Dietmar (eds.): *Umzug ins Offene. Vier Versuche über den Raum.* Wien, New York 2000.

Fielding, Raymond: "Hale's Tours: Ultrarealism in the Pre-1910 Motion Picture." In: *Cinema Journal,* Vol. 10. No. 1 (Autumn 1970) pp. 34–47. 1970 [1968–69]. pp. 17–40.

Fiske, John: "Surfalism and Sandiotics: The Beach in Oz Culture." In: *Australian Journal of Cultural Studies.* Vol. 1 No. 2, September 1983.

Flusser, Vilém: *Medienkultur.* Frankfurt/Main 1997 [1993].

Foucault, Michel: "Of Other Spaces." In: *Diacritics 16* (Spring 1986 [1967]) pp. 22–27.

Franzen, Brigitte: *Die vierte Natur. Gärten in der zeitgenössischen Kunst.* Köln 2000.

Fulton, Hamish: *Walking Artist.* Düsseldorf 2001.

Gamper, Michael: *"Die Natur ist republikanisch." Zu den ästhetischen, anthropologischen und politischen Konzepten der deutschen Gartenliteratur im 18. Jahrhundert.* Würzburg 1998.

Gänshirt, Christian: "Entwerfen und Forschen. Architektur und die Idee der Universität." In: *Wolkenkuckucksheim,* 5. Jg., Heft 2, Dezember 2000. Cottbus Web 26.9.2002: http://www.tu-cottbus.de/BTU/Fak2/TheoArch/Wolke/deu/Themen/002/Gaenshirt/gaenshirt.html.

Geertz, Clifford: *The Interpretation of Cultures.* New York 2000 [1973].

Gesellschaft für Theorie & Geschichte audiovisueller Kommunikation e.V. (ed.): *montage AV* 17/2/2008. Themenheft: Immersion.

Gesellschaft für Theorie & Geschichte audiovisueller Kommunikation e.V. (ed.): *montage AV* 19/1/2010. Themenheft: Erfahrung.

Gibbons, Michael; Nowotny, Helga, et al.: *The New Production of Knowledge. The Dynamics of Science and Research in Contemporary Societies.* London 1994.

Gibson, James J.: *The Ecological Approach to Visual Perception.* Boston 1979

Giersch, Ulrich: "Im fensterlosen Raum—das Medium als Weltbildapparat." In: *Sehsucht. Das Panorama als Massenunterhaltung des 19. Jahrhunderts*. Frankfurt/Main 1993. pp. 94–104.

Ginzburg, Carlo: "Clues: Roots of an Evidential Paradigm." In: Id.: *Clues, Myths, and the Historical Method*. Berlin 1989 [1979]. pp. 96–125.

Girot, Christophe: "Four Trace Concepts in Landscape Architecture." In: James Corner (ed.): *Recovering Landscape: Essays in Contemporary Landscape Architecture*. New York 1999. pp. 59–67.

Girot, Christophe: "Movism." In: Girot, Christophe; Schwarz, Marc (eds.): *Cadrages I. Carnet Video*. Zürich 2002.

Girot, Christophe: "Landschaft und Szenografie." In: *Pamphlet 4*. Zürich 2005. pp. 9–23.

Goldberg, Marcy: "Gehen, denken, drehen." In: *Cinema 50*. Marburg 2005. pp. 72–75.

Gombrich, Ernst: "The Renaissance Theory of Art and the Landscape." In: *Norm and Form. Studies in the Art of Renaissance*. London 1966. pp. 107–121.

Graham, Rhys: "Just Hold Still: A Conversation with Jem Cohen." In: *Senses of Cinema*. Issue 9, Sept.–Oct. 2000. Melbourne 2000. Web 15.5.2007: http://www.sensesofcinema.com/contents/00/9/cohen.html.

Greene, Linda Wedel: *Yosemite: The Park and its Ressources. A History of the Discovery, Management and Physical Development of Yosemite National Park*. Denver 1987.

Groh, Ruth; Groh, Dieter: *Weltbild und Naturaneignung. Zur Kulturgeschichte der Natur*. Frankfurt/Main 1991.

Groh, Ruth; Groh, Dieter: "Kulturelle Muster und ästhetische Naturerfahrung." In: Jörg Zimmermann (ed.): *Ästhetik und Naturerfahrung*. Stuttgart 1992.

Gruenter, Rainer: "Landschaft. Bemerkungen zur Wort- und Bedeutungsgeschichte." In: Alexander Ritter (ed.): *Landschaft und Raum in der Erzählkunst*. Darmstadt 1975 [1953]. pp. 192–207.

Gustafsson, Henrik: *Out of Site. Landscape and Cultural Reflexivity in New Hollywood Cinema*. 1969–1974. Stockholm 2007.

Hahn, Achim: "Die Lesbarkeit der Landschaft. Sozialwissenschaftliche Überlegungen zum Kontext von Bild, Leitbild und Planung." In: *Wolkenkuckucksheim 4/2*, Februrar 2000. Cottbus Web 2.2.2007: http://www-1.tu-cottbus.de/BTU/Fak2/ TheoArch wolke/deu/Themen/992/Hahn/hahn.html.

Haraway, Donna: "Situated Knowledges: The Science Question in Feminism and the Privilege of Partial Perspective." In: *Feminist Studies*, Nr. 3, 1988. pp. 575–599.

Hard, Gerhard: *Die "Landschaft" der Sprache und die "Landschaft" der Geographen. Semantische und forschungslogische Studien*. Bonn 1970.

Hard, Gerhard: "Geographie als Spurenlesen. Eine Möglichkeit, den Sinn und die Grenzen der Geographie zu formulieren." In: *Zeitschrift für Wirtschaftsgeographie*, Jg. 33 (1989), Heft 1/2. Frankfurt/Main pp. 2–11.

Hard, Gerhard: *Spuren und Spurenleser. Zur Theorie und Ästhetik des Spurenlesens in der Vegetation und anderswo*. Osnabrück 1995.

Hebdige, Dick: "Reeling in Utah: The Travel Log Trilogy." In: *Afterall* No 8. London, Los Angeles 2003. pp. 11–31.

Hein, Birgit; Herzogenrath, Wulf: *Film als Film, 1910 bis heute*. Stuttgart 1977.

Heisenberg, Werner: "Modern Physics View of Nature." In: *Universitas 7*, 1965 [1954]. pp. 273–287.

Herzog, Werner: *Of Walking in Ice. Munich–Paris. 23 November–14 December 1974*. New York 2007.

Hirschfeld, Christian Cay Lorenz: "Ueber die Verwandtschaft der Gartenkunst und der Malerey." In: *Gothaisches Magazin der Künste und Wissenschaften*. Band 1. 1776. pp. 41–58.

Hirschfeld, Christian Cay Lorenz: *Theory of Garden Art*. Philadelphia 2001 [1779–85].

Hunt, John Dixon: "The Idea of the Garden, And the Three Natures. Band 1." In: Joachim Wilke (ed.): *Zum Naturbegriff der Gegenwart. Kongressdokumentation zum Projekt "Natur im Kopf"*. Stuttgart 21.–26. Juni 1993. Stuttgart 1994. pp. 305–326.

Huhtamo, Erkki: "Encapsulated Bodies in Motion: Simulators and the Quest for Total Immersion." In: Simon Penny (ed.): *Critical Issues in Electronic Media*. New York 1995. pp. 159–186.

Jackson, John Brinckerhoff: *Discovering the Vernacular Landscape*. New Haven, London 1984.

Jackson, John Brinckerhoff: *A Sense of Place, A Sense of Time*. New Haven, London 1994.

Jäggi, Urs: "Entmythologisierung der Alpenwelt—Zu Kurt Gloors Film Die

Landschaftsgärtner." In: *Zoom*, März 1971. Zürich p. 9.

Janson, Alban: "Architektur ist Entwurf." In: *Wolkenkuckucksheim*, 4. Jg., Heft 1, Mai 1999. Cottbus Web 26.9.2002: http://www.tu-cottbus.de/BTU/Fak2/TheoArch/Wolke/deu/Themen/991/Janson/janson.html.

Johnstone, Barbara: *Stories, Community, and Place. Narratives from Middle America.* Bloomington 1990.

Keiller, Patrick: "The Dilapidated Dwelling." In: *Architectural Design*, Vol. 68 No 7/8, July–August 1998.

Keiller, Patrick: *Robinson in Space*. London 1999.

Keiller, Patrick: "The Poetic Experience of Townscape and Landscape and Some Ways of Depicting It." In: Nina Danino and Michael Mazière (eds.): *The Undercut Reader: Critical Writing on Artists' Film and Video*. London 2003. pp. 75–83.

Keiller, Patrick: "Atmosphere, Palimpsest and Other Interpretations of Landscape." In: Nina Danino and Michael Mazière (eds.): *The Undercut Reader: Critical Writing on Artists' Film and Video*. London 2003. pp. 204–208.

Kienast, Dieter: "Zur Dichte der Stadt." In: *Topos* 7/1994. p. 103–109.

Kienast, Dieter: "Stadtlandschaft." In: *ZOLLtexte*, 2/1995. Wien

Kienast, Dieter: *Dieter Kienast—Die Poetik des Gartens. Über Chaos und Ordnung in der Landschaftsarchitektur*. Basel 2002.

Klein, Norman: "The Politics of Scripted Spaces." In: Andreas Lechner; Petra Maier (eds.): *stadtmotiv**. Wien 1999. pp. 80–95.

Kleinspehn, Thomas: *Der flüchtige Blick. Sehen und Identität in der Kultur der Neuzeit.* Reinbek 1989.

Knorr-Cetina, Karin: *The Manufacture of Knowledge. An Essay on the Constructivist and Contextual Nature of Science*. Oxford 1981.

Koch, Gertrud (ed.) in: *Umwidmungen. Architektonische und kinematographische Räume.* Berlin 2005.

Koolhaas, Rem: "The Generic City." In: Rem Koolhaas; Bruce Mau: *S,M,L,XL*. 1995.

Kowarik, Ingo: "Stadtbrachen als Niemandsländer, Naturschutzgebiete oder Gartenkunstwerke der Zukunft?" In: *Geobotanisches Kolloquium* 9, 1993. pp. 14–16.

Kracauer, Siegfried: *Theory of Film. The Redemption of Physical Reality.* London, Oxford, New York 1960.

Lant, Antonia: "Haptical Cinema." In: *October* Vol. 74, Autumn 1995. pp. 45–73.

Latour, Bruno; Woolgar, Steve: *Laboratory Life. The Social Construction of Scientific Facts*. Berverly Hills 1979.

Latour, Bruno: "Drawing things together." In: Michael Lynch, Steven Woolgar (eds.): *Representation in Scientific Practice*. Cambridge MA, London 1990. pp. 19–68.

Le Corbusier: *Aircraft*. London 1935.

Lefebvre, Henri: *The Production of Space*. Oxford 1991 [1974].

Lefebvre, Martin (ed.): *Landscape and Film*. New York 2006.

Linde, Charlotte ; Labov, William: "Spatial Networks as a Site for the Study of Language and Thought." In: *Language* 51, 1975. pp. 924939.

Löw, Martina: *Raumsoziologie*. Frankfurt/Main 2001.

Lowry, Stephen: "Film—Wahrnehmung—Subjekt." In: *Montage/av. Zeitschrift für Theorie & Geschichte audiovisueller Kommunikation*. 1/1/92. Berlin 1992. pp. 113–128.

Lukinbeal, Chris: "Cinematic Landscapes." In: *Journal of Cultural Geography*. Fall/Winter 2005. pp. 3–22.

Lynch, Kevin: *The Image of the City*. Cambridge 1960.

MacDonald, Scott: "Exploring the New West. An Interview with James Benning." In: *Film Quarterly*, Vol. LVIII, 3 (2005). pp. 2–15.

MacDonald, Scott: "American Dreams." In: *Film Quarterly*, Vol XL, 4 (1987). pp. 16–20.

MacDonald, Scott: *A Critical Cinema. Interviews with Filmmakers, Band 2.* Berkeley 1992.

MacDonald, Scott: *The Garden in the Machine. A Field Guide to Independent Films About Place*. Berkeley 2001.

Marks, Laura U.: *The Skin of the Film*. Durham 1999.

Marks, Laura U.: *Touch: Sensous Theory and multisensory Media*. Minneapolis 2002.

Marot, Sébastien: "The Landscape as Alternative." In: *Het Landschap/The Landscape*. Antwerpen 1995. p. 9–36.

Meinig, Donald W.: *The Interpretation of Ordinary Landscapes. Geographical Essays.* Oxford 1979.

Merleau-Ponty, Maurice: *Phänomenology of Perception*. London, New York 2002 [1945].
Merleau-Ponty, Maurice: "Eye and Mind." In: Galen A. Johnson (ed.): *The Merleau-Ponty Aesthetics Reader. Philosophy and Painting*, Evanston 1993. p. 121–149.
Metz, Christian: *The Imaginary Signifier. Psychoanalysis and the Cinema*. Bloomington 1982 [1977].
Metz, Christian: "Images subjectives, sons subjectives, 'point de vue.'" In: *L'énonciation impersonnelle, ou, Le site du film*. Paris 1991.
Mitchell, W.J.T.: "On Narrative." In: *Critical Inquiry*, 7.1 (1980). Chicago, London 1981.
Mitchell, W.J.T. (ed.): *Landscape and Power*. Chicago 1994.
Mitchell, W.J.T.: *Picture Theory*. Chicago 1994.
Mitscherlich, Alexander: *Die Unwirtlichkeit unserer Städte. Anstiftung zum Unfrieden*. Frankfurt/Main 1965.
Mittelstrass, Jürgen: "Das Absolute und das Relative." In: Michael Astroh; Dietfried Gerhardus; Gerhard Heinzmann (eds.): *Dialogisches Handeln*. Heidelberg 1997. pp. 77–89.
Mittelstrass, Jürgen: *Die Häuser des Wissens. Wissenschaftstheoretische Studien*. Frankfurt/Main 1998.
Moore, Rachel: "James Benning's California Trilogy: A Lesson in Natural History." In: *Afterall* No 8. London, Los Angeles 2003. pp. 35–42.
Morin, Edgar: *The Cinema, or The Immaginary Man*. Minneapolis 2005 [1956].
Müller, Ulrich: "Die Bildhaftigkeit der Natur." In: Olaf Breidbach (ed.): *Natur der Ästhetik—Ästhetik der Natur*. Wien, New York 1997.
Mulvey, Laura: *Death 24 × a Second. Stillness and the Moving Image*. London 2006.
MVRDV (Winy Maas): *Costa Iberica*. Barcelona 2000.
Natali, Maurizia: *L'Image-paysage. Iconologie et cinéma*. Saint-Denis 1996.
Nichols, Bill: "The Voice of Documentary." In: Bill Nichols (ed.): *Movies and Methods*. Vol II. Berkeley 1985.
Nichols, Bill: *Representing Reality. Issues and Concepts in Documentary*. Bloomington 1991.
Nichols, Bill: *Blurred Boundaries. Questions of Meaning in Contemporary Culture*. Bloomington 1994.
Nieding, Gerhild: *Ereignisstrukturen im Film und die Entwicklung des räumlichen Denkens*. Berlin 1997.
Norberg-Schulz, Christian: "Ort?" In: Id.: *Genius Loci*. London 1980. pp. 6–23.
Nowotny, Helga: *Es ist so. Es könnte auch anders sein*. Frankfurt/Main 1999.
Nowotny, Helga; Scott, Peter; Gibbons, Michael: *Re-Thinking Science. Knowledge and the Public in an Age of Uncertainty*. Oxford 2001.
Odin, Roger: "Lecture documentarisante, film documentaire." In: *Cinémas et Réalités*. Saint-Etienne 1984. p. 263–78.
Pichler, Barbara: *Landscapes of the Mind. The Idea of Landscape in Patrick Keiller's London and Andrew Kötting's Gallivant*. London 1998 (unpublished manuscript).
Pichler, Barbara; Pollach, Andrea (eds.): *Moving Landscapes. Landschaft und Film*. Wien 2006.
Pichler, Barbara; Slanar, Claudia (eds.): *James Benning*. Wien 2007.
Plantinga, Carl; Smith, Greg M. (eds.): *Passionate Views. Film, Cognition, and Emotion*. Baltimore 1999.
Plath, Nils: "Blicke auf Landschaften." In: *Augenblick, Marburger und Mainzer Hefte zur Medienwissenschaft, No. 37*. Marburg 2005.
Polanyi, Michael: *The Tacit Dimension*. London 1966.
Potteiger, Matthew; Purinton, Jamie: *Landscape Narratives: Design Practices For Telling Stories*. New York 1998.
Prominski, Martin: *Landschaft entwerfen. Zur Theorie aktueller Landschaftsarchitektur*. Berlin 2004.
Rakatansky, Mark: "Spatial Narratives." In: John Whiteman; Jeffrey Kipnis; Richard Burdett (eds.): *Strategies in Architectural Thinking*. Chicago 1991.
Reynaud, Bérénice: "James Benning the Filmmaker as Haunted Landscape." In: *Film Comment XXXII/6* Nov–Dec 1996. pp. 76–79, 81.
Ritter, Joachim: "Landschaft. Zur Funktion des Ästhetischen in der modernen Gesellschaft." In: Gert Gröning; Ulfert Herlyn (eds.): *Landschaftswahrnehmung und Landschaftserfahrung. Texte zur Konstitution und Rezeption von Natur als Landschaft*. München 1990 [1963]. pp. 23–41.
Robnik, Drehli: "Körper-Erfahrung und Film-Phänomenologie." In: Jürgen Felix (ed.): *Moderne Film Theorie*. Mainz 2002. pp. 246–280.
Rodaway, Paul: *Sensuous Geographies. Body, Sense and Place*. London, New York 1994.

Ropohl, Günter: "Das Ende der Natur." In: Lothar Schäfer; Elisabeth Ströker (eds.): *Naturauffassungen in Philosophie, Wissenschaft, Technik.* Freiburg 1996.

Rosa, Hartmut: *Beschleunigung. Die Veränderung der Zeitstrukturen in der Moderne.* Frankfurt/Main 2005.

Roth, Wilhelm: *Der Dokumentarfilm seit 1960.* München 1982.

Schama, Simon: *Landscape and Memory.* New York 1995.

Scharoun, Hans: Eröffnungsvortrag zur Ausstellung "Berlin plant. Erster Bericht." In: Vittorio Magnago Lampugnani; Katja Frey; Eliana Perotti (eds.): *Anthologie zum Städtebau. Vom Wiederaufbau nach dem Zweiten Weltkrieg bis zur zeitgenössischen Stadt.* (Band III). Berlin 2005. pp. 39–48.

Schaub, Martin: "Die eigenen Angelegenheiten." In: *Cinema Jahrbuch: die eigenen Angelegenheiten. Themen, Motive, Obsessionen und Träume des neuen Schweizer Films 1963–1983.* Basel 1983.

Schiemann, Gregor: "Phänomenologie versus Naturwissenschaft. Zum Verhältnis zweier Erkenntnisweisen." In: Gernot Böhme (ed.): *Phänomenologie der Natur.* Frankfurt Main 1997. p. 213–231.

Schivelbusch, Wolfgang: *The Railway Journey. The Industrialization of Time and Space in the 19th Century.* Berkeley 1979 [1977].

Schlappner, Martin: "Kinobilder—Bilder der Schweiz." In: Schweizerisches Filmzentrum (eds.): *Vergangenheit und Gegenwart des Schweizer Films (1896–1987).* Basel 1987. pp. 7–73.

Schlögel, Karl: *Im Raume lesen wir die Zeit.* München 2003.

Schmidt, Aurel: *Gehen.* Frauenfeld 2007.

Schmidt, Widdicombe; Naimark, Michel; Bradley, Ruth: "Landscape and Place" (Special Issue). In: *Wide Angle* XV/4, Dec 1993. pp. 1–84.

Schön Donald: *The Reflective Practitioner: How professionals think in action.* London, 1983.

Schumacher, Christina: "'Dogged by the model of science.' Ist Architektur Wissenschaft? Ein wissenschaftssoziologischer Beitrag zu einer hundertjährigen Debatte." In: *tec21,* Heft 13, 2001. Zürich pp. 25–28.

Seel, Martin: *Eine Ästhetik der Natur.* Frankfurt/Main 1991.

Shaviro, Steven: *The Cinematic Body.* Minneapolis 1993.

Shaviro, Steven: "The Cinematic Body REDUX." In: *Parallax 14:1,* 2008. pp. 48–54.

Sieferle, Rolf P.: *Rückblick auf die Natur. Eine Geschichte des Menschen und seiner Umwelt.* München 1997.

Sieferle, Rolf P.: "Die Totale Landschaft." In: Franz Oswald; Nicola Schüller (eds.): *Neue Urbanität—Das Verschmelzen von Stadt und Landschaft.* Zürich 2003. pp. 59–76.

Sieverts, Thomas: *Cities without Cities. An Interpretation of the Zwischenstadt.* London, New York 2003 [1997].

Simmel, Georg: "The Philosophy of Landscape." In: *Theory Culture Society,* Vol. 24 (7–8). Los Angeles, London, New Delhi, Singapore 2007 [1913]. pp. 20–29.

Sitney, P. Adams: "Structural Film". P. Adams Sitney (ed.): *Film Culture Reader.* New York 1970. p. S 326–349.

Sitney, P. Adams: "Landscape in the cinema: The Rhythms of the World and the Camera." In: Salim Kemal; Ivan Gaskell (eds.): *Landscape, Natural Beauty and the Arts.* Cambridge 1993. pp. 103–126.

Sitte, Camillo: *City Planning According to Artistic Priciples.* London 1965 [1889].

Smith, Anthony D.: *National Identity.* London 1991.

Smith, Greg M.: *Film Structure and the Emotion System.* Cambridge 2003.

Smith, Murray: *Engaging Characters: Fiction, Emotion, and the Cinema.* Oxford 1995.

Smithson, Robert: *The Collected Writings.* Berkeley 1996.

Sobchack, Vivian: *The Address of the Eye. A Phenomenology of Film Experience.* Princeton 1992.

Sobchack, Vivian: "What My Fingers Knew: The Cinesthetic Subject, or Vision in the Flesh." In: Vivian Sobchack: *Carnal Thoughts. Embodiment and Moving Image Culture.* Berkeley 2004. pp. 53–84.

Sobchack, Vivian: "Breadcrumbs in the Forest. Three Mediations on Being Lost in Space." In: Vivian Sobchack: *Carnal Thoughts. Embodiment and Moving Image Culture.* Berkeley 2004. pp. 13–35.

Sobchack, Vivian: "The Scene of the Screen. Envisioning Photographic, Cinematic, and Electronic 'Presence.'" In: *Vivian Sobchack: Carnal Thoughts. Embodiment and Moving Image Culture.* Berkeley 2004. pp. 135–162.

Soja, Edward: *Postmodern Geografies. The Reassertion of Space in Critical Social Theory.* London 1989.

Sontag, Susan: *On Photography* (electronic edition). New York 2005 [1973].

Sternberger, Dolf: *Panorama. Oder Ansichten vom 19. Jahrhundert.* Hamburg 1955.

Stoffler, Johannes: *Gustav Ammann. Landschaften der Moderne in der Schweiz.* Zürich 2008.

Sturm, Gabriele: *Wege zum Raum. Methodologische Annäherungen an ein Basiskonzept raumbezogener Wissenschaften.* Opladen 2000.

Sudjic, Deyan: *The 100 Mile City.* London 1992.

Tan, Ed S: *Emotion and the Structure of Narrative Film: Film as an Emotion Machine.* Mahwah, 1996.

Testa, Bart: *Spirit in the Landscape.* Toronto 1989.

Tode, Thomas: "Unfrohes, fahles Licht. Über einige Landschaftsfilme von Rüdiger Neumann." In: *Cinema 47. Landschaften.* Zürich 2001. p. 117–125.

Tröhler, Margrit: "Filmische Authentizität. Mögliche Wirklichkeiten zwischen Fiktion und Dokumentation." In: *Montage/av. Zeitschrift für Theorie & Geschichte audiovisueller Kommunikation.* 13/2/2004. Berlin 2004.

Truniger, Fred: "Spurensuche im Kreisverkehr." In: *Cinema 47. Landschaften.* Zürich 2001. pp. 16–25.

Truniger, Fred: "Raum-zeitliche Verdichtungen des Raums. The Work of Director Michel Gondry". In: *werk, bauen + wohnen*, 09/04. p. 66–67.

Truniger, Fred; Trolle, Kristina: "Komplexe Landschaft." In: Barbara Pichler; Andrea Pollach (eds.): *moving landscapes. Landschaft und Film.* Wien 2006. pp. 57–70.

Truniger, Fred ; Kamensky, Volko: "Filme machen mit brüchiger Argumentation. Ein Gespräch zwischen Fred Truniger und Volko Kamensky." *Kultur & Gespenster*, Heft Nr. 4, 2007. pp. 142–153.

Truniger, Fred: "Wenn Filme Landschaften erzählen." In: Udo Weilacher et al. (eds.): *Neuland. Landschaft zwischen Wirklichkeit und Vorstellung.* Basel, Boston, Berlin 2009. pp. 22–35.

Truniger, Fred: "Bilder akkumulieren. Eine filmische Deutung der englischen Landschaft." In: Eduard Heinrich Führ (ed.): *Wolkenkuckucksheim. Zum Interpretieren von Architektur. Konkrete Interpretationen* (Onlinepublikation, Mai 2009). Zugriff via: http://www.cloud-cuckoo.net/.

Truniger, Fred: "Rhythm as approach to the landscape experience at high speeds." In: *'scape. Landscape architecture and urbanism.* 1/2010. pp. 29–33.

Truniger, Fred: "1000 Steps. A Landscape Narrates." In: Christophe Girot; Sabine Wolf (eds.): *Blicklandschaften—Landscapevideo. Landscape in Movement.* Zurich 2010. pp. 45–49.

Truniger, Fred: "Learning to See Landscape." In: Filmgalerie 451; Arsenal – Instutute for Film and Video Art; Maike Mia Höhne (eds.) *Archive of Gazes. Films by Rüdiger Neumann.* Hamburg 2010. pp. 12–26.

Tuan, Yi-Fu: *Topophilia. A Study of Environmental Perception, Attitudes, And Values.* Englewood Cliffs 1974.

Tuan, Yi-Fu: *Space and Place: The Perspective of Experience.* Minneapolis 1977.

Tuan, Yi-Fu: "Thought and Landscape. The Eye and the Mind's Eye." In: Donald Meinig; J. B. Jackson (eds.): *The Interpretation of Ordinary Landscapes.* New York 1979. pp. 89–102.

Venturi, Robert; Scott Brown, Denise; Izenour, Steven: *Learning from Las Vegas: The Forgotten Symbolism of Architectural Form.* Basel 1997 [1972].

Vidler, Anthony: "The Explosion of Space: Architecture and the Filmic Imaginary." In: *Assemblage*, No. 21. (Aug. 1993). Cambridge 1993. pp. 44–59.

Virilio, Paul: "Véhiculaire." In: *Cause Commune: Nomades et Vagabondes.* Paris 1975.

Vöckler, Kai: "Psychoscape." In: Walter Prigge (ed.): *Peripherie ist überall.* Frankfurt/Main 1998. pp. 277–287.

Haller, Albrecht von: *The Alps.* Dübendorf 1987 [1729].

von Plessen, Marie-Louise: "Der gebannte Augenblick. Die Abbildung von Realität im Panorama des 19. Jahrhunderts." In: Id.: *Sehsucht. Das Panorama als Massenunterhaltung des 19. Jahrhunderts.* Frankfurt/Main 1993. p. 12–19.

Waldenfels, Bernhard: "Gänge durch die Landschaft." In: Id.: *In den Netzen der Lebenswelt.* Frankfurt/Main 1985. p. 179–193.

Wees, William C.: "The Cinematic Image as a Visualisation of Sight." In: *Wide Angle*, Vol. 4, Nr. 3. 1981. pp. 28–37.

Weihsmann, Helmut: *Cinetecture. Film, Architektur, Moderne.* Wien 1995.

Weilacher, Udo: *Visionäre Gärten. Die modernen Landschaften von Ernst Cramer.* Basel 2001.

White, Hayden: *Tropics of Discourse. Essays in Cultural Criticism.* Baltimore, London 1978.

White, Hayden: "The Value of Narrativity in the Representation of Reality." In: W.J.T. Mitchell: *On Narrative. Critical Inquiry, 7.1.* Chicago, London 1980. pp. 5–27.

White, Hayden: *The Content of the Form. Narrative Discourse and Historical Representation.* Baltimore 1987.

Winkler, Hartmut: "Der Zuschauer und die filmische Technik. Apparatus-Theorien, Frankreich 1969–75." In: Knut Hicketier; Hartmut Winkler (eds.): *Filmwahrnehmung.* Berlin 1990. pp. 19–25.

Winkler, Hartmut: *Der filmische Raum und der Zuschauer. "Apparatus"—Semantik "Ideology."* Heidelberg 1992.

Winston, Brian: "Documentary: I Think We Are In Trouble." In: Alan Rosenthal (ed.): *New Challenges for Documentary.* Berkeley 1988. pp. 21–33.

Wulff, Hans J.: "Flow. Kaleidoskopische Formationen des Fern-Sehens." In: *Montage/av. Zeitschrift für Theorie & Geschichte audiovisueller Kommunikation.* 4/2/1994. Berlin 1994. pp. 21–39.

Wulff, Hans J.: "Empathie als Dimension des Filmverstehens. Ein Thesenpapier." In: *Montage/av. Zeitschrift für Theorie & Geschichte audiovisueller Kommunikation.* 12/1/2003. Berlin 2003. pp. 136–161.

Yarbus, Alfred L.: *Eye Movements and Vision.* New York 1967.

Zimmer, Oliver: "In Search of Natural Identity: Alpine Landscape and the Reconstruction of the Swiss Nation." In: *Comparative Studies in Society and History.* Vol. 40, No. 4, Oct. 1998. Ann Arbor. pp. 637–665.

Zimmermann, Jörg (ed.): *Das Naturbild des Menschen.* München 1982.

ACKNOWLEDGEMENTS

The author would like to thank Annemarie Bucher, Christine Noll Brinckmann, Christophe Girot, Tereza Smid, Lucas Hugelshofer, Marc Schwarz, and Kristina Trolle for their help, support, and critical reading of this text.

I am also grateful to Alexander Horwath, Georg Wasner, and the people at the Filmmuseum in Vienna for giving me not only the right to use their scans of James Benning's film frames, but also providing them from old digital sources.

The images in the chapter "Traveling in Images" are reproduced with the kind permission of BFI/BBC.

Finally, this book would hardly have been possible without the filmmakers, who allowed me to work with their films and who kindly gave their time for discussions. I extend to them my sincere gratitude.

IMPRINT

© 2013 by jovis Verlag GmbH
Copyright for the texts by the author.
Copyright for the images by the photographers/holders of the picture rights.
All rights reserved.

Translation: Lynette Widder
Proofreading: Inez Templeton, Lynne Kolar-Thompson
Graphic design: Willi Schmid & Radim Peško
Typefaces: Landscript Condensed (radimpesko.com), DeVinne
Paper: Reaction 310g (cover) and Planoart 115g
Printing and binding: Gugler GmbH

Bibliographic information published by the Deutsche Nationalbibliothek
The Deutsche Nationalbibliothek lists this publication in the Deutsche
Nationalbibliografie; detailed bibliographic data are available on the Internet at
http://dnb.d-nb.de

jovis Verlag GmbH
Kurfürstenstraße 15/16
10785 Berlin

www.jovis.de

ISBN 978-3-86859-211-5